MONASTIC WI[illegible]

Eugene Boylan, OCSO

# Partnership with Christ

*A Cistercian Retreat*

## MONASTIC WISDOM SERIES

Patrick Hart, OCSO, General Editor



MW1 Cassian and the Fathers: Initiation into the Monastic Tradition
*Thomas Merton, OCSO*

MW2 Secret of the Heart: Spiritual Being
*Jean-Marie Howe, OCSO*

MW3 Inside the Psalms: Reflections for Novices
*Maureen F. McCabe, OCSO*

MW4 Thomas Merton: Prophet of Renewal
*John Eudes Bamberger, OCSO*

MW5 Centered on Christ: A Guide to Monastic Profession
*Augustine Roberts, OCSO*

MW6 Passing from Self to God: A Cistercian Retreat
*Robert Thomas, OCSO*

MW7 Dom Gabriel Sortais: An Amazing Abbot in Turbulent Times
*Guy Oury, OSB*

MW8 A Monastic Vision for the 21st Century: Where Do We Go from Here?
*Patrick Hart, OCSO, editor*

MW9 Pre-Benedictine Monasticism: Initiation into the Monastic Tradition 2
*Thomas Merton, OCSO*

MW10 Charles Dumont Monk-Poet: A Spiritual Biography
*Elizabeth Connor, OCSO*

MW11 The Way of Humility
*André Louf, OCSO*

MW12 Four Ways of Holiness for the Universal Church: Drawn from the Monastic Tradition
*Francis Kline, OCSO*

MW13 An Introduction to Christian Mysticism: Initiation into the Monastic Tradition 3
*Thomas Merton, OCSO*

MW14 God Alone: A Spiritual Biography of Blessed Rafael Arnáiz Barón
*Gonzalo Maria Fernández, OCSO*

MW15 Singing for the Kingdom: The Last of the Homilies
*Matthew Kelty, OCSO*

MW16 Partnership with Christ: A Cistercian Retreat
*Eugene Boylan, OCSO*

MONASTIC WISDOM SERIES: NUMBER SIXTEEN

# Partnership with Christ

*A Cistercian Retreat*

by

Eugene Boylan, OCSO

Edited with a Preface by

Chaminade Crabtree, OCSO

Introduction by

Nivard Kinsella, OCSO

Cistercian Publications
www.cistercianpublications.org

LITURGICAL PRESS
Collegeville, Minnesota
www.litpress.org

A Cistercian Publications title published by Liturgical Press

**Cistercian Publications**
Editorial Offices
Abbey of Gethsemani
3642 Monks Road
Trappist, Kentucky 40051
www.cistercianpublications.org



1 2 3 4 5 6 7 8 9

**Library of Congress Cataloging-in-Publication Data**

Boylan, Eugene, 1904–1964.
Partnership with Christ : a Cistercian retreat / by Eugene Boylan ; edited with a preface by Chaminade Crabtree ; introduction by Nivard Kinsella.
p. cm. — (Monastic wisdom series ; no. 16)
ISBN 978-0-87907-016-8 (pbk.)
1. Spiritual retreats—Catholic Church. 2. Spiritual life—Catholic Church. 3. Christian life—Catholic authors. I. Crabtree, Chaminade. II. Title. III. Series.

BX2375.B69 2008
269'.6942—dc22 2008013426

# TABLE OF CONTENTS

# PREFACE

In January 1958, Dom Eugene Boylan, OCSO, author of the Christian classic, *This Tremendous Lover*, gave a ten-day retreat at Our Lady of the Holy Spirit Abbey in Conyers, Georgia. Our senior monks still consider the retreat as one of the best. They speak fondly of Dom Eugene's energetic personality, his conviction about the contemplative vocation, and his encouragement to place confidence in God's love.

The retreat took place during a period of transition for the eighty monks at Conyers. Their beloved abbot, Dom Robert McGann, had died suddenly on October 3, 1957 shortly after he arrived in France for the general chapter. Dom Augustine Moore, who was the English-language definitor at the time, was elected abbot on October 22. The community was finishing the construction of a permanent monastery, one which was built by the monks themselves with a skilled lay-foreman overseeing their efforts.

Our Lady of the Holy Spirit Abbey was one of several American monasteries graced with the knowledge and wisdom (and humor) of Dom Eugene in 1958. Dom Augustine, who as definitor visited several European abbeys, had developed a friendship with Dom Eugene and was instrumental in getting him to come to the United States. Previous to Conyers, Dom Eugene conducted a retreat at Mepkin Abbey in South Carolina. He would also give retreats at Gethsemani Abbey in Kentucky, Genesee Abbey in New York, and Saint Joseph's Abbey in Massachusetts.

In 1955, Dom Eugene was appointed superior *ad nutum* at the Cistercian monastery on Caldey Island, off the coast of Wales. His task was to bring economic and communal stability to a community that consisted of several nationalities. In 1958, Caldey Abbey was a year away from becoming an autonomous monastery having demonstrated that they could be self-supportive through financial stability and having a solid number of men in solemn vows. Dom Eugene was able to make the journey to America to share his spiritual teachings. He was already well-known through his books *Difficulties in Mental Prayer* (1943) and *This Tremendous Lover* (1947).

I am told by our seniors that the only notes Dom Eugene used during the retreat were those in a small notebook of quotes from his novitiate days under Father Malachy Brasil (later to be elected abbot at Mount Saint Bernard). Dom Eugene's presentation was fluent, direct, and entertaining. The stories from his life—boyhood days, studies in Vienna, novitiate at Mount Saint Joseph Abbey in Roscrea, and superior at Caldey Abbey—gave his talks a personal flavor that aided the listeners in receiving the good news of God's love, mercy, and compassion given to us through Jesus Christ.

I first heard about Dom Eugene's retreat from my novice master, Father Alberic, in 1996. It was the week before our annual community retreat which would be my first as a novice. Father Alberic told me of how one of the monks had been profoundly influenced by a retreat, namely the one given by Dom Eugene. Community retreats are a time of grace, Father Alberic said, and even of conversion to a deeper love of God and subsequently a strengthening of one's vocation as a Cistercian monk.

I discovered that Brother Alphonse was the monk referred to by Father Alberic. Normally a quiet person, Alphonse enthusiastically related to me his impressions of that 1958 retreat. Alphonse even quoted Dom Eugene directly. Other monks shared with me their remembrance of the retreat.

It was fortunate that someone had the foresight to record Dom Eugene's retreat. Originally recorded on a reel-to-reel recorder, the talks were later transferred to cassette tapes. *Partnership with Christ: A Cistercian Retreat* is a transcription of those tapes. My editing is minimal and only as needed to put spoken language into a book format. For example, I spelled out contractions except when used by Dom Eugene in stories. I did my best to locate the exact source for the quotes used by Dom Eugene, although the book editions may differ from those referred to in 1958. Dom Eugene used many biblical passages in his talks, mostly from his memory. I have taken the liberty to "correct" these memorized passages by using the exact passage from the Catholic translation closest to the time—the Confraternity edition (New York: Catholic Book Publishing, 1957).

The vibrancy of Dom Eugene words, whether heard on tape or read in a book, brings the message that the contemplative vocation is lived in partnership with Jesus Christ. May Dom Eugene Boylan continue to inspire us today to daily walk with our Lady and her divine son, our Lord Jesus Christ.

Finally, I end with gratitude to Dom M. Basil Pennington, ocso. It was during his time as our abbot that I shared with him the transcriptions of Dom Eugene's retreat talks. Dom Basil, who himself knew Dom Eugene, encouraged me to submit the talks for publication. With my limited skills in such an endeavor, Dom Basil guided me with his suggestions. When he resigned as our abbot in 2002, I put the manuscript aside. Shortly before the car accident in March 2005 which eventually took his life (June 5, 2005), Dom Basil again expressed how much he would like to see Dom Eugene's talks be a part of the Cistercian Publications. I express my deep thanks to Dom Basil for his encouragement. May his prayers be with you, the reader, as you make a retreat with Dom Eugene Boylan.

Brother Chaminade Crabtree, ocso
Our Lady of the Holy Spirit Abbey
Conyers, Georgia

# INTRODUCTION

Dom Eugene Boylan, ocso (1904–1964)
by Fr. Nivard Kinsella, ocso
Monk of Mount Saint Joseph Abbey
Roscrea, County Tipperary, Ireland

## Early Years—Education

Richard Kevin Boylan was born on February 3, 1904 in Bray, County Wicklow, twelve miles south of Dublin. His youth was spent in Derry, northern Ireland, where his father was a bank manager. He had two brothers, Stephen and Gerard, and two sisters, Moyra and Kathleen. All but Gerard would one day be religious. For his secondary schooling, Kevin as he was known then (later Eugene in religious life and the name I will use henceforth) attended the famous O'Connell School in Dublin run by the Christian Brothers. His father, Richard, was a graduate of the school. During the school term, Eugene lived with his uncle in Dublin and spent the holidays at home in Derry.

Eugene used "R.K." for a signature and was known as "Orky" in his later school years and at the university. He did not particularly like the nickname.

His mother, Agnes Colclough-Boylan, was musically gifted as would be her children. Local priests often gathered at the Boylan house for an evening of music with Mrs. Boylan at the piano. Thus, Eugene grew up in a family atmosphere where priests frequented the house, and where music and cultural interests played a considerable part in the family's own entertainment and leisure activities.

After his father retired and the family moved to Dublin, Mrs. Boylan taught music and singing, mainly plainsong, in the schools. She was well-known in musical circles. She also had a great love for theater, herself being a flamboyant personality. There is no doubt that Eugene took after her in this regard. He always spoke warmly and affectionately of his mother and readily expressed his admiration of her. He especially enjoyed telling stories in which she figured as causing surprise or astonishment to passersby. Eugene's father was a quiet, devout man whom Eugene would later refer to as the "Saint Joseph of our house."

**University**

Eugene entered the archdiocesan seminary at Clonliffe College, Dublin. From there he attended University College Dublin, as was the custom for all students for the priesthood. His brother Stephen, two years older than Eugene, was studying for the priesthood as well. After two years in the seminary, Eugene decided that the diocesan priesthood was not for him. He left the seminary but continued at University College to study science.

Eugene excelled in the sciences and maths. He was keen on debating and joined the university's debate club. Here he honed his natural flair for public speaking. With his excellent voice and the foundation laid in the debate club, he developed a powerful and commanding delivery which served him well throughout his life.

Coming from a musical family, Eugene played the piano with flair, was a very fine singer, and had a first-class ear for music. He enjoyed sports as well, particularly swimming. He competed in national swimming events and developed the barrel chest of a powerful swimmer. His gait was slightly awkward; he tended to roll in his walk.

Eugene was remembered by contemporaries as pleasant and easygoing. He was attentive to the uncertainty and shyness of students who were only just beginning their time at the university. One student remembers Eugene writing "NBG" on a piece of faulty equipment. When the student took this for some arcane scientific reference and asked what it meant ("no bloody good"), Eugene laughed and told him he would have to learn that mathematical formula quickly or else be in trouble. Eugene excelled in his studies. Upon graduation he earned a Rockefeller traveling scholarship which enabled him to study abroad for two years. He elected to study in Vienna.

## Vienna

The city of Vienna had emerged from the First World War intact, but with the Austro-Hungarian Empire gone. While slowly adjusting to the changes in its fortunes and history, it still held much of the magic of the old Vienna in the pre-1914 years. For Eugene, fresh from the insularity of Ireland and the smallness of Dublin, it was a place of wonder.

Eugene was in a world capital, one of the most cultured cities of Europe, and he made full use of it. He regularly attended the opera and the great orchestral concerts. However, like all students, he was often short of cash, so he and a friend would buy one score between them and follow the music from it. Despite their being banned by law, duels still took place occasionally between members of the student fraternities. Eugene recalled some of his adventures in this area, acting as second on one occasion to a former cavalry officer, who left his opponent, a fraternity bully, neatly pinstriped with saber cuts from neck to waist. (Perhaps some of the stories grew with the years.) The beer cellars, the *heurigen* (wine taverns) with their new wines, skiing and mountain climbing, the fellowship of a large international student body—all delighted him.

A small detail that emerged during his time in Vienna was his genuine phobia about snakes. One evening, he and his friend from Dublin stopped at a fashionable shoe shop to admire the window display with snakeskin shoes grouped around two large stuffed snakes. As soon as Eugene saw these, he took off in terror and did not stop until he was a block away. When his friend caught up with him, Eugene was shaking and unable to speak—the mere sight of the snakes having such an effect on him.

More important than the cultural attractions of Vienna was the intellectual stimulation of working with professors leading the world in the fields of science and mathematics. It has been asserted by some that Eugene was associated with the beginnings of the Atomic Age by working with Ernest Rutherford (1871–1937) on atomic fission. No evidence supports this. Eugene's published papers were about atmospheric ionization rather than anything to do with atomic fission.

Returning to Dublin, Eugene took up a lectureship at University College and quickly settled into the academic life. Had he remained there he most likely would have become a department head.

## Change of Direction

For several years Eugene yearned for something more than secular life could give him. He was a member of the "conventional" Catholic societies—the Sodality and the Vincent de Paul Society—but there was something more which he was seeking. Eugene had a Jesuit spiritual director who recommended that he go to Mount Saint Joseph Abbey in Roscrea to test a possible vocation to the Cistercian life. It should be noted that Stephen had entered the Carthusians at St. Hugh's Charterhouse in England, and Moyra was a nun in the order of Marie Reparatrix. In 1932, Kathleen would join the Cistercians (Trappistines) at Glencairn, Ireland.[1] His family's support for the religious voca-

1. Father Stephen Boylan was born on October 25, 1906. He was ordained a diocesan priest on May 18, 1930. He professed solemn vows on August 9, 1935 at St. Hugh's Charterhouse at Parkminster, England. He died on April 6, 1987.

Moyra Boylan joined the order of Marie Reparatrix. Her name in the order was Sister Mary of St. Fintan. She made her vows on February 1, 1931 and died in Cincinnati, Ohio on April 15, 1967.

Kathleen Josephine Boylan was born in 1909. She entered the Cistercian monastery of Glencairn [Ireland] on September 8, 1932. Her religious name was Sister Mary Magdalen. She professed solemn monastic vows on February 3, 1938 and died on January 2, 1982, in her fiftieth year as a Cistercian. "I lived with Sr. Magdalen for 20 years here in Glencairn. She loved music [and] was very careful in her work. She was sacristan when I was a young nun, and I remember her absolutely gorgeous flower arrangements for the sanctuary on big feasts. She was honest and truthful and a very humble person in the nicest way. She had Parkinson's disease for some years before her death, but she was very independent and insisted on continuing to fend for herself as much as possible." Sister

tion had an effect on Eugene. In addition, the Irish society at the time was markedly Catholic in its outlook and ethos. Devotionalism and a strong moral sense marked the Irish Church.

Eugene entered the abbey at Roscrea on September 8, 1931 and received the novice habit on October 11. He had come to the monastery with excellent recommendations from all sides—a brilliant and gifted young university lecturer, well-traveled, and the son of a devout and well-known family. He also was manifestly renouncing a promising academic career.

The novice master at Roscrea was Father Malachy Brasil, who later became abbot of Mount Saint Bernard in England.[2] Although Father Malachy was at Roscrea only during the time of Eugene's novitiate, his moderation and kindness inspired the young man. Eugene often quoted Father Malachy up to the end of his life. In addition to his duties as novice master, Father Malachy was prior of the monastery. His assistant, Father Camillus Claffey (later abbot of Roscrea) had more to do with the novices on a day-to-day basis than the novice master himself. It is probably true that Father Camillus never understood the brilliant young man who had entered the monastery. Indeed, he was overawed by Eugene. As a result, Father Camillus tended to be defensive in his relations with Eugene. Yet, Eugene had a great and lasting veneration for the older monks, and his admiration for them had fueled the fires of his own resolve and perseverance.

After two years in the novitiate, Eugene professed simple monastic vows and came under the care of Father Columban

---

Veronica Gertrude Kelly, Glencairn Abbey, "Sister Magdalen," June 28, 2006, personal email (June 29, 2006).

The youngest member of the Boylan family, Gerard, married and died in Dublin.

2. Dom Malachy Thomas Brasil was born in 1883 and entered Roscrea Abbey in 1905. He was elected abbot of Mount Saint Bernard in 1933 and served until 1959. He spent his last years at Sancta Maria Abbey (Nunraw, Scotland), the daughterhouse of Mount Saint Joseph (Roscrea) where his former novice, Dom Columban Mulcahy, was abbot. Dom Malachy died on July 28, 1965 and is buried at Nunraw. Dom Malachy attributed his love for the contemplative way of life to a retreat given at Roscrea Abbey by Dom Columba Marmion at the beginning of 1914.

Mulcahy, later the abbot of Nunraw in Scotland.[3] Father Columban was strict (somewhat military in his exercise of authority) and totally devoted to the monastic ideal. Father Columban and Father Malachy both positively influenced Eugene. In them, he found kindred spirits to whom he could talk and unburden himself.

Eugene professed solemn monastic vows on October 15, 1936. At that time, all choir monks were destined for ordination to the priesthood. Brother Eugene took eagerly to study. He read widely and avidly, even reading the entire *Summa Theologica* of Saint Thomas. He always held that this stood to him as nothing else in his studies.

Eugene was appointed to teach in the secondary school attached to the monastery. Scarcely a success in the classroom—Eugene was more of a university lecturer than a teacher of teenage boys—he was still popular with the students. This was partly due to the tales he could tell about life in Vienna.

Eugene was ordained a priest on May 9, 1937 and appointed to teach philosophy to the young monks. Ecclesiastical studies followed a carefully planned path at that time; there was little room for originality. Eugene taught with an enthusiasm which he passed on to at least some of his students. Eventually, he was appointed to teach moral theology.

In addition to his teaching duties, Eugene was one of the confessors in the public church of the abbey. Frequent confession was the norm at the time and four priests were regularly assigned to hear confessions. Eugene gained a reputation for kindness and understanding. His wide reading and comprehensive theological knowledge stood him in good stead. He had many requests for spiritual direction, particularly from the religious and

3. Dom Columban Mulcahy, born in 1901, entered Roscrea in 1924 at age 23. In 1948, he was elected the first abbot of Sancta Maria Abbey in Nunraw, Scotland, founded by Mount Saint Joseph (Roscrea) in 1946. He died on July 15, 1971, several weeks after a cerebral hemorrhage. He played a key role in the ecumenical movement in Scotland between 1961 and 1966.

priests in the active ministry. It was from this experience that he decided to write his first book, *Difficulties in Mental Prayer*.

**Teaching on Prayer**

*Difficulties in Mental Prayer*, published in 1944, was an immediate success. Some thought the title unfortunate, but most found that it showed them how they might solve problems in their prayer lives. Endless requests came for Eugene to give retreats, but in the climate of the time, these were invariably refused. It was only much later that he would give retreats in Australia and the United States of America.

Eugene had two outstanding charisms as a spiritual director and confessor. He could meet any account of a situation or a problem with a sympathy. He was non-judgmental and inspired enormous confidence in others. While it was clear in his own mind about where right and wrong lay, he never condemned anyone or turned anyone away. Secondly, he could see where a course of action was leading, long before the one seeking advice. He had great common sense and brought this to bear on any problem he encountered.

In his theology classes, Eugene frequently quoted a statement of Saint Alphonsus, who said that he had never refused anyone absolution. Eugene proposed this as the ideal for any confessor. He also firmly believed in the virtue of "keeping your mouth shut." He repeated this as an axiom for the counselor, embellishing the phrase with suitable adjectives. Years later, shortly before leaving Australia, he gave conferences on confessional practice and spiritual direction to the priests of the monastic community at Tarrawarra. He returned to the same admonitions: do not judge people, never express surprise at anything, realize your own weakness and sinfulness, one's own need of mercy, and above all, "keep your mouth shut" unless you see some positive good to be done by talking.

Eugene had read the Cistercian Fathers (mostly in Latin), but they had not really influenced his own work on prayer. He found the schemata and clearly defined divisions and distinctions of Father Adolphe Tanquerey's *The Spiritual Life* (1930) attractive, so he taught spirituality along the same lines.[4, 5] No doubt his scientific training and mathematical mind found this approach congenial, but he always held the person and not the method as primary. Therefore, he was never satisfied with a mechanical or stereotyped presentation on prayer.

> Now, prayer, especially from the individual's point of view, can often be very indefinite and quite unclassifiable. Further, even if there does exist a well-marked ladder of prayer for each individual, it is by no means necessary, at least as a general rule, to know on which rung one is standing. The important thing is to avoid standing still, and to keep on climbing.[6]

Eugene's writings and teachings could certainly be applied to monks and nuns living in the cloister, but one wonders if it could really be classified as monastic spirituality. There are two main reasons for this. First, Eugene was writing for priests and active religious. They were the ones who consulted him and sought his spiritual direction, thus *Difficulties in Mental Prayer* was written. The articles he wrote for religious magazines and reviews catered to a similar audience. Eugene would eventually write two books especially for priests: *The Spiritual Life of the Priest* (1949) and *The Priest's Way to God* (1963). Secondly, the spirituality of the Irish Cistercian monasteries in the 1940s was pervaded by the Sulpician spirituality of the 19th century. This spirituality was geared toward the formation of priests and con-

4. *The Spiritual Life: A Treatise on Ascetical and Mystical Theology*, 2nd ed. and trans. Herman Branderis (Desclée, Belgium: Society of Saint John the Evangelist, 1930; Westminster, Md.: Newman, 1947). "This work [*The Spiritual Life*], which has been translated into English, is a mine of information on every part of the spiritual life, and should be in the library of every religious house, even of those who have not been trained in theology. It is the outstanding work of reference in the spiritual life." Eugene Boylan, *Difficulties in Mental Prayer* (Westminster, Md.: Newman, 1946), p. 75.

5. Father Adolphe Tanquerey (1854–1932), a French Sulpician, was a celebrated scholar who wrote on dogmatic, moral and ascetic theology. His work in dogmatic theology is presented in a two-volume *Manual of Dogmatic Theology* (New York: Desclee, 1959).

6. Boylan, *Difficulties in Mental Prayer* (Westminster, Md.: Newman, 1946), p. xiii.

tained strict observances and regulations (such as self-abnegation and silence) also found in Cistercian-Trappist monasteries.[7] Eugene was influenced by this French school and frequently quoted Cardinal Pierre de Bérulle (1575–1629) and Father Charles de Condren (1588–1641) in his conferences.[8] Writers such as Dom Columba Marmion and Odo Casel were only beginning to influence the spiritual life of the cloister.[9]

Critics of *Difficulties in Mental Prayer* were severe on Eugene for patronizing the diocesan clergy. Such criticism was misplaced. Eugene was trying to encourage all priests to take prayer seriously and consider themselves called to the highest states of prayer. His book was used in novitiates and seminaries not only

7. In 1642, Jean-Jacques Olier (1608–1657), a disciple of Cardinal Pierre de Bérulle, founded the Society of St. Sulpice, dedicated to the education of priests. This religious association was responsible for the establishment of seminaries in France, Canada, and the United States. "Sulpician spirituality" became the norm for the spiritual formation of seminarians prior to Vatican II.

8. "Let us note that the doctrine of our association with the mysteries of Christ's life is used as the foundation for the teaching of one of the finest schools of spirituality we have: that, namely, which is founded in the writings of Berulle, Condren, Father Olier, and Saint John Eudes." Eugene Boylan, *The Mystical Body* (Westminster, Md.: Newman, 1948), p. 62.

These words should be balanced with comments made by Dom Eugene in a talk to religious sisters of the Society of the Sacred Heart of Jesus in 1960: "Even that wonderful school of spirituality that is associated with St. John Eudes, M. Olier, Conderon, Berulle is contaminated with a hated of the flesh, of the human person as consisting of a soul locked up in a vile body. Heresy! And it makes the Incarnation inexplicable. A human person consists of a body and a soul, and our bodies are just as much part of our person as our soul is. Both have to be sanctified and both are holy." Sisters of the Society of the Sacred Heart of Jesus, mimeographed transcription of talks by Dom Eugene Boylan at Duchesne College of the Sacred Heart and convent, Omaha, Nebraska, March 24–27, 1960, talk 4, p. 1. Hereafter cited as "Boylan, talk to Sisters" followed by the talk number, page number.

9. Blessed Columba Marmion, (1858–1923) was beatified on September 3, 2000 by Pope John Paul II. He was a prolific writer on spirituality. His famous trilogy is *Christ in His Mysteries* (1919), *Christ the Ideal of the Monk* (1922), and *Christ the Life of the Soul* (1917).

Odo Casel (1886–1948) was a Benedictine monk of the Abbey of Maria Laach in Germany, near Bonn. He developed mystical theology in *The Mystery of Christian Worship* (1932).

in Ireland but throughout the English-speaking world. It was translated into the main European languages and went through several editions. *Difficulties in Mental Prayer* established Eugene as a spiritual teacher of the first rank. In the opinion of some, it was his best book. While he used the writings of the great masters of the tradition, he rarely quotes them in the book. Rather, he made their teaching his own. He most often quoted the New Testament—his two favorite writers being Saint Paul and Saint John. The commentaries he used most for Saint Paul was *The Theology of Saint Paul* by Fernand Prat, SJ (1857–1938) and *The Whole Christ* by Emile Mersch, SJ (1890–1940).[10, 11]

Eugene's approach to Scripture was that of his period. He was writing at the time when Pope Pius XII's encyclical *Divino Afflante Spiritu* (On the Promotion of Biblical Studies, 1942) was making an impact. For Eugene, the Gospels were the vivid retelling of what it was like to know Jesus Christ, but it was in Saint Paul's epistles where he found two central ideas that he used in his talks and writings—the all sufficiency of Christ, and the Church as Christ's Body.

Eugene frequently spoke in his conferences to the Roscrea community on how Christ alone was the glory of the Father. If we would please God, it must be through our entering into Christ and putting on Christ. In his later years, he cultivated a habit of ending sermons and conferences with, "Through Him, with Him, in Him in the unity of the Holy Spirit, is all the glory of the Father."[12] He emphasized the repeated word *Him*, so that it came out as a ringing affirmation of a profound theological truth. This was all the more effective in those days of the Latin Mass when

10. Fernand Prat, SJ, *The Theology of Saint Paul,* trans. John L. Stoddard, 11th French ed., 2 vols., (Westminster, Md.: Newman, 1956). Also by Prat: *Jesus Christ: His Life, His Teaching, and His Work* (Milwaukee: Bruce Pub. Co., 1950).

11. Emile Mersch, SJ, *The Whole Christ,* trans. John R. Kelly, SJ, 2nd French ed., Religion and Culture Series (Milwaukee: Bruce, 1938). The first French edition was published in 1933. Also by Mersch: *The Theology of the Mystical Body* (St. Louis: Herder, 1951).

12. In four of his books—*Difficulties in Mental Prayer, The Mystical Body, The Spiritual Life of the Priest,* and *This Tremendous Lover*—Boylan concludes with the doxology.

the phrase was not heard as frequently as it is today. (On the other hand, it could become rather tiresome after awhile, and when listening to his conferences one sometimes wondered when it was going to be said!)

A subject to which he applied this truth was the Divine Office. He spoke of how the Office is the prayer of Christ. He had read Saint Augustine's *Ennerationes* on the Psalms and loved to quote the saint saying that when the Church prays, the one voice of Christ is heard throughout the world.[13] He considered the Breviary as the prayer of the Church and central to the spirituality of the priest.[14] Eugene would, for example, defend a priest who turned immediately to his Breviary after saying Mass. He held that this often showed a humility and an awareness of the profound meaning of the "prayer of Christ."

### *This Tremendous Lover*

*This Tremendous Lover* was published in 1946. It was his *summa* of spirituality. One of the first quotations in the book is from Saint Augustine: "There shall be one Christ, loving himself."[15] Eugene used this statement repeatedly in his sermons and conferences to sum up the culmination of the life of faith. As the Christian "puts on Christ" he becomes one with him, and so Augustine's

13. Saint Augustine's commentary on Psalm 54 and 85.

14. "Now the Divine Office is an entering into the prayer of Christ; it is a putting-on of the prayer of Christ; it is an identification with the prayer of Christ; it is an abiding in the Vine. Therefore, when the priest opens his Breviary, he 'enters into' the prayer of Christ in a much more real way than a monk, coming into choir where the office is being sung, 'enters-in' to the prayer of the community. It is the prayer of Christ that the priest is praying. Christ is praying in him; he is praying in Christ. He is praying in the name of Christ and in the name of each of His members." Eugene Boylan, *The Spiritual Life of the Priest* (Westminster, Md.: Newman, 1949), p. 38. Dom Eugene is writing to priests, but his words can be applied to all Christians devoted to the Divine Office.

15. In Latin: *Et erit unus Christus seipsum amans.* Saint Augustine, Homily 10 on the Epistle of St. John (1 John 5:1-3) in The Works of St. Augustine, *Nicene and Post-Nicene Fathers*, vol. 7, first series, ed. Philip Schaff (1888; reprint, Peabody, Mass.: Hendrickson, 1995), p. 521.

vision is realized. This could be called the major theme of the book.[16]

**Australia**

Roscrea Abbey founded the monastery of Sancta Maria at Nunraw, Scotland in 1946. With the monks at Roscrea still numerous, consideration was given to founding a monastery in Australia. One of the monks, Father Ignatius Keneally, had worked as a priest for some years in the goldfields of Kalgoorlie and often urged the community to begin a foundation in his beloved Australia. He was in touch with Archbishop Mannix of Melbourne who favored the project as well. However, the uncertainty of the international situation, so soon after World War II, made emigration into Australia difficult.

In June 1952, Cardinal Gilroy of Sydney visited Roscrea Abbey and urged the community to proceed with plans for a foundation in Australia. Dom Camillus sent Eugene to Australia to look for potential sites. Eugene arrived in Sydney on September 15, 1953. He was unsuccessful in locating property in the hinterland of Sydney, so he went south to Melbourne where Archbishop Mannix welcomed him. Finally, Eugene found property at Tarrawarra, Yarra Glenn (30 miles north of Melbourne). Dom Camillus came to verify the suitability of the property and subsequently 1,000 acres were purchased for the monastery which would be called at the time Notre Dame (today Tarrawarra Abbey).

Father Cronin Sherry was appointed superior of the new monastery; Eugene was procurator. Perhaps Eugene felt disappointed

16. "The whole Christian life, then, is Christ and His love. We ourselves live and love no longer, it is Christ who lives and loves in us. In us Christ loves the Father, and the Father loves Christ in us. Christ in us loves our neighbour, and in our neighbour we love Christ. Christ in the husband loves the wife, and in the wife the husband loves Christ. So also Christ in the wife loves the husband, and in the husband the wife loves Christ. Christ is our supplement, our complement, our All in fact, both in loving and being loved. 'And there shall be one Christ loving Himself.' For 'Christ is all and in all' [Lk 9:41-42]." Eugene Boylan, *This Tremendous Lover* (Westminster, Md.: Newman, 1947; Notre Dame, In.: Ave Maria Press, 1964), p. 333. This and subsequent quotes from *This Tremendous Lover* are used with permission from Ave Maria Press.

at not being appointed superior, but it did not seem so to the other members of the foundation. The superior would be in office for a few years and then there would be an election for the first abbot. If the community wanted him then, they could elect him. Also, it was hardly to be expected that Dom Camillus would have appointed him superior. Eugene was not a man with whom he would be totally sympathetic.

Eugene had reveled in the job of searching for the site of the foundation. He had given lectures and conferences to priests and religious in the eastern Australian dioceses. He could talk grandly of acquiring property, of borrowing large sums of money, of doing this and achieving that. He had deadlines to meet and appointments with government ministers and members of the hierarchy to keep. This was the life he loved. In addition, he was in at the very beginning of a great and historic venture—the foundation of the first Cistercian community in Australia.[17]

The main group arrived in Melbourne at the end of September 1954.[18] They were met by Eugene, along with Dom Camillus and two other Roscrea monks who had flown out ahead of them. The house at Tarrawarra was not ready for occupation, so they lived for several weeks in a house owned by the Sisters of Charity.

Shortly after the founding monks arrived, an incident took place which was typical of Eugene. A group of monks were standing one evening talking to Dom Camillus when a car, a Jaguar sports model, roared in the driveway and the driver, clearly not expecting to meet anyone, swerved quickly around them and disappeared behind the house. Moments later, Eugene emerged humming nonchalantly. Dom Camillus looked at him and asked, a little uncertainly, if that was a new car, as he had not seen it before. Eugene replied breezily that it was not new. It was second hand, a bargain, had only cost so much, and really its purchase was a matter of saving money and so forth. In the end no one quite knew

17. The foundation made by the French Cistercians at Beagle Bay in Western Australia in 1890 had not survived.

18. The formal opening of Notre Dame Abbey was December 19, 1954. On November 29, 1958, Father Kevin O'Farrell, who was novice master at Mount Saint Joseph (Roscrea), was elected the first abbot. He served until September 17, 1988.

why he had bought it or what it had cost. The real reason, however, was that it is much more exciting to drive a Jaguar than a half-ton pickup truck, which was what was needed. This fascination with cars and speed stayed with Eugene until the end of his life.

No sooner had the main party arrived in Australia than Dom Camillus announced that the abbot general, Dom Gabriel Sortais, had appointed Eugene as superior *ad nutum* for the monastery on Caldey Island in Wales.[19] The community there was in some difficulty and needed strong leadership to bring about both economic stability and unity within the community. Eugene would be superior of the monastery for an indefinite period until the community was in a position to elect an abbot. Eugene could not leave Tarrawarra immediately since he was committed to speak at the first Australian National Liturgical Congress in January 1955.[20]

The diocesan clergy expressed their best wishes to Eugene. He was very much a "man's man" and well liked by the many priests who had gotten to know him. His monastic community, too, was losing a well-known figure who did much in establishing the Cistercians in Australia.

## Caldey Island

Caldey Island, about three miles by one mile in extent, is situated off the Welsh coast in the Bristol Channel. It had been a monastic settlement since early Christian times. In the last century, the island had been the place of the re-foundation of the monastic life, under the leadership of Father Aelred Carlyle, in the Church of England. In March 1913, the majority of this Anglican community was received into the Roman Catholic Church. Eventually, they found that the economics of life on an offshore

19. As a point of interest, Dom Eugene preached a retreat to the Caldey monastic community in 1950.

20. The title of his paper at the Congress was "The Liturgy and Personal Holiness." His definition of holiness is worth quoting: "Holiness consists in receiving and making our own the holiness we derive from Christ, rather than in the mere perfecting of ourselves . . . until we are filled with him, until nothing is wanting to us in any grace." He then went on to show how the liturgy draws us into Christ, changes our prayer pattern, and rids us of self-centered piety.

island was too difficult, so they left in October 1928 and resettled at Prinknash, near Gloucestershire.[21]

The Holy See asked the Cistercians to take over the island in order that it might remain a monastic settlement. In response, the community of the Abbey of Scourmont in Belgium established a Cistercian monastery on the island in 1929.[22] The community remained firmly Belgian until after World War II. It was a bit awkward for young Englishmen joining a monastery located in their native land to find a lifestyle more European than English. The reading in the refectory, for example, was in French. In addition to this tension between nationalities was the economics of a monastery located on an island. The superior since 1946 was Father Albert Derzelle.[23] In September 1954, Father Albert, exhausted mentally and physically, tendered his resignation. Eugene was subsequently appointed superior *ad nutum*.[24] His mandate, although never spelled out, was to anglicize the community and make it economically viable.

21. A history of the Benedictine monks on Caldey Island is given by Peter F. Anson, *The Benedictines of Caldey: The Story of the Anglican Benedictines of Caldey and Their Submission to the Catholic Church* (London: Catholic Book Club, 1940).

22. The community at Scourmont Abbey voted on the Feast of Saint Benedict, March 21, in 1928 to establish a foundation on Caldey Island. The founders arrived on the island on January 2, 1929, but the official foundation date is January 6, 1929, the feast of the Epiphany. See Roscoe Howells, *Total Community: The Monks of Caldey Island* (Tenby [Great Britain]: H.G. Walters, 1975).

23. Father Albert Derzelle was prior at Chimay Abbey (Belgium) when he was appointed prior of Caldey on February 12, 1946. He subsequently was elected as prior. On September 14, 1954, he resigned due to physical and mental exhaustion. In 1957, he went to Notre Dame des Mokoto in what was then Zaire (now Democratic Republic of Congo). He was superior there from March 9, 1967 to December 31, 1981. He was then chaplain at La Clarté-Dieu, Murhesa (also in Zaire) from 1985 to 1991. He died on April 11, 1993 at La Clarté-Dieu where he is buried.

24. Until Dom Eugene arrived at Caldey in February 1955, Dom Godefroid Bélorgey filled-in as superior. A Frenchman, Dom Godefroid Bélorgey, entered Scourmont Abbey in Belgium at the age of 30. He was novice master and prior before serving as auxiliary abbot of Cîteaux from 1932 to 1952. He spent two years at Caldey (1953 to 1955). He then was chaplain at the Trappistine monastery of Our Lady of Peace in Chimay (Belgium). He returned to Scourmont in April 1964 and died six months later on September 15. He wrote several books. *The Practice of Mental Prayer* was translated into English in 1952 (Westminster, Md.: Newman Press).

Many of Eugene's friends wondered how he would fare now that he had a house of his own to govern. The verdict must be that he was not entirely successful. He failed to have himself accepted by the Belgians in the community, although some of the other monks liked him very much, finding him congenial and helpful. To some extent this was true of Eugene wherever he went—people either loved him or found him "hard to take." Perhaps this is the case with any strong personality.

The economy of Caldey was parlous when Eugene was appointed superior. Living on an island required the transportation to and from the mainland every item for sale or purchase. The cost of living was high. Transport charges limited the profits of farm produce. The greatest opportunity for developing a self-sufficient community (financial stability) came from tourism, especially during the summer months.

An attempt was made to come up with a product made by the monks that could be sold to visitors. In 1953, two years prior to the arrival of Eugene, a perfume made from lavender and other flowers growing wild on the island was sold for the first time. With the help of a Polish pharmacist and perfumer, Henry Kobus, hand lotion made from natural ingredients as well as other perfumes were added to the monastery's products. Eugene was friendly with one of the leading Irish *couture* designers who publicized the perfumes and lotion. The perfume enterprise made headlines. Shops for Caldey products, which now included soaps and cosmetic items, were opened in the resort town of Saundersfoot and in London. Both shops have since been closed, but the perfume industry at Caldey continues as a small part of the monastic income.

Even with the demands of his position as superior, Eugene spoke at universities and Catholic meetings. There was no shortage of invitations, and he enjoyed speaking before groups. These speaking engagements publicized Caldey, but whether it brought postulants to the monastery is less certain.

Eugene had been superior of the monastery on Caldey Island for four years. His greatest contribution, apart from the guidance he gave to individuals in their vocation and spiritual lives, was assisting the community in finding an identity for itself. By 1959, the community had become financially self-supporting for the first time. With this economic stability and an adequate number of solemn professed monks, Caldey was promoted to the status of an abbey and preparations were made for an abbatial election.

Eugene emphasized to the community the necessity of electing someone from within their ranks, preferably an Englishman. Eugene, of course, was not permitted to vote since he was a monk of Roscrea Abbey. The community did as he suggested when they elected 38-year-old Father James Wicksteed.[25] Shortly after the election, Eugene returned to Roscrea. Did he expect to be elected as abbot of Caldey? It is likely that he did, despite his exhortations to the community. He never referred to the election in Caldey as a disappointment, but several in the community were convinced that he anticipated being elected as the community's first abbot.[26]

When Eugene left Wales to return to Ireland, he left many friends behind him. Volunteers, men and women, had spent summers during his time at Caldey working for the monastery—staffing the souvenir shops and serving in the guesthouse and tea rooms. His friends remained loyal to him. Even when they criticized him, they did so with affection and admiration.

Returning to Roscrea after the years in Tarrawarra and Caldey, Eugene settled into the work in the confessional and giving retreats. He enjoyed both, but it was the retreat work for which he became popular. It was not easy for the abbot of Roscrea Abbey to continue refusing requests for retreats by Eugene. Diocesan priests and religious in the United States invited Eugene to give retreats and conferences. His retreats were inspirational and his books, especially *This Tremendous Lover* and *Difficulties in Mental Prayer*, continued in popularity.

25. Dom James served as abbot until March 14, 1980.

26. "The Irish monks seemed to think that Dom Eugene had not been fully appreciated. They gained the impression, however, that it had come as a relief to him not to have been chosen as Abbot. He said to some of them, 'The big problem was that my mother had bought a new hat in readiness for the occasion'—which seems to suggest that he took it in the right spirit. And this indeed is the truth of the matter, because he was undeniably very disappointed but demonstrated that, if he did have some shortcomings, he was a 'big' man." Roscoe Howells, *Total Community: The Monks of Caldey Island*, p. 171.

## Abbot of Roscrea Abbey

Dom Camillus Claffey, in his eighteenth year as abbot of Roscrea Abbey, tendered his resignation in 1962.[27] Eugene, 58 years old, was elected as Roscrea's fourth abbot by a narrow majority on July 11, 1962. He received the abbatial blessing on August 5. The community looked forward to having Eugene as their abbot for at least ten years, but less than eighteen months later he would be dead. Many felt that Eugene had not an adequate opportunity to achieve anything significant or to leave his mark. Eugene did, however, make a notable contribution to the community. He continued to offer monks spiritual guidance through his conferences, and he was ready to allow people the freedom he preached.

Shortly before he died, Eugene expressed to one of the monks his disappointment at how little impact he had made on the community. He expected that by virtue of his teaching, which was certainly of the first order, people would change. Communities are probably the same the world over—a net full of mixed fish as in the Gospel. Some monks are eager and enthusiastic, others less so. It was naïve of him to think that in a little over a year he would have changed people much. He believed in the goodness of people. If they were given the lead through his preaching and teaching, he thought an early harvest would result. This did not happen. The monks remained much as they were and life went on.

What then was his legacy at Roscrea? His entry in 1931 opened up the monastery to a wider world than it had known up to then. In the early 1930s the community was introverted, and knew little of life outside Ireland, or indeed outside the political categories of the time. Not only did the politics of the Civil War (1922) still dominate, but the idea that there was a completely different way of looking at things had not made much headway.[28] Whether

27. Dom Camillus was elected abbot of Mount Saint Joseph (Roscrea) on September 25, 1944. His resignation was accepted on February 21, 1962. He died on July 28, 1971.

28. "The Irish Civil War (June 28, 1922–May 24, 1923) was a conflict between supporters and opponents of the Anglo-Irish Treaty of December 6, 1921, which established the Irish Free State, precursor of today's Republic of Ireland. Opponents of the Treaty objected to the fact that it retained constitutional links between

the monks came from Dublin or the rural areas, the struggle for national independence, in which some of them had taken part, characterized their thinking. The Irish Church outside the monastery had little impact on it. Moreover, as a strict Trappist community, they had little to do with what they sincerely regarded as dangerous and alien to themselves—"the world." That mold was broken by this man with university credentials and a wealth of experience in the world. The very fact that Eugene persevered and professed solemn vows in 1936, in itself, opened the community to wider horizons.

Eugene's second contribution to Roscrea, and to the countless others who came to him seeking help and direction, was to break away from the legalistic spirituality of the time and lead people into a new freedom. The spirituality of the monks (as of the then Church) was one of merit, of observance, and of law, and thus rather minimalist. That it sanctified many cannot be doubted, but that it was the fullness of the Gospel of Jesus Christ as the Redeemer cannot be asserted without qualification either.

Into this climate of duty and legalism came Eugene Boylan with his incisive mind, his eagerness for knowledge, and his voracious appetite for reading. He quickly saw that it was in the New Testament—particularly in Saint Paul's epistles—that one could find a true Christian spirituality, and he went straight to that. He also read widely in the history of spirituality. Pourrat's four volume *Christian Spirituality,* which even today remains an influential work, delighted him.[29] From it he went to the Fathers, notably Saint Augustine and Saint Thomas, and eventually to the best available commentaries on Saint Paul. With such reading it was impossible that he would not come to see the weakness of the current spirituality, and without criticizing it, go beyond it to what he was to call over and over again "partnership with Christ."

---

the United Kingdom and Ireland, and that the six counties of Northern Ireland would not be included in the Free State. The Civil War cost the lives of more than had died in the War of Independence that preceded it. It left Irish society deeply divided and its influence in Irish politics can still be seen to this day" Wikipedia, "Irish Civil War," <http://en.wikipedia.org/wiki/Irish_Civil_War>.

29. Pierre Pourrat, ss, *Christian Spirituality,* 4 vols. (1927; Westminster, Md.: Newman, 1953).

> The whole plan of our spiritual life is a loving union and intimate partnership with Jesus in which we return Him love for love. We can picture that union in three ways: as the life of Christ in us; as our life in Christ; or as what we might call a "shoulder-to-shoulder" partnership with Jesus, a constant companionship of two lovers sharing every thought and every deed. Each of these pictures corresponds to a true aspect of the reality, the intimacy of which is so extraordinary that it defies description.[30]

Thus he changed the spirituality of many and led them from the half-light of a feared and fearful God to the splendors of the Risen Christ.

A third aspect of Eugene's legacy is that he definitely "opened the windows" of Roscrea to admit change. No doubt some were not ready for this. Formed in the over-regulated regime of the 1930s and 40s, they found the liberty of the 1960s beyond them and unacceptable. This is true, but it is equally true that the change had to come. It came best from a man who believed in it totally himself, rather than someone who gave way only reluctantly to the pressures of the time. Eugene, however, believed in freedom and felt that if he gave people responsibility they would act responsibly.

It may be asked how he would have dealt with the changes that came in the wake of the Second Vatican Council. He would probably have resisted some of them, for he was conservative in many ways. For example, he repeatedly opposed the unification of choir monks and lay brothers in the Cistercian Order when this was proposed in the early 1960s. He felt this would be a mistake and that it would exclude a certain type of vocation from the monasteries. He was convinced that in Ireland, at least, there were men who wanted a simple form of life and who would feel excluded if they had an intellectual sort of formation in the monastery. (This view would still attract some support today.) It is doubtful, however, if he was really in touch with the rapid secularization of Irish society. Moreover, free secondary education for all in Ireland became effective only after his time.[31]

30. Boylan, *This Tremendous Lover,* p. 310.

31. For another glimpse on how Dom Eugene might have viewed the changes brought about by Vatican II, we can turn to his 1960 talk to the sisters of the Society

To the end, Eugene retained a somewhat idealized notion of monastic life and community. There existed in him, alongside the remarkable gift he had for understanding other people and being in sympathy with them, the difficulty which a city-dweller has in understanding the countryman. Eugene tended to think that if the facts were set before people, they would react to them in much the same way as he himself did. Nothing could have been further from the truth.

It might also be noted that after he became abbot his restless intellect sought outlets it did not find. He felt the day-to-day trivia of the office to be tiresome and boring. He undoubtedly had a restless nervous energy for which he did not always find outlets in monastic life. (He would try to work off his frustrations by going out and chopping wood!)

**Death**

It was December 1963. Traditionally, on the day the College of Roscrea closed for Christmas holidays, the parents of the boys attended the school play. The abbot was expected to make a speech and greet the parents afterwards. Eugene had been up

---

of the Sacred Heart of Jesus. "There is one thing you have got to do—you and I and every one of us. Every fifteen years a new generation comes into the Society [of the Sacred Heart of Jesus]. You have got to adapt yourself to them. If you do not do that, the Society will cease to go on. Do not stand too rigidly on the "spirit of our Holy Mother [foundress]" or "our Holy Father [founders]." I am quoting from the pope. I was present at two conferences of major religious superiors, one in Sydney and the other in London. We were addressed both occasions by the delegate. He said, "Now, Reverend Fathers, I am not speaking in my name. To make it clear to you I am going to read what I have to say to you. Please remember that it is the pope who is speaking to you." We were exhorted to reconsider our constitutions, our customs, and the general habit of our life, including our habit, our robes, and everything else—our practices. And not to consider so much what our Holy Father or our Holy Mother did so many hundred years ago—what they said, did, and thought. But, what they would say and think and do if they were alive today, if they had the intelligence to understand the needs of today and the courage and the virtue to adapt themselves to it. That is the Holy Father's opinion. Now, to some extent, we have to adapt ourselves to a newer generation." Boylan, talk to Sisters, 5,7.

early that morning and busy all day. After the play, he entertained a group of distinguished guests to dinner in the guesthouse and then got ready to drive to Sligo, about a three-hour drive from Roscrea. He was to attend the funeral the next day in County Donegal of Bishop William MacNeely, the bishop of Raphoe, who had died on December 11. Normally he would not have gone so far to a funeral, but it was a special occasion since the late bishop had been a priest in Derry when Eugene was a boy and had been a family friend. Eugene felt an obligation to attend.

I was the last one to speak to him before he left. The guests had departed, and we stood on the front steps of the guesthouse. I suggested that since he had had a long day, he should go to bed and start early in the morning. He replied that by going to Sligo he would have three quarters of the journey over and would make it easily to the cathedral the next morning without having to start too early.

I further suggested he should bring someone with him, either to drive or just to help keep him awake by talking. With a characteristic gesture he put his arm around my shoulder and said, "Don't worry about me, son, I'll be alright." It was the last time I saw him alive.

It can scarcely be doubted that Eugene fell asleep driving. The car left the road on a long straight stretch and went nose first into a deep ditch. Eugene was thrown out of the car through the passenger door and lay seriously injured on the ground. It was not until a passing motorist saw the rear lights of the car shining toward the sky that help came. Eugene was rushed to a hospital where he died three weeks later. A seven-inch tear in the pericardium (the membrane surrounding the heart) went unnoticed by the medical staff because the tight strapping around his seven broken ribs prevented bleeding into the heart cavity. When the strapping was removed on January 5, 1964, Eugene died from a heart attack. His death came as a shock. The Roscrea community had been told that he was making a good recovery. The fact was that he had very little chance of survival.

**Assessment**

Eugene had started an autobiography, which still survives among his papers. It covers only a few years of his youth but contains nothing of particular significance. In contrast, he wrote an article in 1961 on Cistercian spirituality for the Dublin-based Dominican magazine *Doctrine and Life*. He expounded his views on the monastic vocation and was, in its own indiscreet way, quite self-revelatory. Eugene's article was a part of a series called "Paths to Holiness." Having often heard him speak in community conferences of the temptation of what he called "careerism" for the monk, I have no doubt that this article distills Eugene's most exact thoughts on what it meant to him to be a Cistercian.[32]

Eugene begins by describing the regulated life which the monk lived at that time. He continues with what he says is most essential—for the monk is to realize that he is seeking God.

> Nothing less will do. His aim is neither perfection, nor the service of God, nor any lesser good. . . . It takes the young monk a long time to see this truth . . . its realization only comes at the end of a long process when the monk realizes that the monastic life is organized to give God not so much the monk's service as the monk's own self. (287)

What God does for the monk, Eugene continues, is infinitely more important than what the monk does for God.

> In his early days the young monk tends to seek what might be called a monastic career. His outlook is like that of the soldier, determined to achieve distinction in his country's service. (287)

Eugene points out that stories from the lives of saints encourages a notion of "achieving" great deeds for the Church. For the common, ordinary religious monk or nun, he cautions, this "achieving," even though it may be a genuine quest for holiness, can be tinged with a self-seeking. He notes that many people

32. The quotes from Dom Eugene's article, "Paths to Holiness, [Part] V: The Cistercians" in the January 1961 issue of *Doctrine and Faith* are used with permission from Dominican Publications, 42, Parnell Square, Dublin 1, <www.dominicanpublications.com>.

regard holiness as they regard, perhaps, one's giftedness in music or painting. One has a natural aptitude for it, and one must work at that.

> But the holiness to which we are called is something that does not correspond to any natural disposition we may have . . . it is a participation in the holiness of Christ, who sanctifies us by communicating to us a share in his own holiness. (288)

This idea of the centrality of Christ and our coming to God only through identification with him is emphasized by Dom Eugene. It took him a long time to learn it.

> Early in his life the monk begins to see the spiritual life as a partnership with Jesus, and if he is willing to make the sacrifices such a partnership involves, he will soon find that Our Lord is generous in manifesting his love and interest in return. (288)

This, too, ends, and the monk enters the desert. Eugene uses the image of the Exodus, which he considered "illustrates and typifies very closely the behavior of the monk at this stage."

> The monk feels that God has led him out into the desert and in some way has abandoned him. He can no longer pray as he used to . . . The monastic life tends to become a monotonous treadmill without meaning or purpose . . . compared with what he could do for souls outside, his present life seems fruitless. For a time perhaps he tries to escape into intellectual studies or into some other interesting occupation. Even if he finds satisfaction in them, it is short-lived. The limitations of his library and the lack of intellectual contact put an early limit to any development in this field, and the general limitations and obligations of the monastic life frustrate most of his efforts to achieve success in any other direction. Providence seems to have abandoned him; in some mysterious way difficulties with superiors arise; his health begins to cause added difficulties, and temptations may renew their attractive promise of an escape from the very displeasing contemplation of himself. For, frequently the monk is his own cross. He is faced with one of the greatest mortifications in the spiritual life—the complete acceptance of himself as he is, even as he has made himself. This becomes harder as his own limitations and insufficiency become more and more apparent. He begins to cry out

> with Saint Paul—"Who will deliver me from this body of death?" (Rom 7;24). (289)

What is the answer?

> Some day, when the time is ripe, and when he has been finally cured of his tendency to put his own name on all that God does for him, he hears the voice of the Lord: "My grace is sufficient for you" (2 Cor 12:9). (289)

The message may not be clear at first, he notes, and it may take a long time to be understood. But when it is finally grasped, the monk turns to God and says that he will glory in his infirmities so that that power of Christ may dwell in him. This is "The Promised Land." Eugene then links this with Saint Benedict's Rule.

> The monk is no longer called to live himself but Christ lives in him . . . his very prayer is the prayer of Christ, and his claims on the Father are those of the Beloved Son. By emptying himself and laying hold of Christ through doing the will of God in humility and love, the monk reaches his vocation which is to love God with the love the Holy Spirit pours into his heart and to live so that Christ lives in him. (290)

It is worth noting that Eugene ends this article with the formula "through Christ and with Christ and in Christ is all the glory of God."

Through his reading of the New Testament, Eugene Boylan had broken out of the ascetical/achievement-based spirituality of the time. He had come to an understanding of the true asceticism that is self-acceptance and total poverty in the presence of God. He had come to understand the true meaning of "putting on Christ"—only when we shed selfishness does the power of Christ come into our lives. This, he said, is the work of a lifetime.[33] It had been the pattern of his own life. He had found

33. "Let us then take as our slogan the words of St. Paul, '*I live, now, not I, but Christ liveth in me*' (Gal 2:20). Let us try to put this into practice. It means forgetting ourselves and remembering Christ. It means giving up our own petty narrow interests and assuming those of Christ. . . . It means that we give up the dream of making of ourselves and our lives something wonderful of our own creation,

intellectual satisfaction in study, but that period had ended with the publication of his books. He had been working desultorily at a book on the Mother of God for a long time, but it may be doubted whether it would have been completed. He had neither the intellectual stimulation nor the library facilities for producing a magisterial work. Yet, this is what he was aiming at, as he considered much of the writing about the Blessed Virgin to be second-rate.

Eugene went to Australia to start a new foundation and was brought back by the abbot general to serve as superior to the community at Caldey Island. The harvest he helped sow in Australia would be reaped by others. It was the same in Caldey—he was not elected, and it can scarcely be doubted that this was a serious blow to his self-esteem, despite his protestations to the contrary.

Eugene returned to Roscrea, and as he wrote this article for *Doctrine and Life*, he must have been trying to come to terms with all this. In one sense there was little achievement in his life. To anyone who is seriously seeking God in a life of prayer, books published or people helped do not add up to achievement, as he realizes that others could do the same and do it better. This is in no way to belittle either the work itself or its importance. What we are talking about is the way it appears to the person doing it, in any assessment of his own life.

Even when he was elected as abbot of Roscrea, he found his impact on the community was less than he had hoped. At age 60, he probably died somewhat a disappointed man. This indicates a certain unreality in him, but it was always there. If one could meet him as an equal, one was "in." If not, then, to some extent, one felt left outside. It is doubtful if anyone got really close to him; he often felt isolated in the community. His tendency was to dominate a relationship, but I believe he was unaware of this.

---

in which we can take pride; instead, we now leave it to Christ to communicate to us and to form in us a beauty that is a reflection of His own and that is of His making. It means complete abandonment to Christ, and complete self-surrender." Boylan, *The Spiritual Life of the Priest*, p. 150.

Any shadows, however, should not be over-emphasized. He was as happy a person as the next. He integrated all that happened to him into an intense spiritual life, but still faced the "ups and downs" of life like the rest of humankind. Eugene was, to use the timeworn phrase, "a man before his time." He helped an enormous number of people, and he did, in fact, change the community in which he lived. He retained to the end a sort of boyishness, shown by his delight in fast cars, in visiting his old university whenever he got the chance, and in the fondness of his recollections of Vienna. There he had walked in Arcady, and he never forgot it.

Eugene's legacy endures in a Christ-centered spirituality, in freedom of spirit, and in his approach to the life of prayer. He saw these as central not only to the life of the monk but to anyone seeking God.

> Now the whole of God's will has only one purpose, to re-establish all things in Christ. Therefore if our wills are conformed to the will of God, the whole of our history, with every single thing that happens to us, is part of a plan—a plan which is being carried out by the omnipotent power of God—to unite us to Christ and sanctify us in Him.[34]

Certainly, whether Eugene realized it or not, what Saint Paul talks about—counting everything as naught when compared with Christ—had happened in his own life.[35] Despite the disappointments, in the one place where it mattered his achievement had been great. Perhaps the best conclusion to this account of him is what he wrote himself in the article that appeared in *Doctrine and Faith*:

> In retrospect the long weary road seems but a short passage . . . in actual fact it was much longer, much more difficult and even dangerous. But it had its brighter moments. When most needed, God came to the aid of his servant to encourage him and strengthen him. Looking back one sees that God did everything, and was always at work, even when he seemed furthest away. Looking

34. Boylan, *This Tremendous Lover*, p. 175.
35. Phil 3:7.

back one sees that the most absolute need is total confidence in the infinite goodness of God . . . for he has said "He who believes in me though he die, shall live" . . . and we have all received of his fullness, for he is given to us that nothing may be wanting to us in any grace . . . everything is simplified, everything is peaceful, everything is organized, everything leads to Christ. His (the monk's) own nothingness, his own poverty, his own powerlessness is his joy—for so Christ may be all. (290-291)

## CONFERENCE ONE:
# HUMILITY

### Christ Dwelling in Us

Most people say that if you are humble, you can be confident. I say the opposite. You cannot be humble unless you have confidence. First, you cannot have confidence unless you have some idea of the goodness of God. Second, you must realize the immense treasure and power that is placed at our disposal by the merits of Christ. Only then can we break the barriers between God and us.

God's goodness comes to us through his Son, Jesus Christ. At baptism, Christ himself came to dwell in our souls. He entered with the Holy Trinity and will remain there as long as we remain in a state of grace. He comes with zeal to glorify his Father. He wants to make all of our acts meritorious and pleasing to his Father as well as to share in our actions.

The Lord desires intimacy with us because he has a personal love for us. His love was why he instituted the Eucharist; he wanted to unite himself with us. The reception of Holy Communion is a sacrament, a sign of a God's union with us.[1] We come to Jesus with love for him and he gives himself to us because of his love for his Father and us.

In the *Summa Theologica,* Saint Thomas says—and it is the teaching of the Church—that by baptism the passion and death of Christ are communicated to the person baptized as if he

1. "Our own personal part in the work of our salvation commences with baptism and the Blessed Eucharist. By these sacraments, we are incorporated into Christ, and receive His grace, His strength, His help—His very self. We receive also His example, and, in fact, in some mysterious way, we are mystically conformed to His death and resurrection. He gives us both a plan and the means to carry it out. He is our model, and our partner. He is our wisdom and He is our strength." Boylan, *The Mystical Body*, p. 68.

himself had suffered and died.[2, 3] The merits of our Lord are ours.[4] We stand before God exactly as if we had suffered the agony in the garden and had been crucified on Calvary. In essence, everything that Christ had is ours as if we ourselves had undergone it. This is our confidence.

## Christ Welcomes Sinners

Jesus comes into our souls not because we are good but because he is good. He made it quite clear that he did not come to look for saints. He has come to look for sinners. *"I have not come to call the just, but sinners, to repentance"* (Lk 5:32).[5] The one thing I have in common with our Lord is what was said against him, *"This man welcomes sinners and eats with them"* (Lk 15:2). That should be the motto of everyone who hears confessions.

Our Lord has a special soft spot for sinners. Our past sins are no barrier to our union with God. Our present sins, when we repent of them, are no further barrier. The only thing that comes between you and God is a deliberate decision to continue offending him. Regardless of your sins, the Lord our God himself told us, *If your sins be as scarlet, they shall be made as white as snow* (Is 1:18).

2. *Summa Theologica* part III, question 49, article 1, objection 4: "Christ's passion, the universal cause of the forgiveness of sins, has to be applied to individuals, if they are to be cleansed from their sins. This is done by baptism and penance and the other sacraments, which derive their power from the passion of Christ"; III, 49, 3, obj. 2: "In order to benefit by Christ's passion, one must be likened to him. We are sacramentally conformed to him by baptism, for *we were buried with him by means of Baptism into death* (Rom 6:4)." St. Thomas Aquinas, *Summa Theologiæ*, vol. 54, *The Passion of Christ (3a. 46–52)*, trans. Richard T. A. Murphy (London: Eyre and Spottiswoode; New York: McGraw-Hill, 1965; copyright Blackfriars, 1965), pp. 97, 103.

3. *Catechism of the Catholic Church* [hereafter cited as CCC] (Vatican City: Liberia Editrice Vaticana, 1994, 1997; Washington, D.C.: United States Catholic Conference, 1997) 1010.

4. CCC 2009–2011.

5. See also the parables of the Lost Sheep (Lk 15:4-7) and Lost Coin (Lk 15:8-10).

Saint Paul tells us, *Now we know that for those who love God all things work together unto good . . .* (Rom 8:28). Yes, says Saint Augustine, even our sins.[6] God is so good that he will use your sins to make you holier. There is no reason to hesitate in going to God, no matter what our weaknesses or how weak we feel.

## Saint Benedict on Humility

Why, then, cannot God—or our Lord, if you prefer to look at Christ in our hearts—do all that he wants to do with us? Why are we not saints? One answer: because we are not humble. The perfection to which we are called is a perfection of charity. There is no other perfection in the Christian economy. We monks, like

6. The phrase "even our sins" was not used by Saint Augustine but is a phrase used to summarize his thought that "even sin" serves God's purpose. In *This Tremendous Lover,* Boylan surmises the phrase from the *Summa Theologica*, III, I, 2 of Saint Thomas Aquinas who is expounding upon the words of Saint Augustine. Henri Marrou, however, in *Saint Augustine and His Influence Through the Ages* (trans. Patrick Hepburne-Scott, New York: Harper, 1962, pp. 142–143), provides the source of "even our sins." Marrou explains that *etiam peccata* (even sin) was used by French poet and dramatist Paul Claudel (1868–1955) in *Le Soulier de Satin* ("The Satin Slipper," 1931). Marrou provides three works of Saint Augustine to substantiate the summation *etiam peccata.*

1) Saint Augustine, *Enchirdion*, chapter III, 11: "As even infidels admit, the omnipotent God, primal power of the world, being Himself supremely good, could not permit anything evil in His works, were He not so all-powerful and good as to be able to bring good even out of evil." Louis A. Arand, trans. *St. Augustine: Faith Hope and Love*, vol. 3 of Ancient Christian Writers (Westminster, Md.: Newman, 1947), p. 18.

2) Saint Augustine, *De Correptione et Gratia*, chapter 24: "To such as love Him, God co-worketh with all things for good; so absolutely *all* things, that even if any of them go astray, and break out of the way, even this itself. He makes to avail them for good, so that they return more lowly and more instructed [emphasis retained]. Benjamin B. Warfield, trans. "A Treatise on Rebuke and Grace," in *Saint Augustin's Anti-Pelagian Works*, vol. 5 of the First Series of Nicene and Post-Nicene Fathers (Peabody, Mass.: Hendrickson, 1995), p. 481.

3) Saint Augustine, *De Libero Arbito*, chapter 9, 26: "Hence, if the soul only becomes happy through sin, *our sins must be necessary* for the perfection of the whole creation which God has made" [emphasis added]. Dom Mark Pontifex, trans. *St. Augustine: The Problem of Free Choice*, vol. 22 of Ancient Christian Writers (Westminster, Md.: Newman, 1947), p. 167.

all Christians, are called to that perfection of charity.[7] In the end, it is the only virtue that matters. In practice however, the only virtue that matters is humility. If you have humility, as Saint Benedict tells us, you have perfect charity. "When, therefore, a monk shall have ascended these various grades of humility, he shall presently attain to that perfect love of God which casteth out fear."[8]

The secret of the spiritual life, and the whole secret of the heights of mysticism, is in humility. Saint Benedict knew it. There was no need for him to write a treatise on the mystical life. Rather, he wrote his rule to regulate the life of the monastery in order to lead monks to humility. You might say that the one spiritual chapter he gives us is the chapter on humility.

Saint Benedict's fourth degree of humility is significant:

> ". . . to keep patience in the exercise of obedience, and not to lose it or depart from it, either because of the difficulty of the thing commanded or the injuries to which one may be subjected, agreeably to what is said in Scripture: *He that shall persevere to the end shall be saved* (Mt 24:13); and again, *Let thy heart take courage, and wait thou for the Lord* (Ps 26[27]:14)."[9]

### Dependence on God

The only obstacle to the work of God in your soul is pride. It is removed through humility. God has told us that he will not give his glory to another. *For my own sake, for my own sake, will I do it, that I may not be blasphemed; and I will not give my glory to*

7. "All Christians in any state or walk of life are called to the fullness of Christian life and to the perfection of charity." The Roman Catholic Church document *Lumen Gentium* 40§2, quoted in CCC 2013, 2028.

8. *The Holy Rule of St. Benedict, Revised Translation for the use of The English Speaking Religious of the Order of Cistercians of the Strict Observance* (Dublin: M. H. Gill, 1934), p. 20. Cross referenced with *The Rule of St. Benedict in Latin and English with Notes*, ed. Timothy Fry (Collegeville, Mn.: Liturgical Press, 1981) chapter 7, verse 67. Quotations used by Dom Eugene in the conferences will be from *The Holy Rule of St. Benedict* (Dublin, 1934) edition with biblical references added to the text. The chapter and verse of the Rule given in the footnote will be that of *The Rule of St. Benedict* (Collegeville, 1981) hereafter cited as RB.

9. RB 7,35–43.

*another* (Is 48:11). Yet, what do we do? We seek to glorify ourselves and make ourselves above God, or as a god. In Scripture, we find God mourning us. God resists the proud and gives grace to the humble.[10]

Because of pride we desire to claim credit for every good thing we do or see in ourselves; we refuse to admit that we are dependent on God. All the good we do, have, are, or find in ourselves comes from God.

My understanding of the spiritual life comes from both being in love and metaphysics. In metaphysics, you eventually come to understand that we do not exist of ourselves. We had to be created, and we have to be kept in existence. When I stop talking, my words cease. If God stopped thinking about us, we would cease to exist. God has to keep us in existence. Every human action, even the ones that we do not have to think about, like the process of digestion, God has to think about and provide. If God does not cooperate with all these, they cease. That is true in the natural order. That is why our first duty to God is adoration.

In the supernatural order, we have been lifted into a new state of life. We are partakers of the divine nature and called to share in the life of the Holy Trinity. However, we are completely dependent on God for this new life and need the grace that comes from God.

The craze for liberty and independence is so illogical that it makes men refuse to admit their dependence on God. You see it happening in Europe now. For a long while Christian principles were the basis of law, government, and the customs of society. Several European nations have discarded Christianity and substituted law as a source of human rights. All human rights, or natural rights, have been legislated away. Man is now seen as merely a creature of the state. He has no one to appeal to nor a basis on which to appeal and justify his individual rights and liberty.

The only person who can protect the dignity of human nature and the freedom of the individual person is God and the knowledge of God. Our dependence on God is the basis of our freedom.

10. 1 Pt 5:5-6.

However, we must admit our dependence. The trouble is that we want to sign our names to things. We want the glory for ourselves, so we refuse to admit dependence on God.

**Confidence in God**

An obstacle to being humble is lack of confidence. We must know the goodness of God and have assurance that God will do the job. Saint Peter recommends that we cast our burden on the Lord.[11] Unless we realize and know that it is his goodness that is the source of our existence and all that we do, we dare not admit to ourselves anything that lessens our self-esteem. If the truth about ourselves is forced home on us by a failure, a comment, a criticism or anything else, we grasp at every straw to justify our faith in ourselves because we have no one else to hope in. The worse off we seem—the lower we are forced to admit ourselves—the less hope we have in God because our hope is not based on God's goodness.

Once we realize that the reason for hoping is in God and his goodness then we begin to see that it does not matter how small we are, how weak we are, or how bad we are. In fact, we begin to realize that it is all the better to be weak, all the better to be poor, all the better to be without merit. Why? Because we can trust in God.

Why do we believe in God? Why do we love God or why should we love God? Why do we hope in God? Because God is good—infinitely good. Therefore, there is no limit to our faith, love, and hope in God because none of them depends on our goodness.

If anyone of us were to fall into mortal sin, we would repent of it. We have as much reason to hope in God after the sin as before it. In fact, I have more reason to hope in God's mercy when I have sinned because God came to save sinners.[12]

11. 1 Pt 5:7.
12. 1 Tm 1:15.

**God's Mercy**

For Saint Benedict, everything a monk does must be for the glory of God: "In selling goods, let them not be influenced by the evil promptings of avarice, but let such goods be sold at a somewhat lower rate than they would be by seculars, that God may be glorified in all things."[13]

God created this world for his glory. How did he decide to glorify himself? God glorifies himself by his justice in the next life. But in this life, God glorifies himself by his mercy. The whole of this plan of the economy of creation is based on the redemption of sinners.

God's plan was that where sin abounded, grace might more abound.[14] The whole plan of his design for glory is based on mercy. The more mercy he shows, the more glory he gets. Therefore, logically, the less claim you have on God's goodness, the more glory he gets from giving you mercy.

Our Lord summed it up: *Blessed are the poor in spirit, for theirs is the kingdom of heaven* (Mt 5:3). If we only knew the gift of God's mercy. The worse we are, the more reason for having confidence in God our savior. That sounds startling, but it is true.

In the revelations of Saint Mechtild of Magdeburg, our Lord appeared to her and found her weeping because she had been unfaithful.[15] He reaffirmed the blessedness of those who are poor because of suffering.

13. RB 57,7-9.

14. Rom 5:20.

15. Mechtild (also spelled Mechthild or Mechtilde) (1210?–1282) entered the monastery of Helfta at the end of her life after living in Magdeburg and having already experienced mystical states. When she was in her mid-30s, on the advice of her Dominican confessor, Mechtild recorded her visionary experiences. *Flowing Light of the Godhead* is divided into seven books which contain not only her visionary experiences but letters of advice and criticism, allegories, reflections, and prayers.

Mechtild of Magdeburg should not be confused with Mechtild of Hackeborn (1241–1298) who was also a nun of the monastery of Helfta. Also, Helfta is often incorrectly referred to as a monastery of the Cistercian order. The monastery followed a Cistercian way of life and was formed by the writings of Saint Bernard of Clairvaux, but it was never officially affiliated with the order.

> When I, a sinner and inert, went to my prayer one day, it seemed as if God would not give me the slightest inclination of his grace. I bewailed my human frailty which seemed to me a hindrance to my spiritual life. "Ah! No!" said my soul. "Think rather of the faithfulness of God and praise him for it. *Gloria in excelsis Deo.*"
>
> And in this praise a great light appeared to my soul and in the light God himself in great glory and unspeakable clearness. And our Lord lifted up two golden chalices in his hands and both were full of living wine. That in the left hand was the red wine of suffering, that in the right, the white wine of sublime consolation. Our Lord said: "Blessed are they who drink this wine; for although I offer both in Divine Love, yet is the white wine nobler in itself; but most blessed are they who drink both, the white and the red."[16]

Once you realize that, you begin to realize that the best policy is to be as poor as you can. Get rid of everything. Accept the truth about yourself. Saint Paul was forced to accept it. *Unhappy man that I am! Who will deliver me from the body of this death?* (Rom 7:24). What hope have I? Who is going to keep me up if I jump in the ocean? What straws are there that I can grasp at?

God said to Saint Paul, and he says to me, *"My grace is sufficient for thee, for strength is made perfect in weakness"* (2 Cor 12:9). Now what does grace mean? The best translation of grace is: My *mercy* is sufficient for you. What does Saint Paul do? Saint Paul, of course, saw the point immediately. *Gladly therefore will I glory in my infirmities, that the strength of Christ may dwell in me* (2 Cor 12:9). There is the whole theology of Saint Benedict's humility and the whole theology of our supernatural life. Gladly will we glory in our infirmities in order that the power of Christ may dwell in us.

**Faith in God**

Our function as monks is to have Christ dwelling in us and to offer him to God every moment of the day. We do that by humility. The section of the rule on humility deals with the whole

16. Lucy Menzies, trans., *The Revelations of Mechthild of Magdeburg* (London: Longmans, 1953), p. 37.

spiritual life and the whole of mystical life. It is all there, and it is all yours.

The spiritual life is often considered as something fearfully complicated or difficult. People are quite surprised to find that it is simple. Our Lord himself told us that his burden is light and his yoke is easy, but we do not believe him.[17]

If our Lord came here at the moment to speak in his own person, the only comment he would have to make against us: *"O thou of little faith, why didst thou doubt?"* (Mt 14:31). We would like to say he would pat us on the back and tell us we are far better than we think we are doing. The only complaint he has to make against us is our lack of confidence. That was his agony in the garden. It is not our sins that broke his heart but the lack of confidence in his mercy.

Jesus had done ninety-nine percent of what is necessary to make us saints. He is quite prepared to do the other one percent, but we will not let him. What did he cry for over Jerusalem? *"Jerusalem, Jerusalem, thou who killest the prophets, and stonest those who are sent to thee! How often would I have gathered thy children together, as a hen gathers her young under her wings, but thou wouldst not!"* (Lk 13:34). That is our trouble. We will not be gathered under his wings. We want to be big fellows. We want to have something big on our tombstone: This man did so and so. We will not trust our Lord. We will not accept the truth about our weaknesses and admit that we need our Lord. In every other walk of life, progress is associated with independence. The more competent you are, the more independent you are. The one exception is the spiritual life. The more you progress in the spiritual life, the more completely dependent you become on God. But how many of us resent that dependence?

## Grace

In the beginning, for example, God gives a certain reserve of grace. You feel you have got some assurance. As time goes on, he cuts that down. He only gives you the grace for the present

17. Mt 11:30.

moment. If you start trying to carry tomorrow's cross with today's graces, you fall into discouragement.

You ask yourself, What would I do if I was going to be martyred? If you want to bluff yourself, you would certainly say profess the faith and let them do what they liked. I know I would not, but on the other hand, I know I must. I know further that I have a claim to that grace from confirmation. I have no need to worry. When an issue arises, it is me plus the grace that is needed to deal with it, therefore I do not worry. I will be quite capable of handling any issue that comes my way.

You only get grace according to the needs of the particular moment. Once the need is past, you are back to your original weaknesses. We are as useless before God without grace as a  lamp is without electricity. God gives the power to meet the needs of the situation. When the extraordinary demand for power arises because of personal crosses or special needs, the power is supplied immediately. Once it is over, it is reduced, and we have to accept it. We are then faced with our own shortcomings. In fact, the whole of the spiritual life and the whole of God's providence are directed to showing us our shortcomings so that we see the power of God's grace. That is the secret of the whole spiritual life: *"My grace is sufficient for thee, for strength is made perfect in weakness"* (2 Cor 12:9).

## CONFERENCE TWO:
# POVERTY OF SPIRIT

### Blessed Are the Poor in Spirit

In the Sermon on the Mount, the Lord gave us a fundamental principle: *Blessed are the poor in spirit, for theirs is the kingdom of heaven* (Mt 5:3). Although he could be referring to material poverty, our Lord is speaking of a spiritual poverty called humility. Dom Marmion writes:[1]

> Who are those whom our Lord calls *pauperes spiritu* [poor in spirit]? Those who own nothing either in mind or heart or will, who wish to have nothing except from God. Daily they lay down their own judgment, their manner of seeing things, their will, everything, at the feet of Christ; they say to him: "I do not want to have anything of myself; I want to have only what comes from Thee, to do only that which, from all eternity, Thou, as the Word, hast decided for me: to realize Thy own divine ideal for me." They can make their own words which literally belong to Saint Paul: *Vivo autem, jam non ego; vivit vero in me Christus.* [It is now no longer I that live, but Christ lives in me.] (Gal 2:20)[2]

1. "Hardly any spiritual author of recent times has made such a universal appeal or produced so widespread an effect as Abbot Columba Marmion. There is no religious order of which the members cannot find rich food for their spiritual life in his works. Even among the laity there are many who are enthusiastic about his writings, and any Catholic, lay or religious, who wishes to live the Catholic life in its fullness can find in Dom Marmion's pages the light, the instructions, and the encouragement he needs." Eugene Boylan, "Benedictine Influence in the Doctrine of Abbot Marmion," in *Abbot Marmion: An Irish Tribute*, trans. monks of Glenstal (Cork: Mercier, 1948), p. 45.

2. Dom Columba Marmion, OSB, *Christ, the Ideal of the Monk: Spiritual Conferences on the Monastic and Religious Life*, 8th ed. (London: Sands, 1926), p. 207.

Of course, we need grace and self-abnegation in order to have poverty of spirit. The life of our soul must be entirely subject to the Divine and must have no movement that does not come from the Holy Spirit. We do not have to build up a picture for ourselves of ourselves—of our riches. On the contrary, we must be prepared to meet our own poverty because we are rich in Christ.[3]

Our Lord told Sister Josefa to tell souls that the basis of his work in them is their nothingness and their imperfection.[4] It is not because he told Josefa that I am accepting it, it is what he said himself, *"Blessed are the poor in spirit, for theirs is the kingdom of heaven."*

### Christ, Our Holiness

"If I should be asked," Marmion once said, "in what does a spiritual life consist? I should answer: Christ."[5, 6, 7] Holiness and

3. "Too often our confidence in God is based on an illusory sense of our own merits. But true theological hope is based on the goodness of God, who is sufficiently good to overlook our lack of merit, and to be infinitely merciful to our poverty and nothingness. When a man realizes this truth, which is one of the most fundamental of all the truths of the spiritual life, he feels an urge to strip himself completely of all pretended possessions of it is when we are poor in ourselves that we are most rich in God." Eugene Boylan, *The Priest's Way to God* (Westminster, Md.: Newman, 1963), p. 127.

4. "I will make it known that My work rests on nothingness and misery—such is the first link in the chain of love that I have prepared for souls from eternity. I will use you [Sister Josefa] to show that I love misery, littleness, and absolute nothingness." *Christ's Appeal for Love to His humble Servant Josefa Menéndez, Religious of the Sacred Heart*, trans. L. Keppel (London: Sands, 1951; reprinted Rockford, Il.: TAN, 1975), p. 82.

5. "As for me, if you asked me in what the spiritual life consists, I should say, 'It is very simple, it is resumed in one word: Christ.'" Undated letter of Dom Marmion in Dom Raymond Thibaut, *Union With God According to the Letters of Direction of Dom Marmion*, 3rd ed., trans. Mary St. Thomas (St. Louis, Mo.: Herder, 1957), p. 51.

6. "It all amounts to this—loving Jesus Christ." Dom Marmion letter to the Abbess of Maredret, Louvain (Belgium), October 28, 1902, in M.M. Philipon, *The Spiritual Doctrine of Dom Marmion*, trans. Dom Matthew Dillon (Westminster, Md.: Newman, 1956), p. 65.

7. "We must never forget this capital truth of the spiritual life: all is summed up, for the monk as for the simple Christian, in being united, in faith and love

the Christian life were for Dom Marmion nothing else than the complete acceptance of the Incarnation with all its consequences. For Jesus Christ is the gift which God makes of himself and his holiness to humanity. It is a gift of holiness to all in proportion as they are incorporated in Christ. All holiness is derived from the Father who communicates this infinite holiness through his Son who is our justice, our holiness, and our redemption. Christ is our holiness. It is not something that we do for ourselves. It is something we get from Christ.

Holiness consists in receiving Christ through faith in the divinity of Christ, through reception of his sacraments, and through carrying out of his commandments, especially the commandment of love.

Our Lord spoke to Saint Mechtild:[8, 9]

---

to Christ Jesus in order to imitate Him. Christ being the very "form" (cf. Rom 7:29) of our predestination, is at the same time the ideal of all holiness for us. He is the centre of monasticism as of Christianity: to contemplate Christ, to imitate Him, to unite our will to His will in order to please His Father, that is the sum total of all perfection. The Father has placed all things in His beloved Son; we find in Him all the treasures of redemption, justification, sanctification; for us everything lies in contemplating Him and drawing near to Him. For the thought of Jesus, the looking upon Jesus, are not only holy, but sanctifying." Marmion, *Christ the Ideal of the Monk*, p. 317.

8. Saint Mechtild of Hackeborn (1240–1298) (sometimes referred to "of Helfta") was one of three saintly women who lived in what is now the ruins of the monastery of Helfta in Germany. The other two were Saint Mechtild Magdeburg and Saint Gertrude the Great. Mechtilde's spiritual "graces" come to us today as the *Book of Special Graces* whose main compiler is actually Saint Gertrude the Great, novice of Saint Mechtild of Hackeborn. The book serves as a guide to Christian living through revelations of both Jesus and his mother Mary. Mechtilde and her pupil were early proponents of devotion to the Sacred Heart of Jesus.

There is no American English translation of *The Book of Special Graces* (*Liber Specialis Gratiae*). A Middle English copy of the book is available from the Pontifical Institute of Mediaeval Studies (1979) under the title of *The Booke of Gostlye Grace of Mechtild of Hackeborn*. The text of the *Book of Special Graces* is on microfiche while the print volume by Teresa A. Halligan includes notes, glossary, indexes, and a historical background.

9. For more on the life of Mechtild of Hackeborn, see Ann Marie Caron, "Taste and See the Goodness of the Lord: Mechtild of Hackeborn," in *Hidden Springs: Cistercian Monastic Women, Book Two* (Cistercian Publications, 1995), 509–524.

> In what does the praise of God consist if not in the lamentation of the soul that can never praise Him as it desires? All it desires is a sorrowful lamentation. And when I come to supply for it myself, I heal it of all wounds.[10]

Christ supplies for our shortcomings. This is fundamental in Saint Paul's doctrine. "Do not be troubled. I will pay all your debts. I will supply for all your negligences," says the Lord.

What did the Lord say to Mechtild when she could not be consoled for having squandered the gifts of God? Which one of us here has not squandered the gifts of God? By sin? By cowardice in the monastic life? By lack of courage? By lack of confidence? By lack of fidelity? Here is the answer:

> Even if you were perfectly faithful to me, you would instantly prefer that my love would repair your negligences rather than that you should do it. So that my love may have all the honor and glory.
>
> It is a great joy to me that men expect great gifts from me. If any of them expected to receive from me greater rewards than he had deserved after this life, and if in consequence he thanked me for them during this life, he would give me so much pleasure that no matter how great his faith or extraordinary his confidence, I would reward him beyond his merits. It is impossible that a man should not receive what he has believed and hoped for. Therefore, it is good for a man to hope much and in me to place all his confidence.

## Allowing God to Work in Our Life

Our sanctification is already complete. It is completed in Christ. It is only a question of transferring it to us. The only obstacle to that transference is ourselves. All we have to do is to get out of God's way and give him a clear road. Stop shoving him out of the driver's seat. Be a passenger and let him drive the

10. This and the following two quotes are from *The Book of Special Graces.* Dom Eugene could have used two possible sources from which he translated into English: 1) Mechtild of Hackeborn, *Liber specialis gratiae*, vol. 2 of *Revelationes Gertrudianae ac Mechtildianae*, ed. monks of Solesmes (Poitiers-Paris, 1877); 2) *La livre de la grâce spéciale: Révélations de Sainte Mechtilde Vierge de l'Ordre de St. Benoit*, trans. nuns of Wisques (Tours: Mame, 1928).

car. One of the troubles of the monastic life is our tendency to drive instead of being God's passengers.

A man who has established himself with success in a profession comes into monastic life. He has learned his own limitations and accepted them. He accepts himself as he is. Once he is instructed in the spiritual life and appreciates the spirit of community, you can put him anywhere in the house. He is happy washing dishes in the kitchen. He is happy if you ask him to take charge of the abbey. It is all the same to him.

A young man comes to the monastery from home where he has been squashed. He lacks maturity. For the first time in his life, he has a certain amount of freedom, but he has never found himself. He has never undone the work of humiliation. Whether it is his mother or father or his school teacher, or whoever it is. But he has been kept down by being "under a governor," as Saint Paul says.[11]

Compassion, understanding, and charity say to give that fellow a chance. Give him a job. He will do it, he thinks, for God, but it is really to satisfy himself. In one sense he is wasting his time. In another sense, he is not because it is a necessary psychological preparation before God can make him humble. He has got to satisfy himself that he could do something before he admits that he can do nothing. Therefore, pick a job that you know the young monk likes doing even though you know there will be a lot of natural motives in it.

### Receiving the Riches of Christ

I was appointed superior [of Caldey] quite suddenly. I had no experience in being superior. I walked into a troubled community. There are ten nationalities in our community. Not ten nationalities born in England but ten different origins: China, Spain, Norway, Poland, and, of course, a few Irish. Obviously, I knew I was going to make mistakes, but the abbot general [Dom Gabriel Sortais] came over some time afterwards to make the

11. Acts 13:38-39. Apostle Paul speaks of the Jewish people being under a governor—"under the law of Moses"—and guarded by the law.

first visitation.[12] I do not speak French very well, and he does not speak English at all. However, as you know, he is an extraordinary man.

I met him when he came across on the boat and I said to him, "You know, most Reverend Father, it was a great mistake to appoint me to this monastery. First of all, I'm Irish. It's not fair to an English house to have an Irish superior. There are three houses in England that have Irish superiors. With the best will in the world the good English people must be fed up with us Irish priests. I've gone out of my way to avoid trouble, and I think we get along quite well. But far from that, Reverend Father, I have no experience of being superior. I am not that type. I have not an even temperament. I dodge decisions, and when I do make them, they're rash. I can't control my tongue. I say too much or too little. I really should not be in this job at all."

He said, "Father, you have exactly what I've got to rule the order. Say no more. No less. You have your daily Mass and your union with God. No superior has anything else."

That is true of each one of us. All we want is to be saints. We have our daily Mass and all that it supplies. We have our union with God through humility and obedience. We want no more than that. God is our sufficiency. As Saint Paul put it: *May my God supply your every need according to his riches in glory in Christ Jesus* (Phil 4:19). We are rich with the riches of Christ provided we accept it. That is why we must get rid of this attitude of mind—it is an attitude rather than an act, that is called pride.

## Pride

Pride is the belief that any good we do is done by us independent of God and as the result of our own effort. It is the tendency to put our name on everything we do. You have this conviction

12. Dom Gabriel Sortais was abbot general for the Cistercian Order of the Strict Observance from November 7, 1951 until his death on November 13, 1963 at age 61. He entered Abbey of Our Lady of Bellefontaine (south of Paris, France) on August 4, 1924 at age 22. He was ordained on June 29, 1931 and the following year was appointed prior. Three years later, he was elected abbot on May 6, 1936.

that you were born for great things. We have our ambitions, too. Be careful. We tend to think that even though we can not reach anything, that it should be given to us. That it is our own right. In the back of our heads is this notion: What are they going to do about me? It is time they gave me my rights, put me up on a pedestal somewhere. That is in all of us, more or less. That is the pride we have got to get rid of.

The answer is humility. The way to achieve humility is by humiliations. One might say, "I've never achieved humility through humiliations. All I've achieved by humiliations is being humiliated." This is quite a different thing from being humbled, I can assure you. There is tremendous danger in tying to humiliate a man. It is what I call the technique of the father master of the old school where you try to break a fellow down, comment on his awkwardness and make things difficult for him. That is a mistake. You must first give a man confidence in God. Otherwise, he is not true to himself if he accepts humiliations. If he has not confidence in God, the only thing left is for him to have confidence in himself. And if he lacks that confidence, he has no reason for staying in the monastery. You must, first of all, give him confidence in God. Then pray that he can get the grace of humility.

**Humility**

Humility is primarily a gift from God. Certainly, we can help by trying to build up our confidence in God. Secondly, we make up our mind to face the truth about ourselves. It is not so bad after all. We have one tremendous value: "Look, O God, on thy servant for whom the Lord Jesus Christ, thy Son, did not hesitate to hand himself over to the hands of the torturers and to undergo the torment of the cross." That is my value. God thinks enough of me to undergo the torture of his passion and crucifixion. That is our value and hope. That is why our hope must be built up on God's goodness and not on our own.

Further, God's goodness is in our poverty of spirit. Where sin abounds, grace does more abound.[13] The more sin we have to

13. Rom 5:20.

offer to God, the more he can glorify himself by his mercy in making us saints. Marmion says: "This way is *sure*. Nothing glorifies God as much as the triumph of His grace in a soul that acknowledges her misery, her weakness, her unworthiness, and that hope for *all* from His power and His goodness. This is the *Laus gloriae gratiae suae* [cause of our praise and glory of his grace] which St. Paul speaks."[14]

**Offering God Our Sins**

Saint Jerome (347–419) lived in a cave and had apparently detached himself from everything. He was praying and offering the Infant Jesus, to whom he had a great devotion, everything he could think of. Still, it was obvious that our Lord was not satisfied. Jerome said, "What more can I offer you, Lord? What is there that I have not offered You?"

"Give me your sins. Give me your sins," said the Lord.[15]

Did you even think of offering to God your sins? Put them before God. The technique consists in sharing your wounds and needs. There is no good in going to the Lord and saying, "I've practiced such and such a virtue" or "I've put up with the abbot the last twenty years." That is not the way to bring down God's grace.

Tell him, "I haven't practiced obedience for twenty years. I haven't put up with your Providence. I've committed sin. I'm the sort of guy that you've become man to save. The sort of man you're looking for."

A doctor at a medical university, who specializes in a specific disease like leprosy, tries to find a cure by being attentive to cases

14. [Emphasis retained.] Raymond Thibaut, *Union With God According to the Letters of Direction of Dom Marmion,* trans. Mother Mary St. Thomas (St. Louis, Mo.: B. Herder, 1957), p. 262.

15. "God is more anxious to save us than we are to save ourselves. There is a story told to the effect that one day Our Blessed Lord appeared to Saint Jerome, saying to him, 'Jerome, what will you give Me?' Jerome answered, 'I will give you my writings,' to which Our Lord replied that it was not enough. 'Then,' said Jerome, 'what shall I give you? My life of penance and mortification?' But the answer was, 'Even that is not enough!' 'What have I left to give Thee?' cried Jerome. Our Blessed Lord answered, 'Jerome, you can give Me your sins.'" Bishop Fulton J. Sheen, *Seven Last Words* (New York: D. Appleton-Century, 1942), pp. 17–18.

of leprosy that will aid his research. Here is God who became man to provide a cure for humankind.[16] And here I am, a person to be saved. I am an obvious case for our Lord. The tougher the case I am, the more interest he has in the job. The more difficult it is to make me a saint, the more glory he gets from the power of his grace.

God planned this world to be glorified by his mercy and grace. His grace is almost synonymous with his mercy. Merit and justice belong to the next life. This life is a time for mercy. I would go so far as to say, and I would not like to be quoted theologically on this because it needs proper expression, that God never punishes individuals in this life. Rather, he only corrects them. He will come down on you like a ton of hot bricks sometimes, but it is not just to take it out on you. It is to correct you and to give you a chance for making up for what you lost.

His punishments in this life, if we can call them that, are always corrective and medicinal. They are planned to repair what you have lost by your infidelity or your sins. He never judges us in this life; he saves us. Our whole union with God in this life is based on the fact that we are sinners and he is saving us from our sins. I dare to say that your sins are the most effective means you have of affecting divine union. They draw down the mercy of God.

Our Lord insisted that he came to look for sinners, not for saints.[17] For lost sheep.[18] For prodigal sons.[19] I think you can find some of those headings in which you could put yourself.

We have to be humble and admit the truth about ourselves. By refusing to admit this truth, we put ourselves outside the special enclosure where God is looking for us. It is only when we have labeled ourselves as sinners and people to be saved, that he can get at us.[20]

16. Mt 1:21.

17. Mk 2:17.

18. Lk 15:3-7.

19. Lk 15:11-32.

20. "We must, then, try to correspond fully with our vocation. No sense of our unworthiness or our incapacity, no consciousness of our coldness, our tepidity or even our sinfulness should deter us from seeking intimate friendship with

## Our Lady, an Example of Humility

Now, of course, the tremendous obstacle to his work in our souls is putting our name to what we do. Humility is truth. If you have the grace of contemplation, or if you can do miracles, it is not humility to deny them. You may be under an illusion about your grace of contemplation. Generally, I find that the people who have infused prayer do not know it. They may suspect it sometimes, but even then they are afraid of being under an illusion. If they do miracles, and I have met people who do miracles, they cannot possibly ascribe it to themselves.

Our Lady is a perfect example of humility. You have this classic case of the *Magnificat*. Her cousin reminds her that she is the mother of God, the greatest person God ever made.[21] Mary responds by saying it is wonderful because it magnifies God.[22] *"My soul magnifies the Lord, and my spirit rejoices in God my savior"* (Lk 1:46-47). She did not see it as magnifying herself. She could not see good in herself without also seeing it in the same glance as coming from God. That is humility.

You and I who are priests say, "This is my Body," and we adore the host as the Body of Christ. It never crosses our mind for a second to ascribe that power to ourselves. This is the attitude that must extend to every action of our spiritual life. It is the attitude of humility.

## Giving God the Glory

I heard many confessions when I was at Roscrea Abbey. I was supposed to be an easy mark, a refuge to sinners. One dark December night—the sun goes down in Ireland at half past three during the winter—a brother came and made signs to me that there were three nuns to see me in the guesthouse. I went and

---

Jesus. It is our nothingness that he wants. The only foundation for his work in our souls is our incapacity, our misery, our futility. He will even accept our sins, for his is our Savior, come to save us from our sins." Boylan, *The Priest's Way to God*, p. 96. Although Dom Eugene is writing to priests, his words are applicable to all religious.

21. Lk 1:41-42.

22. Lk 1:46-47.

found the three having tea and plum cake. "Well, Father, we didn't really want to see you," said one of them. "We wanted to go to confession."

I said, "Very well. I'll be down in the box when you come down." This good lady came in, made her confession, and said, "I am hesitant about speaking to anyone about this but Reverend Mother wants me to talk with somebody. Your name was suggested, so we came down to see you."

I said, "Well, what's the trouble, dear sister?"

She said, "Father, it's about my prayer." I just shrugged my shoulders.

"Whenever I go into the oratory I used to feel our Lord was present and in love with me. It used to feel that it was as if his arms were around me."

I said, "That could easily be just an illusion. In any case, a feeling doesn't get us anywhere. It often gets us to the wrong place."

"Recently, however," she said, "that's all stopped. When I crossed the threshold of the monastery, I experienced a fierce, indescribable and unbearable pain in my head. I can't tell you how terrible it is."

"Sister," I said, "I'm terribly suspicious of pains and feelings associated with special places or things. They're nearly always heretical in origin."

Normally I would have stopped there, but looking back afterwards, I realized that I had been impressed by one thing about this woman. She hated talking about herself. I could sense that immediately. It was not that she was objecting to talking to me, but that she did not want to talk about herself.

"I have to admit that God sometimes uses them for his own purposes," I said.

She said, "That's just what I was afraid of. I felt that God was really angry with me for something and was showing his anger in this way."

"Well, that's easily settled," I said. "Why should he be angry with you?"

She said, "Oh, because I might be refusing him something."

"If God is angry with you because you are refusing him something, it's not just something he asked you for in a passing second, and you didn't say yes on the spot. On the contrary, it'd be something he's been nagging at you and made it quite clear to you what it is he wants and that he wants it. Second, you've been equally definite in saying no each time. Are you refusing our Lord anything?"

"Father," she said, "How could you refuse our Lord anything?" It was said with sheer simplicity. No affectation at all. With complete conviction.

"Well, what's this trouble then, sister?" I said.

She said, "I was worried, and I went to Reverend Mother."

That pleased me very much, too. When you find people opening their minds to other people like that, they are generally on a safe wicker, as we say in England.

I went to Reverend Mother and told her about the whole thing. I said, "I'm terribly worried lest I incurred the anger of God. I want to make some reparation to him. I want your permission to do something. I suggest that you let me look after Sister So-and-So."

Sister So-and-So is one who had a very difficult character, being Irish. She had an ulcer on her head, which is particularly nasty. No one liked doing the job, and no one liked having anything to do with the old lady because she was a tough old board. Sister asked for permission to look after her.

"Right you are," said Reverend Mother.

"I went to the nun," she said, "and I talked to her and washed her ulcer. And I kissed it."

I said, "Sister, I don't like that sort of thing. It is a heroic thing to do, and I'm sure you'll have your reward, but please don't do anything like that again. In fact, never do anything out of the ordinary without either asking Reverend Mother or a confessor. The more you stick to the ordinary common routine of life in any religious house, the holier you will be. All these departures from the normal are to be suspect, especially abnormal penances. I frequently find they come from some perverted natural motive. Anyway, you'll have your reward for it."

She said, "That's alright then."

"But what's the trouble, sister?" I said.

"Well, the next morning," she said, "I went back to the sister to dress the ulcer and there was no ulcer there."

I took it all in stride.

"Sister," I said, "I don't think you need worry about God being angry with you, but I think you should make hay while the sun shines. It is not going to shine for very long. I think you are a victim-soul." That is an expression I hardly ever use, yet I told her that.[23]

"I think you are a victim-soul," I said. "And you had better prepare yourself for tribulation." She asked me a few questions, and I answered them the best I could.

About seven or eight months afterwards, a voice appeared on the other side of the grille. "Father, do you recognize me?"

I said, "I think your voice is familiar. I seem to remember you're the woman who goes around bandaging ulcers and things like that."

She said, "Father, you may or may not know that you are more than a priest. You're a prophet. I was here about seven months ago, and you told me that the sun was going to go out. That I should prepare for some tribulations. You are a true prophet, Reverend Father. They made me Reverend Mother, and I have had to take over the novices because the mistress of novices was ill. Three novices left. Two nuns have applied for dispensations. One has publicly refused me obedience. There's an epidemic in the convent. There's a lawsuit going on, and with that is

23. "To be a victim necessarily implies immolation, and as a rule atonement for another. Although strictly speaking one can offer oneself as a victim to give God joy and glory by voluntary sacrifice, yet for the most part God leads souls by that path only when He intends them to act as mediators: they have to suffer and expiate for those for whom their immolation will be profitable; either by drawing down graces of forgiveness on them, or by acting as a cloak to cover their sins in the face of divine justice. It stands to reason that no one will on his own initiative take such a role on himself. Divine consent is required before a soul dares to intervene between God and His creature. . . . He Himself chooses these persons, and because they are free He asks them for their voluntary co-operation. Those who accept put themselves at His mercy, and He then makes use of them as by sovereign right. . . . And because of this identification with Christ, the victim-soul shares in His dolorous Passion and undergoes, to a greater or lesser degree, and in various but generally superhuman ways, the torments and agonies that were His." H. Monier Vinard, introduction to *The Way of Divine Love* (Westminster, Md.: Newman, 1954), pp. xix–xx.

bankruptcy. For me, God is not angry with me. As far as I know, he doesn't exist."

I laughed.

"Oh, but it's easy for you to laugh," she said. "You haven't had to put up with it."

"Sister," I said, "if you go around kissing ulcers, you've got to take it on the chin."

Well, I did more than that. I tried to console her. She was one of the most humble women I know. She was raised to a high degree of union with God and a high degree of prayer. She was paying a terrible high price for it. She was utterly incapable of ascribing any good to herself. She would no more tell me that she had worked a miracle or claimed the power of miracles than I claim the power to launch a Sputnik.[24] That is the type of humility that we need. When we have it, extraordinary graces are possible for us.

## Being Wary of the Extraordinary

However, as Cistercians, we should be wary of anything extraordinary. Our vocation is to be ordinary.[25] Solo flights are not encouraged in this order. We fly in formation. It is a job of keeping your wingtips so many feet behind the other fellow's, keeping him on your side all the time. That applies even to our interior life.

In our order you will generally find that even in the great souls of high degree of prayer and high union with God, there is still nothing extraordinary. When you have to reach up to the top of

24. Sputnik refers to the Soviet Union's launch of unmanned space missions in the late 1950s to show the usefulness of artificial satellites. The United States responded with its own satellite launches.

25. "The organisation of the monastery is directed to bringing the monks into close union with Christ, since it is only through the experience of personal love for the Lord Jesus that the specific gifts of the Cistercian vocation can flower. Only if the brothers prefer nothing whatever to Christ will they be happy to persevere in a life that is ordinary, obscure and laborious. And may he lead them all together into eternal life." *Constitutions and Statutes of the Cistercian Order of the Strict Observance* (1990), C.3.5. Hereafter cited as *Constitutions and Statutes*.

the chapter room to pull a man down from the ceiling, that sort of thing does not belong to normal Cistercian piety.

Humility is the one thing we need, and Saint Benedict knew it. If you get humility, God can pour all his graces into your soul. Our Lord can live his life in you. God can look down at you in everything you do and say, *"This is my beloved Son, in whom I am well pleased; hear him"* (Mt 17:5).

## CONFERENCE THREE:
# HUMILITY AND OBEDIENCE

### Humility

There is no secret to our sanctification. It has already been accomplished by Christ. All that is needed is the removal of obstacles preventing Christ from living his life in us. These obstacles, mainly pride, are removed by humility and obedience.

*Way of Humility*

How, then, are you to become humble? Faith and confidence in God are necessary prerequisites. Through prayer and meditations on God's goodness and his love for you, you face and accept the truth about yourself. Namely, that you are a weak being in need of God's mercy.

Our God is merciful. He is waiting in anticipation to help his children. It is not so much the truth about yourself (all your faults) that we must know but the truth about God, who is a loving father. You learn more about yourself and about humility by knowing and adoring God's wonderful goodness than focusing only on your own shortcomings. Before you realize how much God loves you and how much hope can be placed in that love, you fight against every manifestation of the truth about your limitations. But after you experience God's love and admit your dependence on him, you accept the truth about yourself because you realize that your poverty is a claim on God and the kingdom of heaven. By filling up the gaps in your soul and supplying for your needs, God gets the glory.

As you grow in love of our Lord you even begin to relish your shortcomings. You begin to glory in them so that the power of Christ may dwell in you. And even further is to appreciate, with a certain amount of reserve perhaps, the fact that other people know your limitations. When God does great things in you, no one will think that it is your doing. God will get the glory. Remember this the next time you are in despair because of your neighbor's faults. It is for God's glory that these faults exist in those whom he is raising to high sanctity in a monastery.

When a monk dies in our monastery, others say that he was a good monk like the rest of the good monks. Eventually it comes out with a word here and there that he was an extraordinary man of God. However, you never saw it while he was living. "I lived with that monk and never saw anything extraordinary in him." The same was said of Saint Thérèse of Lisieux (1873–1897) and the same will be said of many of you.[1] God hides his work. You need not expect to see it yourself. Above all, you need not expect your brethren to see it. They will accept your oddities and shortcomings with a kindly smile, and they will say a prayer for you. With your perseverance in the ways of God, one day they will believe that you were a saint.

*Acceptance*

Humility is the basis of all God's work. He makes us humble *if* we cooperate. If it is his will, accept it. If it is God's plan that includes our history, our past, our present, everything else, accept it generously and fully. That is what makes us humble. It is what makes us saints.

Curiously, our Lord only asks us to imitate him in one thing. *"Take my yoke upon you, and learn from me, for I am meek and humble of heart. . ."* (Mt 11:29). He drew our attention to the virtue of imitating him in meekness and humility. Our Lady, too, sang the

1. "One day, when lying in her cell during recreation in order to allay the pain of this cruel cauterization, she heard a Sister in the kitchen speak about her as thus: 'Soeur [Sister] Thérèse de L'Enfant Jésus will soon die, and in truth, I ask myself what can our Mother [Superior] say of her after her death? She will be embarrassed for this little Sister, amiable though she is, has surely nothing worth recounting.'" Monseigneur Laveille, *St. Thérèse de L'Enfant Jésus*, 3rd ed., trans. Rev. M. Fitzsimons (Dublin: Clonmore and Reynolds; London: Burns, Oates and Washbourne, 1951), p. 296. The sister is referring to the Mother Superior sending a death notice (or obituary) to Carmelite convents.

praises of humility in the *Magnificat*.[2] We cannot say that we have not been shown the way.

There is a quotation from the Cistercian abbot, Blessed Guerric, a disciple of Saint Bernard:

> Humility is the greatest of all virtues, although it does not know itself to be a virtue. It is the root and seed-bed, the tinder and incentive, it is the summit and peak, the custody and discipline of almost all virtues. From it they begin, through it they make progress, in it they are perfected, by it they are preserved. It is humility that makes all the virtues what they are, and if any one of them is lacking or less perfect it is humility that compensates for the loss since it profits by the other's absence.[3]

"Paul," said the Lord, "my grace is sufficient for you."[4] Be convinced that the words to Saint Paul from the Lord are meant for you and me. The freely given grace of God, for which we have no claim or no right, is all that we need to be great saints. Until we accept that liberality on God's part and put our trust in it, we will never be what we should be. We will never have peace of mind.

Humility is the one virtue that can take defects and shortcomings and turn them into the gold of merit and holiness. When you fail, when you find your day is not as well spent as it should have been, accept it. Tell God you are sorry you have not given him what he deserves, but as far as you are concerned: That is the truth about me. And that very acceptance of the truth will more than supply by an increase of humility for the virtues and the merits and the other things you would have gained by spending the day perfectly. You have to be content with the second best. We can never do more than our second best. We should intend to do our best but, in fact, we never achieve it. It is just as well we do not.

2. Lk 1:46-55.

3. "Sermon 21: Sermon for the Saturday of the Second Week of Lent," *Guerric of Igny: Liturgical Sermons*, trans. Mount Saint Bernard Abbey, Cistercian Fathers Series 8 (Spencer, Mass.: Cistercian Publications, 1970), p. 144.

4. 2 Cor 12:9.

What is important is that we accept the truth about ourselves and, if possible, relish it. It is not enough to be poor in spirit. It is not enough to know your own infirmities. You must accept them and look at them as a source of glory to God. You must relish them.

*Saint Benedict's Ladder of Humility*

We who follow the Rule of Saint Benedict have no excuse for not knowing the way to humility—acquiring and developing it. In Chapter Seven of the Rule, we have Saint Benedict's ladder of humility that contains wisdom, sanctity, service of God, sacrifice, and holiness. Saint Benedict tells us what is at the end of the ladder: "When, therefore, a monk shall have ascended these various grades of humility, he shall presently attain to that perfect love of God which casteth out fear."[5] That is the perfection of life.

The first two rungs on Saint Benedict's ladder of humility are really the progress in virtue that brought you into the monastery. "The first degree of humility, then, is always to have the fear of God before our eyes—never forgetting, but always remembering what He has commanded."[6] "The second degree of humility is, that a person love not his own will, nor seek the gratification of his own desires, but shape all his actions according to those words of Our Lord: 'I came not to do My own will but the will of Him that sent Me' (Jn 6:38)."[7] These two degrees of humility cover the conversions of a man from a life of sin, or perhaps the avoidance of sin, to a realization of the importance of God's will. The passing of these two degrees may be considered the preliminary steps which have led us into religious life.

The next five degrees of humility concern interior humility. "The third degree of humility is for a monk to submit himself with all obedience to his Superior for the love of God, after the example of Jesus Christ, of Whom the Apostle saith: 'He humbled Himself, becoming obedient unto death' (Phil 2:8)."[8] There is an

5. RB 7,67.
6. RB 7,10-11.
7. RB 7,31-2.
8. RB 7,34.

importance advance here, for the monk accepts the principle that God's will is shown to us by our superior, in whose authority we must believe and whom we should obey and love. Faith and charity is stressed here and the example of our Lord takes an important place.

The next degree is a testing of the spiritual life and which is a stumbling stone where many come to grief and failure in their life as a religious. "The fourth degree of humility is to keep patience in the exercise of obedience, and not to lose it or depart

from it, either because of the difficulty of the thing commanded or the injuries to which one may be subjected, agreeably to what is said in Scripture: 'He that shall persevere to the end shall be saved' (Mt 24:13); and again, 'Let thy heart take courage, and wait thou for the Lord' (Ps 26[27]:14)."[9] This is where most of us fail to carry out the sacrifice we make of ourselves at our profession. When we notice the human element in our superior, or in our neighbors who try us, or in the trials of life which cause us so much trouble, we cease to take the supernatural view. We set aside our faith and lose our patience and submission. This is a fatal error. Saint Benedict exhorts us in the words of Scripture: *Wait for the Lord with courage; be stouthearted, and wait for the Lord*

(Ps 26[27]:14). It is a reminder that God will come to aid us if we but wait as we are asked to do.

Saint Benedict goes on: "The Scripture furthermore teaches that the faithful servant ought to suffer all things, however repugnant, for the love of his Lord, saying in the person of those who thus suffer, 'For Thee we suffer death all the day long; we are counted as sheep for the slaughter' (Ps 43[44]:23)."[10] Saint Benedict then expects us to rejoice: *But in all these things we overcome because of him who has loved us* (Rom 8:37).[11] The time comes sooner or later when obstacles permitted by God, and even appearing to come from the hand of superiors, may interfere with our vocation as Cistercian monks. A new appointment, a change of duty, a removal of some help can frustrate us. We forget that

9. RB 7,35-37.
10. RB 7,38.
11. RB 7,39.

God has warned us that we are to be purged. We fail to realize that we are being invited to go up higher at the banquet of his love.

Saint Benedict completes the ladder of interior humility in the next three degrees. The fifth degree refers to our need of revealing our interior life to a competent guide who can represent God. "The fifth degree of humility is for a monk to manifest to his Abbot, by humble confession, his evil thoughts and the sins he has committed in secret. To this the Scripture exhorts us in these words: 'Commit thy way to the Lord, and trust in Him' (Ps 36[37]:5)."[12] In this we obtain pardon, light, and strength.

The sixth degree asks us to be content with the poverty and abjection that may fall to our lot, whether interior or exterior, looking upon ourselves as unworthy servants, saying, *I have been brought to nothing, and I knew it not; I am become as a beast of burden before Thee, and I am always with Thee* (Ps 72[73]:22-23).[13]

The seventh degree brings us to the height of interior humility where we sincerely think of ourselves as the lowest of all—*I am a worm, not a man; the scorn of men, despised by the people* (Ps 21[22]:7).[14] This acknowledgement of our nothingness must be absolutely sincere, proceeding from a conviction without a trace of affectation.

The next five degrees are merely the external expression of our interior dispositions, whereby we avoid singularity and observe modesty, not being self-assertive, tending rather to be silent than to speak. When the height of this ladder is reached, Saint Benedict promises us that we shall then "attain to that perfect love of God which casteth out fear, whereby all that we dreaded so much at the outset, we shall begin to do, without any labor—naturally, as it were, and by habit, not through the fear of hell, but for the love of Christ, and because of the delight that attends the practice of virtue."[15]

12. RB 7,44-45.
13. RB 7,49-50.
14. RB 7,51-54.
15. RB 7,67-69.

I would suggest that while each of these degrees in some sense follows one another, they are not exactly like a thermometer. You need not get to the fourth before you get to the fifth. We should not be too worried, for example, if we start practicing the sixth degree of humility and realize that the fifth is by no means perfect. We are called to the closest possible union with God, which means that the monk is called to climb this ladder of humility, there being no other way that leads to God.

Let us pray, then, to Mary, whose humility made her worthy to be the Mother of God, to show us this way of sanctity and divine union and to obtain for us those special graces by which we can leave our self and cleave to God as our all.

## Obedience

Obedience is the infallible way of purification for the monk. It covers all the purifications necessary to reach the height of mystical union. Why? Obedience means cooperating with our Lord. You do not need extraordinary sufferings. Quiet, simple, gentle obedience—the highest prayer known to any of the saints—purifies your soul from all that is in the way of complete union with God. We have the means to this union through obedience in our monasteries. It does not depend on the wisdom of our superiors or our brethren, or even their holiness. Our obedience depends on our selves and on God's grace. All God asks of us is in four words: hope, charity, humility, and abandonment to his will, which is obedience.

I will put it to you in another way: Do what you are told and mind your own business. Your business is the formation of Christ in your soul and nothing else. If you are a superior, your business is the formation of Christ in your own soul and the souls of others. All your temporal administration and appointments must be subject to that. That is why criticism of a superior based on even the most profound technical knowledge, psychology or insights, is beside the point. When all is said and done, when the superior has become cognizant of all the factors involved in a particular job—the need for running a farm properly, the need for running a factory properly, or building properly, whatever it is—he has to subject and subordinate all those considerations to the spiritual good of the community and the sanctification of souls. That is his responsibility ultimately. It is his business, not yours.

The superior should be glad for advice and look for it. At times a monk is bound to give advice to a superior. For example, if you are a novice master and the superior has some views that you regard as mistaken about a novice, the novice master must state the case. If you are the prior who has put the case before the abbot, and the abbot says, "It doesn't matter, Father. We'll carry on as I said," then that is that. At times, however, it is your business to state the case to a superior.

Some superiors do not take it kindly to monks making representations. A superior might have a plan in mind and somebody has come along making representations, even though they are genuine and the monk has a duty to make them. The superior might not be as palpable as one would like. However, many representations made to an abbot are a case of a monk not minding his own business and that monk must be told to do just that, mind his own business.

### *Will of God*

We must not think that there is a special Cistercian perfection. Rather, there is a special Cistercian *way* of reaching perfection. It is the perfection to which all Christians are called.[16] The full perfection of Christianity is charity, union with our Lord Jesus Christ.[17, 18, 19]

16. "All Christians in any state or walk of life are called to the fullness of Christian life and to the perfection of charity." The Roman Catholic Church document *Lumen Gentium* 40§2, quoted in CCC 2013, 2028.

17. "Spiritual progress tends toward ever more intimate union with Christ." CCC 2014.

18. "Now the perfection of charity, in respect of which the Christian life is said to be perfect, consists in our loving God with our whole heart, and our neighbor as ourselves." *Summa Theologica*, IIa IIae, q. 184, a. 3., obj. 3, in St. Thomas Aquinas, *Summa Theologica*, vol. 2, trans. Fathers of the English Dominican Province (New York: Benziger, 1947), p. 1952.

19. "You ask me a way to arrive at perfection. I know only one—Love." Saint Thérèse of Lisieux, letter to her cousin Marie Guérin in 1894, in Monsignor Laveille, *St. Thérèse De L'Enfant Jésus*, p. 196.

For every Christian, perfection consists in doing the will of God. For monks, the obligation to do the will of God as revealed to us through a superior is primary to the other obligations indicated by Saint Benedict, even the obligation of the Divine Office.

With certain limitations, we all tend to have our own idea about how our life should be led. When that particular idea is interfered with, we resent, we murmur, and sometimes we disobey. Our idea is often based on high ideals of what a monastery should be, or what the tradition of the house was, or what an early Cistercian abbot said. We are quite forgetting that our obedience is not to the abbot that lived three hundred years ago, but our obedience is to the man in the job at present and to what he says. Only that will sanctify us.

For Saint Benedict, knowing God's will and doing it leads back to God. "That by pursuing the toilsome path of obedience thou mayest return to Him from whom thou hast departed by the slothful way of disobedience."[20] There is no other way of reaching heaven except the way God has planned. It is madness to think that you can plan your sanctification better than God can. Actually, what has happened is that we lack faith to realize that what is happening is God's will. God's will is never an obstacle in our lives.

I admit that sometimes a man in a state of grace debates with himself and is uncertain of God's will. In the matter of obedience there can be difficult cases. Leaving these cases apart, there is a straight way to heaven and that is doing the will of God.

One of our weaknesses is that we are continually trying to improve on God's will. Each one has a plan for our own sanctification. Especially the planning of the type of saint we are going to be. That is very marked in the case of the younger monks. We older men have got a bit more sense. We are prepared to leave part of the plan incomplete, leaving the details to God. God can decide whether my wings are to be ten feet long or six feet long. I have decided there must be wings and a halo, and a halo presumably of bright gold. But we keep on planning our sanctification and resent God's interference.

20. RB Prol,2.

Another obstacle to doing God's will is resentmen. the manifestation of God's will through a human agent, s. the abbot, especially when it interferes with our own concept . God's will for us.

*Obedience to the Abbot*

God's will is our sanctification. There is no other way to him. In the monastery, God's will is manifested to us through the abbot. A monk, after all, is a man who has chosen to be under an abbot and to walk by the judgment of another person.[21] By our profession of obedience we have announced in public and before God that we are monks who prefer to walk at the judgment of another man. Remember that because it covers a multitude of sins. It covers almost all eventualities that arise in monastic life.

Perhaps most of us prefer a sympathetic confessor. What the confessor says settles it, so I do it. The abbot walks in the chapter in the morning and announces that there will be extraordinary work today and classes are to be dropped. You are the professor of theology, and you have just decided to finish off a tract today. You realize that brother so-and-so had gotten to the abbot. All the brother wants to do is move sand. He could do it quite easily if he only took up a tractor, but he wants the novices and the simple professed to do it. "Why can't the abbot see that he'd been led up the garden path? What about theology?" We are very slow to see the will of God in that.

I dismissed a man under simple vows recently. It is a most unpleasant thing to have to do. It is a long story, but it throws a light on what can happen so I will give you a part of it. He was a convert and somewhat more mature in years. I mention that deliberately. I remember meeting him one day, and I said, "Brother, you're not looking too well."

"Oh, I'm feeling alright," he said.

"Well, you're not looking too well," I said.

"I am a bit worried about certain things," he said.

21. RB 7,34.

"Well, for the next two weeks," I said, "please don't come to vigils. Stay in bed until the Angelus."

So he is down the next morning for vigils. I met him after chapter. "Brother, I was surprised to see you at vigils today. I thought I told you to stay in bed. Is there some kind of misunderstanding?"

"Oh, no," he said. "But after all I have to keep my vows."

"What vow?" I said.

"The vow of obedience," he said.

"Well," I said. "I think I remember the day of your simple profession. And I think I remember that there is a written document promising *me* obedience, not the rule."

"Oh, yes," he said, "but obedience according to the rule. I promised to obey the rule, and I must go to vigils."

The same thing turned up with regards to satisfactions in choir.[22] He was making about ten satisfactions in choir at each Divine Office. Actually I knew what was behind it. He claimed he was reciting too quickly. He wanted to do a meditation on each word. If he had his way we would take three hours to say Office.

I told him in private and in public that he was not to make satisfactions. He went on making them. Because, he said, he was bound by the rule. He even wrote to the abbot general about it.

22. Satisfaction in choir refers to an external gesture made by a monk in recognition of a fault or lack of observance of expectations at the Divine Office. For example, a monk who arrives late to choir makes a satisfaction before occupying his stall. There were three kinds of satisfactions in the Cistercian rite: the great satisfaction which is made by prostrating fully; the moderate satisfaction which consists of going on the knees and bowing in such a way that the knuckles are placed on the ground near the knees; and, the third satisfaction is touching the ground with the knuckles without going on the knees. In addition to lateness to choir, satisfaction was made for a mistake in pronunciation of the text during the Divine Office, the making of disruptive noise, and for the bell ringer who is late to signal the beginning of the Office. These satisfactions were visible, yet symbolic actions indicative of interior conversion—that of admitting one's faults before God and the brethren and making amends for them. Today these external satisfactions of prostrating and bowing on knuckles are no longer in use in Cistercian monasteries. However, the need for admitting one's fault and need for conversion remains, and a monk late to choir, upon his own cognizance, may later apologize to the superior.

I had to dismiss him. That is a typical case. He said, "I want to be a religious." I offered him dispensation, but he would not take it. He said, "I want to be a religious."

"You do, Brother. You want to be a religious," I said, "provided you are your own superior."

"I must obey my conscience," he said.

"I can't claim to be a bishop with the bishop's authority to teach," I said. "But for this monastery, I am the official teacher, and I am telling you bluntly that your conscience is wrong. I am the person who is to temper the obligations of your vows and the rule."

We must train ourselves, as a first reaction, to accept the superior's words. Later, we can then discuss with ourselves the question whether it is prudent, a duty, or desirable to make a representation.[23] We can always do that, having chosen the proper time and the proper way to do it. But our first attitude is a readiness to submit if the superior insists.

### *United with Christ and His Church*

Obedience to God's will is the essence of the monastic life. In accepting the decision of the superior, we are united with Christ and every member of Christ. If we are told to wash dishes and do it with interior submission—without murmuring and for the love of God—we can be certain to be united to Christ, every apostle preaching, every priest saying Mass, every holy soul in this world in their merits and in their prayers, every saint in heaven, and with our Lady in heaven and on earth. We are united not only to all the existing saints but all who were, to the whole history of the Church, the whole body of Christ which extends through time as well as space. It is all ours.

23. "Fidelity to the exact observance of a rule and of regulations is a wonderful thing, provided it is prudent. Prudent means according to custom and according to wisdom. There is one principle, by the way, which I put before you very strongly. It is from Saint Thomas. He says, 'No act of virtue is a virtuous act unless it is also an act of prudence.' In other words, the thing may be good in itself and seem good to do, but unless it is prudent to do it, it is not a good act." Boylan, talk to Sisters, 6,7.

Saint Thérèse [of Lisieux] united herself to the merits of our Lord and all the saints, including, of course, our Lady.[24] We appropriate the good that had been done by other people, and by Christ himself, by uniting ourselves to them through obedience.

The Lord said, *If you love me, keep my commandments* (Jn 14:15). This is the way you abide in him. His commandments are not merely the Ten Commandments, but all these lawful manifestations of his will. They are the infallible means of divine union. In that matter, we have the example of our Lord himself and his mother.

We Cistercians are in a ghastly position. We have no possible excuse on the last day. We cannot say we did not know the way to heaven. We cannot say we did not know the way to high sanctity. We have the privilege of having an inspired guide in Saint Benedict and his rule. Yet, the responsibility of using it is ours. We have no excuse. We cannot tell the Lord on the last day, "Well, I didn't know that," or "I didn't realize that." It is all there in the chapter on humility and the example of the Lord and his mother. All we have to do is to ask both of them to give us the grace to do what they did—to consecrate ourselves to the doing of the will of God.

24. "Since You loved me so much as to give me Your only Son as my Savior and my Spouse, the infinite treasures of His merits are mine. I offer them to You with gladness, begging You to look upon me only in the Face of Jesus and in His heart burning with *Love*. I offer You, too, all the merits of the saints (in heaven and on earth), their acts of *Love*, and those of the holy angels. Finally, I offer You, *O Blessed Trinity!* the Love and merits of the *Blessed Virgin, my dear Mother*. It is to her I abandon my offering, begging her to present it to You" [emphasis retained]. Saint Thérèse of Lisieux, *Story of a Soul*, 3rd ed., trans. John Clarke (Washington, D.C.: ICS, 1996), p. 276.

## CONFERENCE FOUR:
# MONASTIC OBEDIENCE

For Saint Benedict, humility and obedience are closely related; they seem to be different aspects of the same thing. Saint Benedict expresses his concept of obedience in three areas. First, it is obedience to the will of God. Then it is obedience to appointed superiors. Finally, it is obedience to every human superiors. Let us look at our Lord's obedience.

### Consecrated to God

The first moment of God's existence as a human being was at the Annunciation.[1] What did our Lady answer to the angel Gabriel's message? *"Behold the handmaid of the Lord; be it done to me according to thy word"* (Lk 1:38). Do not think for a moment that it was a polite acceptance of a tremendous dignity. Our Lady knew what she was letting herself in for. Not merely would she be the mother of God, she was also to be the companion in the sufferings of the Redeemer. It is in that incident you will see clear evidence of her love for you and me. She saw our need for redemption and consecrated herself completely to the will of God.

Our Lady was certainly the most perfect creature that God ever made. She gave God the most wonderful service and love. She lived the most meritorious life that was ever lived here on earth by a mere human being. Our Lady could see no other way of pleasing God except by consecrating herself to the doing of his will. Such consecration is seen in the words of the prophet David: *"To do your will, O my God, is my delight, and your law is within my heart!"* (Ps 39[40]:9).

1. Lk 1:26-33.

The Annunciation cannot be separated from the mystical union of Christ with all the faithful. In the Annunciation, the union with the human body was only a step to his union with the Mystical Body. From the very first moment of his existence, Jesus, too, saw what he was letting himself in for, if I may speak familiarly of such a tremendous mystery. He saw you and me at our worst. He fitted himself to us and endured all the suffering and shame that we brought to him. Our Lord saw no better way of doing the extraordinary work that he had to do than by consecrating himself, like his mother had done, to the will of God.

## Filled with Christ

What, then, was his life? Saint Paul tells us: *Have this mind in you which was also in Christ Jesus, who though he was by nature God, did not consider being equal to God a thing to be clung to, but emptied himself, taking the nature of a slave and being made like unto men. And appearing in the form of man, he humbled himself, becoming obedient to death, even to death on a cross* (Phil 2:5-8). "He emptied himself" is a tremendous phrase. Our life as monks is to empty ourselves and fill ourselves with Christ. "Taking the nature of a slave." He who knew that it was not robbery to make himself equal to God took the form of a slave and became obedient—"obedient to death, even to death on a cross."

Again, lest we separate obedience from its context, what is the answer? *Jesus is "the stone that was rejected by you, the builders; which has become the corner stone." Neither is there salvation in any other. For there is no other name under heaven given to men by which we must be saved* (Acts 4:11-12).

We have to die daily to obedience just like our Lord did. And if we do, God will raise us up in Christ. It is a waste of time to mortify yourself, to die to yourself, to give up your own will if it does not get you anywhere. These are negative sides of perfection. There is no use in talking about detachment unless at the same time you have some idea of attachment to something else. There is no use in emptying yourself unless you are going to be filled up with something else. That is why you must always balance these things and see them in their perspective. You empty yourself in order to be filled with Christ. You detach yourself from yourself and this world in order to be attached to Christ. You deny yourself in order that literally you can assert Christ before God.

Too many books and preachers stress a negative piety that gets you nowhere. It is depressing, discouraging and not true. God has brought a joyful redemption to us. He took the sorrows on himself, and we now have the joy and liberty of the sons of God. If he asks us to die to our human nature, it is in order that we may rise to the joys of the "divine nature." The phrase is not too strong; Saint Peter used it.[2] We are called to be sons of God, and we are made sons of God by baptism, which is the beginning of our deaths to ourselves. We are baptized into the death of Christ.[3] The work of the redemption is found in the extraordinary way our Lord fitted himself to us and us to himself. He made us part of himself at the Annunciation.

### The Holy Family

To whom did the angels talk when the safety of the Holy Family was threatened?[4] The superior of the house, Saint Joseph. He was the least holy of the three people of the Holy Family. Do not forget that because it is not the holiness of a superior that gives him the right to command. It is, instead, the responsibility given to him by the community and abbot general. But from the point of view of the monk, the superior, with all his frailties, has been given the responsibility by God to lead the monastic community.

It is a terrible responsibility on those of us who are superiors that we have to teach by both word and example. You can understand the fearful strain it is to preach. We are always waiting for someone to stand up in chapter and say, "Very well, Reverend Father. Why don't you do what you're talking about?" Still, anyone who has preached knows that if you had to practice all you say before you preached it, there would be no sermons

2. 2 Pt 1:4.
3. Rom 6:3.
4. Mt 2:13.

preached. The very fact that we do preach virtue is to make up for the harm we have done by our bad example.

Notice that in the Holy Family you have the model of the religious life. Already we have seen how our Lady gave her fiat to God's plan for our redemption. In Saint Joseph, we have the example of obedience. He did exactly what he was told in order to keep his family safe. God came to save the world, found a Church, and convert the nations that were groaning in servitude for deliverance for thousands of years. Yet, our Lord spent thirty years going down to Nazareth and being subject to his parents. To learn obedience, we need not look anywhere else than the Holy Family.

## Jesus: A Model of Obedience

We have a perfect example of obedience in our Lord's life. First, we see his obedience to his Father. Thought by Mary and Joseph to be lost, they went back to Jerusalem and searched three days for him. Where did they find their son? *And it came to pass after three days, that they found him in the temple, sitting in the midst of the teachers, listening to them and asking them questions* (Lk 2:46).

Jesus asserted his obedience to his Father when he said, *"How is it that you sought me? Did you not know that I must be about my Father's business?"* (Lk 2:49).

Then we find in Scripture that Jesus also was obedient to Joseph and Mary.[5] *And he went down with them and came to Nazareth, and was subject to them. . .* (Lk 2:51). You have the whole religious life there. The whole justification and significance of our life is in that one phrase. When we feel that our life is wasted because there is nothing to be written about it, we have not made an impression on the world, we are not distinguished in the

5. "Jesus' obedience to his mother and legal father fulfills the fourth commandment perfectly and was the temporal image of his filial obedience to his Father in heaven. The everyday obedience of Jesus to Joseph and Mary both announced and anticipated the obedience of Holy Thursday: 'Not my will . . .' (Lk 22:42). The obedience of Christ in the daily routine of his hidden life was already inaugurating his work of restoring what the disobedience of Adam had destroyed (cf. Rom 5:19)." CCC 532.

community or anything like that, there is the answer. All they could find to write about the next thirty years of our Lord's life, after the incident of finding him in the temple was, *And he went down with them and came to Nazareth, and was subject to them.*

Jesus went down to Conyers and was subject to the abbot. That is the history of a perfect monk. Perfect means not only outside but inside. That is the snag. As we shall see when we come to examine the details of obedience, you will always have refuge in a little private judgment of your own. There is always a little part of you that stands back and watches the abbot ordering and you yourself obeying. You preserve an independence of judgment and critical admiration of the whole thing. That is the way you save your self-love. You find refuge from the humiliation of obedience in a certain sitting back in intellectual satisfaction in saying to yourself, "Well, of course, I do what I am told. It is the best thing to do. But, still, if I was the abbot, I would do things differently."

Jesus' obedience was a complete emptying of himself. He expects us to do the same: to forget our own will and do the will of the Father. *"Father, if thou art willing, remove this cup from me; yet, not my will but thine be done"* (Lk 22:42). He asks us to stop relying on our own strength and judgment. Instead, he wants us to place our trust in the Holy Spirit.

We cannot say we have not had a perfect example of obedience. Our Lord himself came on earth to give us an example in his life and death. *He humbled himself, becoming obedient to death, even to death on a cross* (Phil 2:8). Our Lady is the same: *"Behold the handmaid of the Lord; be it done to me according to thy word"* (Lk 1:38). There is our vocation. There is our obedience.

### Obedience as a Way to God

The whole of our Christian life is a continual fight. Daily we are given the same choice that the Jews were asked to make: *Pilate said to them, "Whom do you wish that I release to you? Barabbas, or Jesus who is called the Christ?"* (Mt 27:17). For us, it is "This man or Christ?" In this particular moment, am I going to live or is Christ going to live? Am I going to do my will, or am I going to do his?

Obedience is the way to God. The religious life is certainly a means of serving God, but it is more than that. It is a way in which you give yourself to God through obedience. You have the most pregnant expression of Saint Paul in summing up Christ: *It is now no longer I who live, but Christ lives in me* (Gal 2:20).

### Abbot's Role

What does Saint Benedict expect our obedience to be in general? First of all, it must be supernatural. We do not obey the abbot because we like him, he thinks the same way as we do, or we want to get a permission. Obedience is supernatural because we see Christ behind obedience.

We believe, as Saint Benedict tells us, that the abbot plays the part of Christ in the monastery.[6] No matter how familiar you are with the abbot—and everybody should be friends with the abbot—he is our father. On formal occasions you must always be careful to preserve the etiquette of bowing and giving the proper form of address for both your sake and his. It reminds him that everything he says is taken somewhat more seriously than the words of an ordinary man. It reminds you that his words are to be taken with a supernatural significance. Obviously, if it is only general conversation—he is not giving orders, he is not instructing—it still is a contact with somebody who stands in the person of Christ for us. That contact will give us grace if we approach him in faith.

### Prompt Obedience

Our obedience must be prompt, without delay.[7] It is the whole test of and meaning of devotion. It is not senseless feeling. It is not being wrapped in ecstasy. It is a readiness to accept the will of God when it is manifested. Your first reaction to any order or even any suggestion from a superior should be "yes" in your mind.

6. RB 2,2-3.
7. RB 5,1.

However, you may have to make representations. I am in charge of a monastery where farming is of tremendous importance, but I know nothing about farming. Nowadays, you either make a hundred percent job of farming or you lose money. There is no room for mistakes. I go up to Father Alphonsus, who happens to be an Irishman. I make some suggestion or even give some order. He says immediately, "Well, Reverend Father, if you do that to those sheep, you've got to watch the fencing over there. That means five new strands of fences. It means there is a government order about using that land." He may be bound to argue with me in the sense of stressing his case reasonably to assure that I understand. But he should be ready, and I know that this man is ready from the word go, if I insist. Nevertheless, a superior cannot know everything. You have to sometimes put facts before him.

Each man with technical ability has a right to representation, but it must be respectful. You must discern when you need to press your case. Be careful of that part of you that wants its own way.

A monk strives not only for establishing a good relationship with a superior but to "super"-naturalize that relationship. If he cannot, he had better go home. There is no point in staying in the monastery if you cannot see Christ in the abbot. That applies not only to the abbot but to subordinate superiors within the measure of their authority.

## Exact Obedience

The whole of our life is a matter of obedience. Another characteristic of proper obedience: it must be exact. It is the small things that make us saints. If we are waiting for the big things, we never reach sanctity. Cistercian life does not offer you big things. We are sanctified by small things. It requires more virtue and faith to be supernatural in the small things than the big things. Human nature naturally responds to a big occasion. Somehow a big occasion brings out something in us that we did not know we had. It is the little occasions, however, that demand a special virtue and grace.

A monk has to know his superior. No man has the ability to put into words the complete policy that is to be carried out. The abbot will leave something to your judgment. You have got to realize that his words must be judged in human fashion. To a certain extent you have got to know your man—both the superior has got to know his men and the men have to know the superior.

If the superior says in chapter that no one is to do so and so, there are four or five obvious exceptions that he has not even worried to make or even thought about. But where he has laid down a way of doing things definitely, our obedience should be exact and generous.

Suppose it is a question of being asked to do something the way you think is the wrong way. You put your case fairly strong to the superior, and he says, "No, Father, I want it done. . ." Now there is a fearful temptation to do it badly to prove that you are right. The superior will have to give in and let you do it your way in the future. That is the difference between the saint and the "fifty-percent monk." The holy man says, "It is the will of God, and I'll do the best and make a success of it even though it proves I'm wrong." I warn you: The superior may be quite wrong in his ideas, but you will probably find the darn thing will work. I have seen a superior give the most childish instructions. The men carry them out, and they produced wonderful results.

### Interior Obedience

If we are told to plant cabbages upside down, there is no guarantee that they will grow. But it does not matter to you whether they grow or not; it is the will of God that they should be planted upside down. God knows his own business. If it is the will of God that certain things should be wasted, that is his business. God used to insist on the Jews offering their best animals and the first fruits of their crops to him.[8] It is an apparent waste. When you waste things (according to your view) by obedience, you are sacrificing it to God. He has the right to dispose

8. Ex 23:19; Lv 2:4; Nm 18:13; Dt 18:4.

of these things. The unfortunate superior may have to answer to God for waste, but you are offering sacrifice.

The tremendous test of obedience: it must be interior. The man who goes along and does what he is told but with complaining in heart is not practicing religious obedience. It is not obedience to say, "Yes, Father" and then to think, "This is the wrong way to do it. If I had my way, I wouldn't do it that way. He doesn't know what he is asking of me. This will surely fail. What a waste of time." The external obedience is there, but the essential interior obedience is lacking.[9]

## Life through Obedience

The tremendous significance of obedience is in the way we build in ourselves the life of Christ. The good of obedience that Saint Benedict speaks of is Jesus Christ. When we are doing the will of God, Christ is there doing it with us. When we are doing the will of God, Christ is in us identifying himself with us, sharing in everything we do. By doing the will of God, we give Christ birth and share in the maternity of our Lady. With all due reverence, we might even say that to some extent, we share in a remote way in the paternity of the Father. We have the tremendous power to give new life to Christ here on earth—to give him our hands, our hearts, our lips, our whole self, to do the will of his Father. The only condition is that we do God's will through obedience with our heart and hands.

9. "Very often you have to do things badly through obedience. You are not bound to believe that it is the best way of doing them, but you are bound to believe it is the best way of pleasing God. It is the surest way of finding Christ. The surest way of bringing grace down on this earth." Boylan, talk to Sisters, 3,7.

## CONFERENCE FIVE:

# UNITED WITH CHRIST'S PASSION

### Continuing the Work of Christ

Our function as Christians is to continue the life of Christ, and each Christian has a special part of Christ to continue. Priests called to the direct apostolate continue Jesus' public life of preaching. Monks continue not only Jesus' hidden life but his passion and death. We are not called to participate in the direct work of the apostolate except in helping one another within the monastery.

Christ did not save the world by his hidden life, public life, preaching, or by miracles. We are saved by his passion and death. He saved the world when he was absolutely prostrate—nailed to the cross, unable to move a muscle except in the terrible struggles of a tortured body, completely powerless to help himself. This prostration is patron of our life as monks. We continue our Lord's passion by carrying his cross and sharing in his passion, and, above all, his death.

You and I have taken solemn vows to live according to the Rule of Saint Benedict. It is the plan for our sanctification. We read, or hear it read, four times a year. We have no reason to complain, no right to avoid the patron of our life—being on the cross with Christ.

Just as our Lord could not save the world except by the cross, so neither can we be sanctified except by the cross of the fourth degree of humility:

> . . . to keep patience in the exercise of obedience, and not to lose it or depart from it, either because of the difficulty of the thing commanded or the injuries to which one may be subjected, agreeably to what is said in Scripture: "He that shall persevere to the

> end shall be saved" (Mt 24:13); and again, "Let thy heart take courage, and wait thou for the Lord" (Ps 26[27]:14).[1]

If that does not happen to you, if your whole life goes on in sweetness and having your own way, I am afraid you have had it. I am afraid God has set you for less and decided to give your reward here below. If he cannot ask you to carry a cross, then he cannot make you a saint. When things are not going your way, be thankful. If it does go your way all the time, do not say thank you. Ask our Lord, "Is there something wrong?"

We are entitled to expect peace, joy, and happiness, but it is a peace deep down. It is a peace of those who share the cross with Christ.

*He that shall persevere to the end shall be saved* (Mt 24:13). *Let thy heart take courage, and wait thou for the Lord* (Ps 26[27]:14). Allow me to comment on those two texts of Scripture by telling a story.

In the old country, we make butter in a churn constructed of tall cinders of wood. These two frogs fell into a churn of milk that was only half full. They tried to climb up the wall, but it was too slippery. They kept on swimming around. One fellow says to the other after a lot of discussion, "Ah, we may as well give up. There is no point in keeping on swimming. We will never get out of this." He gave up, stopped swimming, and drowned. The other fellow said, "Well, I'll keep on swimming. You never know what will turn up." What happened? He kept on swimming, and, as a result of his swimming, the milk turned into butter and he was able to jump out.

I can assure you from bitter personal experience, there are times in the monastic life when you will feel as helpless as those frogs swimming in the milk. Your only hope is to keep on going, waiting for miracles. During our monastic life, you will meet some situation where someone has got on your nerves or some job you have got drives you to an impossible situation. You will find that it goes on until you are just at a breaking point. Then, God's providence suddenly intervenes. There is a change made

1. RB 7,35-37.

in appointments, or some change made in the monastery. The whole thing is solved. For a moment, you are left in peace. Then it starts all over again. You better get used to swimming in milk, because it is going to be the pattern of your life.

## Patience in Trials

Saint Benedict's fourth degree of humility covers all that Saint John of the Cross (1542–1591) has written about in *The Ascent of Mount Carmel* and *The Dark Night of the Soul.* First, you are going to have hard things happen to you from a superior. It is not that he is an unfair man or wants to take it out on you. Not even that he is planning to crucify you to make you a saint. However, he is a human being and is limited. He cannot see into the depths of your heart. He does not know what suffering he is inflicting on you by a certain appointment. In any case, he is an instrument in the hands of God. Without knowing it, he may produce a condition for you by his appointments where you find what Saint Benedict calls the unjust things—those that are hard and contrary.

The fourth step of humility is that in this obedience under difficult, unfavorable, or even unjust conditions, the monk quietly embraces suffering.[2] And he embraces hardships and unjust treatment with patience. Saint Benedict says, "So patient are they under trials and injuries, that if any man strike them on the right cheek, they turn to him the left. If any man take away their coat, they let him take away their cloak also. If forced to go one mile they go two (Mt 5:39-41); fulfilling the counsel of Our Lord."[3] Saint Benedict also says: ". . . patiently bear one another's infirmities, whether of mind or body."[4]

Wherever patience is spoken of by Saint Benedict, we must refer to the prologue and realize what patience means for him.

> Thus persevering in the Monastery till death, and never departing from the doctrine and guidance of our Divine Master, we shall become, by patience, partakers in the sufferings of Christ,

2. RB 7,35.
3. RB 7,42.
4. RB 72,5.

> and thereby deserve to be co-heirs with Him in His heavenly Kingdom.[5]

Our vocation is to continue the passion of Christ by our patience in adversity. We are to have patience with external and interior difficulties. Patience with the superior, brothers, and even God, patience with the food, patience with the heating arrangement, patience with the ventilating arrangement, patience with the weather, patience with the dryness of our own soul, patience with the lack of the right books, patience with the misunderstandings we have with our confessors. You can multiply the list.

When the superior speaks, it takes heroic patience to say, "*Dominus est.* It is the Lord that speaks." If we always see the human superior speaking, then we are not living by faith. We are told by Saint Benedict that the abbot plays the part of Christ in this monastery.[6]

Suppose the abbot changes your job assignment. Are you prepared to believe that Christ has taken you out of one job and put you in another? If you are not prepared to do that, you have not got the faith that Saint Benedict expects of a monk. There is no use saying, "I've been up at two o'clock every morning. I've never missed an Office. I've been at every common exercise. Why should they treat me like that?" It means all your virtues are directed to the wrong thing. You are satisfying yourself. Here our Lord asks you for this sacrifice, and you will not give it to him.

## Crucified with the Lord

If we want to reign with Christ, we have to be prepared to obey with Christ. We must expect God to prepare us for the tremendous vocation to which he has called us. Through men, bad health, dryness of soul, and other difficulties, we must have a cheerful submission without arguing with ourselves: "Why should I put up with this? What's the reason for this? What have I done? Who's got to the abbot? What on earth has happened?"

5. RB Prol,50.
6. RB 2,2-3.

"*Dominus est*. It is the Lord." After all, I have offered myself this morning at Mass. I told God that he could do what he liked with me. Here I am. I have no right to refuse what the Lord plans for me.

Daily our patience is tested. Bit by bit, we have got to be prepared to die to ourselves, to be crucified and let somebody else do the crucifying. The monastic life has been called a "white martyrdom."[7] Saint Jerome sees monks as martyrs, and Saint Bernard sees our poverty as a martyrdom.[8, 9] That is the point. You are quite willing to put yourself on the altar to be sacrificed provided you can pick up the knife and put it in where you would like. You are perfectly willing to go up to the dorm every morning and scourge yourself. You are perfectly willing to cut down your food to half and have the satisfaction of being a martyr. "Oh, yes, a fine thing. If I'm a martyr, I'm going to be a mystic

7. The origin of "white martyrdom" can be found in early Christian monasticism in Egypt who venerated the Christian martyrs and their "blood witness" to the faith. Regretting that such martyrdom was no longer possible (at that time and locale in history), they saw a "white martyrdom" in dying to the world and flesh with a life of solitude rigorously devoted to prayer, contemplation and worship of God apart from the society.

8. "As martyrs praise the Lord in purity in the region of the living, so also monks who sing the Lord's praises day and night must possess the same purity of the martyrs, because they are truly martyrs themselves. For what the angels do in heaven, that the monks do on earth." Saint Jerome quoted in Maurus Wolter, *The Principles of Monasticism*, trans. and ed. Bernard A. Sause (St. Louis: Herder, 1962), p. 393.

9. "But what means it, most dearly beloved, that the same reward is promised to the poor and to the martyrs? Are we not hereby instructed to look upon voluntary poverty as in the very truth of martyrdom. . . What indeed can you find more wonderful, what martyrdom can be more cruel than to be famished with hunger in the midst of banquets, to shiver with cold, half-clad, in the midst of abundance of costly garments, to be oppressed with poverty in the midst of wealth which the world offers, which the devil displays, which our own cupidity longs for? . . . In fine, the kingdom of heaven is promised alike to poverty and to martyrdom, but whilst it is truly purchased by poverty, it is actually given and given at once to those who suffer for Christ's sake." Saint Bernard in a sermon for the Feast of All Saints in *St. Bernard's Sermons for the Seasons and Principal Festivals of the Year*, trans. priest of Mount Melleray (Westminster, Md.: Carroll Press, 1950), pp. 351–352.

too." But that is not God's way. He is not going to give you the satisfaction of having things always go your way, especially in choosing how you will be martyred. God's way is the formation of Christ in us and the destruction of our selfish self.

The resurrection of Christ came after his crucifixion. With us, both things are happening gradually. Our crucifixion and our dying are bringing us down. At the same time Christ is rising in us. As we die to ourselves, Christ increases in us. Saint John the Baptist put it very neatly, *"He must increase, but I must decrease"* (Jn 3:30). That is a motto for your life, a summary of what you have got to do, what is going to be done to you. We are to receive his body and blood every morning in order that he may increase and we may decrease. Saint Benedict goes on:

> The Scripture furthermore teaches that the faithful servant ought to suffer all things, however repugnant, for the love of his Lord, saying in the person of those who thus suffer, "For Thee we suffer death all the day long; we are counted as sheep for the slaughter" (Ps 43[44]:23).[10]

**Perseverance**

Holding on, do not quit. You will fall down, but it does not matter how often you fall. It does not matter how often you fail in humility. It does not matter how often you fall into sin. It does not matter how often things go wrong. It does not matter how often you are tempted to leave the monastery. Do not quit, but turn back to God. As long as you keep getting up, you cannot be beat. It is not a matter of natural fortitude. It is a matter of faith and confidence in God. You have got to say to yourself, "God knows what he's doing."

All these things arrive when we are in dryness. When you are swimming in grace, and our Lord is present, it is quite easy. There is no trouble at all. "Oh, the abbot's a lovely man. He's not unreasonable at all. He's guided by the Holy Spirit. He's merely given me a cross. Oh, the brethren are difficult, but after all God designed that to sanctify me." It is quite easy. No trouble at all.

10. RB 7,38.

Then, you have a dreary half hour of prayer in the morning. You are thrashing out the Psalms for five hours in the day. You go into the Blessed Sacrament and wonder what is inside up there. Is there a God? God means nothing, no more than being a word of three letters. It is not quite the nice cross the abbot is giving to you. "Who's got at the abbot? What's gone wrong here? What have I done? Why should this happen to me? Haven't I done my best?" You know as well as myself, we are all in the same boat. We all have to learn the hard way.

It is only by many failures that we achieve any degree of success. Remember, it is the last battle that matters. It does not matter how often we are beaten. If we keep on getting up, our Lord supplies for us. Saint Benedict gives the key: "Thus animated with the assured hope of the rewards God has promised them, they go on rejoicing and saying, 'But in all these things we overcome, because of Him that hath loved us' (Rom 8:37)."[11]

**Love for Jesus**

Our motive is the love of our Lord. All this endurance is useless, if it does not come from personal love of Jesus. We Cistercians express our love for our Lord through humility and obedience. It is the way we develop that love.

Love of our Lord makes our monastic life worthwhile. Without that, our life profits nothing and means nothing. Saint Paul said: *And I point out to you a yet more excellent way. If I should speak with the tongues of men and of angels, but do not have charity, I have become as sounding brass or a tinkling cymbal. And if I have prophecy and know all the mysteries and all knowledge, and if I have all faith so as to remove mountains, yet do not have charity, I am nothing. And if I distribute all my goods to feed the poor, and if I deliver my body to be buried, yet do not have charity, it profits nothing* (1 Cor 13:1-3).

Saint Paul also said, *Now we know that for those who love God all things work together unto good, . . .* (Rom 8:28). All these trials and reproofs from our neighbors and ourselves work together for the good. Even our sins, as Saint Augustine says, *if* we love

11. RB 7,39.

God. The reason for loving God is that he has loved us.[12] He is asking us to do nothing else except what he himself had to undergo. We have only to look at the crucifix to realize how our Lord loved us. What he wants from us is a love that will do the same as he did, namely, deliver ourselves to him because we love him. "He loved me and delivered himself for me" sums up our Lord's attitude to us. Can we look at him suffering for us, think of him suffering, and refuse to help him on his cross by patiently enduring the cross he has designed for us—designed deliberately to unite us to himself forever?

12. 1 Jn 4:10.

## CONFERENCE SIX:

# FAITH AND CONFIDENCE IN GOD'S LOVE

### Devotion to Jesus Christ

The word *Christian* implies a relationship of complete dependence on Christ. If you take away that relationship, *Christian* loses meaning. The perfection of a Christian is the perfection of a relationship with Christ which is the perfection of charity—complete dependence and abandonment to Christ. The way to make this relationship with Christ all that it should be is through a personal devotion to the person of our Lord. It is a particular devotion to him under the form that he himself has asked for, namely, to his Sacred Heart.

Our Holy Father [Pope Pius XII] speaks of the personal devotion to the Sacred Heart in the encyclical *Haurietis Aquas*.[1, 2] He warns us against neglecting it under any pretext of pietistic devotion or sentimentality. It contains the essence of all Christianity. It is the remedy for our shortcomings and the needs of our spiritual life. Its devotion is to the love of our Lord for his Father and for us.

> The Church has always valued, and still does, the devotion to the Most Sacred Heart of Jesus so highly that she provides for the spread of it among Christian peoples everywhere and by every

1. Pope Pius XII, Encyclical *Haurietis Aquas* (May 15, 1956).

2. Pope Pius XII, who died on October 9, 1958, is known for his writings that began the theological preparations for Vatican II almost a decade before the Council was convened under his successor, Blessed John XXIII. An ardent devotee of the Immaculate Heart of Mary, Pius XII consecrated the world to the Immaculate Heart in 1942 at the request of Our Lady of Fatima. He established a Feast of the Immaculate Heart of Mary in 1945 and promoted the "Brown Scapular of Our Lady of Mount Carmel" and the "Apostleship of Prayer."

> means. At the same time she uses every effort to protect it against the charges of so-called "naturalism" and "sentimentalism." In spite of this it is much to be regretted that, both in the past and in our own times, this most noble devotion does not find a place of honor and esteem among certain Christians and even occasionally not among those who profess themselves moved by zeal for the Catholic religion and the attainment of holiness.[3]

## Jesus' Love for Us

The first act of devotion to the Sacred Heart is to believe in Jesus' love for us. How often are we in the position of the man in the Bible who said, *"I do believe; help my unbelief"* (Mk 9:23)? We do not believe in the Sacred Heart enough. We are not yet convinced that God really loves us.

Meditation, prayer, reading, and reflection help our faith in God's love and allow that love to influence our lives. How real is God's love in our lives? How much does it affect our lives? How much does it show itself by trust? How much do we still feel that we have to look after our own salvation? Too often, the focus is on what *we* do. *We* have got to arrange providence. *We* have got to arrange our lives. If my little plan is not carried out, God cannot make me a saint. There is a little bit of that in every one of us. Even after 27 years in a monastery, I find it in myself.

We have not yet fully committed ourselves into the hands of our Lord. The reason is that we do not believe in his love. We do not believe sufficiently in his merits. If we believe in his love and merits, we would stop worrying and cast our burden completely on the Lord.

## Faith and Confidence in Our Lord

Faith associated with confidence is the first act of our devotion to our Lord. Look at the trouble he has gone to. It is true that we are not asked to follow private revelations. The Church, however, has made devotion to the Sacred Heart her own and approved of the image that is put before us and the form that is put before

3. *Haurietis Aquas* 8.

us. The symbol of the Sacred Heart is a summary of his love for us: His heart on fire when crowned with thorns, pierced with a lance, shedding its last drop of blood. Is there anything more eloquent? His heart is on fire with love, ready to pour out, as he did, the very last drop of his blood for love of us.

What is our response? To crown that heart with thorns? You do not have to be a big sinner to do that. It is not even so much our sins that crucified our Lord's heart. It is our lack of confidence in him. It is our unwillingness to believe in his readiness to pardon us. It is our unreadiness to take his love at his word. Sins do not worry him. They cost him tremendous suffering, but they do not worry him if we only bring them to him with sorrow. What does worry him, what breaks his heart, and what would have literally killed him in the Garden of Gethsemani, if it was not for the divine power sustaining him, is our lack of confidence.

Our Lord came from heaven to live, suffer, and die for us. Yet, we will not trust him enough. We say, "How could he love me, a great sinner." Or, "I haven't enough greatness to be a great sinner." We find an excuse. We look at the saints and say "I'm not a saint. It's easy for the Saint Thérèse the Little Flower, for example, to trust in God." Well, even Saint Thérèse told us a few things about tremendous sinners when she told us that we should have the *sense* to cast ourselves into the arms of God.[4]

## The Prodigal Son

The story of the prodigal son is a revelation given to us by the Lord himself of God's attitude toward repentant sinners.[5] Anything that contradicts that revelation is heresy. It is the official

4. "The remembrance of my faults humiliates me, leads me never to rely at all on *my* strength, which is only weakness; but the remembrance speaks to me still more of mercy and love. When one casts one's faults into the consuming flame of Love, how could they fail to be consumed past return?" [emphasis retained]. Saint Thérèse letter to Abbé Bellière, June 21, 1897 in *Collected Letters of Saint Thérèse of Lisieux*, ed. Abbé Combes, trans. F.J. Sheed (New York: Sheed and Ward, 1949), p. 348.

5. Lk 15:11-32.

revelation of God's attitude toward sinners. God's way of dealing with sinners is not the angry confessor: "Why did you do that? How on earth could you do that?"

What is God's way?

The picture is painted for us by our Lord of this man who, having got his inheritance from his father, lived riotously until he has nothing left. The son is reduced to the ultimate extreme of misery and degradation for a Jew—to herd swine. He decides that the life of the servants in his father's house is a better one. What does his father do when he starts to return to him? Does he wait for him to come in solid majesty and treat him coldly—"Well it's about time you came back. Of course, you cannot possibly expect to be treated as you were originally. You've had it my friend. You've had your share. Made you bed and got to lie on it." That is the way most Roman fathers would do.

What does God do? *"But while he was yet a long way off, his father saw him and was moved with compassion, and ran and fell upon his neck and kissed him"* (Lk 15:20). That is our Lord's attitude to a repentant sinner. He *runs* to meet you. What does he do? *Embraces you.* That is God meeting a repentant sinner. That is the only picture which we can dare put before ourselves of God dealing with a repentant sinner. Everything else is heresy that contradicts that because that is our Lord's revelation of God's attitude to a repentant sinner.

The only snag in the ointment is the elder brother who is not pleased that his younger brother is getting such a response from their father. Yet, this elder brother, too, has a special place in the Father's heart. *"But he said to him, 'Son thou art always with me, and all that is mine is thine'"* (Lk 15:31).

That is our Lord's revelation to us of how both he and his Father treat repentant sinners. If you think your sins are keeping you back from sanctity, you are denying the revelation of the forgiveness of sins.

### Jesus Forgives Sins

We stand in choir and sing the Nicene Creed with great solemnity. The creed states, "I believe in the forgiveness of sins."

Do you believe your sins are forgiven? Do you believe that when a priest says to you, "I forgive you your sins in the name of the Father, the Son and Holy Spirit," that your sins are forgiven? If you do, forget about them and do not irritate our Lord by reminding him of the times you have offended him. Remind him, if you like, of your need of him. Do not renew the hardness of your heart by insisting that these sins are still between you and the Lord. That is the sin of Judas.

If Judas is in hell, and I am not saying he is, it is not because he betrayed our Lord, bad as it was or worse. It is because he committed the supreme blasphemy of deciding: "My sin is greater than God's forgiveness. I'm such a great sinner that God can't forgive the sins I have committed, can't undo them because God isn't big enough to forgive me my sins. There's a limit to his mercy." That is blasphemy.

If Judas had only had the sense to take our Lord at his word and remember the parable of the Prodigal Son, and cast himself on our Lord's mercy as Saint Peter did, Judas, I hold, would have been the greatest saint in the Church after Saint Joseph. He would have been the saint of our Lord's mercy.

Mercy is the keynote to God's plan for our purification. Therefore, the more sins we have to be forgiven, the better chance we have of reaching the top. Make your sins a source of confidence in God's saving grace. If we have separated ourselves from God in the past by sin, let not those past sins be a present obstacle or separation from him now. It is what breaks his heart that we will not believe in his love and his willingness to forgive our sins. He has gone to endless trouble to assure us that our sins are no obstacle if we only give them to him. He is glad to see us coming and rejoices at the chance of restoring and wiping them out. Our Lord is our complete supplement. He comes to us so that nothing may be wanting to us in any grace. The work of our Lord in saving souls is absolutely a perfect job—nothing was left undone. Trust our Lord.

## Jesus Desires Our Love

Our Lord desires our love because he is in love with us as well as with his Father. He desires our love, first of all, for his Father's sake. Because he sees that it is only by our loving him that he can make us what his Father wants us to be. He desires our love for our sake because he knows that it is only by loving him completely that we will find eternal happiness. He desires our love for his own sake because he has a human heart as well as a divine will. He wants his love returned.

If we would give him half a chance, he would make us tremendous lovers of his own heart. Repeatedly, appeals have been made to us by our Lord for our friendship, for our complete abandonment to him. We need not worry about our sins, our weaknesses, our history, our present temperament, or weakness of character. These things do not matter. We are dealing with infinite power and infinite love. We are dealing with a savior who has the omnipotence of God, the unlimited power to save us and make us what he wants us to be. The only obstacle is our lack of confidence.

What does our Lord himself tell us? What does our Lord want from us? The whole thing is in the Canticle of Canticles [Song of Songs]. *Set me as a seal on your heart, as a seal on your arm; for stern as death is love, relentless as the nether world is devotion; its flames are a blazing fire. Deep waters cannot quench love, nor floods sweep it away. Were one to offer all he owns to purchase love, he would be roundly mocked* (Sg 8:6-7).

You will find it in the Mass and in the most pure heart of Mary. The only other saint to have it in the Church is Saint Mary Magdalene. Our Lord wants us to put him as a seal upon our heart—to keep our heart's love for him and not to waste it on creatures. He does not forbid us to love other people. We must love our parents, family, and brethren. But all those loves must be subordinated to our personal love for him.

## "Prefer Nothing Whatever to Christ"

We cannot quench the love of the Sacred Heart for us. *Deep waters cannot quench love, nor floods sweep it away* (Sg 8:6-8). What is the test of love? To give the whole substance of our house and not to count the cost. Saint Benedict said it, "Let them prefer nothing to Christ."[6] There is a lot in the words, "not to count the cost." We are all quite willing to do heroic things if we can measure up the cost and say to the Lord, "Yes, I love you. It cost me that. I'm going to do it for you."

True love never counts the cost. If you know someone you love wants something, you will get it for them. You do not stop to think of the cost. It is the same way with our Lord. He did not count the cost, and he does not ask us to do it either. When he wants something, give it to him. Do not bargain with our Lord. If you want somebody converted, if you want some favor from heaven, do not go to our Lord and say, "If you do that for me I'll say a rosary every day or I'll offer up this, that, or the other thing." I am not condemning what is a very holy thing to do, but I think there is a better way. Go to God and ask him for what you want. "I want this in the name of our Lord Jesus Christ and I offer up his merits for it." Period. Do not bargain by saying, "Because I love you, I'll do so and so for you." Keep the two things separate.[7]

In all these matters is tremendous liberty. No two people take the same view because the same Holy Spirit produces different works and gifts in each of us. We must be faithful to the work of the Holy Spirit and never to let our own ideas, however holy, interfere with the work of the Holy Spirit in the souls of others.

The Lord brought us to the monastery to give him love with a readiness to share in the sufferings, to comfort him, and to console him. It is the secret of solving all of our difficulties and overcoming all of our weaknesses. It must be based on faith and confidence in him. Most Sacred Heart of Jesus, I trust in Thee.

6. RB 72,11.

7. "You will find nuns saying, 'Now, if you'll convert that soul, I'll say the Stations of the Cross every day. I'll take no butter for breakfast. I'll take no coffee for supper.' They make bargains with God. That is a holy thing and it is not for me to disapprove of it. Personally I would not do it. There is another way that appeals to me better. When I want anything from our Lord, I ask him through his merits—the merits of his own son and his own goodness. And no more. What I do for our Lord, I do without bargaining about what I am to get for it. I ask because of the merits of his son." Boylan, talk to Sisters, 3,9.

## CONFERENCE SEVEN:
# DETACHMENT

### Custody of the Heart

Our first duty in the spiritual life, in regards to the Sacred Heart, is custody of the heart. You will find people trying to keep custody of the eyes, tongue, and ears by going around with eyes cast down and mouths shut. Their hearts, however, are attached to their dreams, imaginations, or some person. That is not devotion. Devotion is primarily the readiness of our heart to do God's will.

Keeping our heart for God does not mean we cannot be attached to our parents and brethren. We are bound to love them. The Lord has a personal love for each one of us and desires our love in return. However, we hurt our Lord by attachment to our own plans, ideas, and ways. You are put into the machine shop, for example, and get attached to the job. The abbot says, "Father, you're to give up the machine shop and you are going to teach theology." What is your reaction? Are you attached to your job? Have you let your custody of the heart down? You can say to the abbot with perfect genuineness and perfect virtue, "Certainly, Reverend Father, if you insist. It is only fair to tell you that I have the type of mind that needs some manual work. Do you mind if I set an hour or two a day for working in the shop?" That is a perfectly reasonable request, but it should be made with detachment. Our first response must be obedience, the willingness to accept God's will because we love our Lord both for his own sake and our sake.

If the monk is working for the love of God, he will be glad to see another man take his job. I was quite annoyed one day when a monk was appointed to play the organ with me. I wanted my way of doing things, so it took me some time to realize that I was being organist to please myself, not our Lord. We have to be wary of the weeds of attachments growing in our heart.

## Purity of Intention

Purity of intention is important in the spiritual life. Be attentive to your actions. What are your reasons for doing things? Once You have got into the monastic run of things—got into step, so to speak—what is the progress we look for? Cutting down your food? Going to bed later and getting up earlier? Taking the discipline extra days? Doing extra penance? The fundamental rule of Cistercian perfection is to be like the others—no more or less. If you want to sleep on the floor, wear iron chains, or do anything like that, go somewhere else. Do not start that in a Cistercian monastery.

The penance of the Rule of Saint Benedict—the penance of obedience—is enough to make a man a saint. We have to do the things we do today and then again tomorrow with greater purity of intention. Purity of intention is living our life more to please God and less to please ourselves.

## "My God and My All"

Poverty in the proper sense of the word is really the foundation of happiness. That is why Saint Francis of Assisi (1181/1182–1226) could go around singing with joy. He had given everything to God and had nothing of his own. There was nothing to interfere with the gift of his heart freely to our Lord. We have to do the same. We are either detached monks or we are not monks at all.

The whole essence of being a monk is being detached from everything else. It would be an absolute waste of energy to detach yourself from the world you left only to spoil the whole thing by getting attached to some five-cent trifle in a monastery. Examine your life and the things to which you are attached. What comes between you and God?

The fearful trouble about attachments, whether it is an attachment to your plan, work, possession, or to a person, is the blindness. Attachments blind us to our own conduct. You can see others as blind, but you yourself hold that there is only one way of doing things. That is blindness in you!

If you want to find all, you have to leave all. Remember Saint Francis of Assisi's ecstasy. It shows you the fundamental pattern of prayer and spiritual joy. Saint Francis' life was: "My God and my all." God was his everything.

The development of prayer starts with: *I* am praying. *My* prayer. And finishes with: My God and my all. In the end, I do not even have a prayer of my own. They are all from God but God is mine. The whole mystical life is that transition from a prayer of my own to nothing of my own but God.

Personal devotion to our Lord cuts at the root of self-seeking. We are to make the Lord the center of our lives instead of ourselves. Our prayer, in fact, is the returning of God's love for us back to the Lord that he has given to us.

**Christ's Sacrificial Death**

Our Lord saw you and me at the beginning of his life here on earth. He saw me with all my sins, temptations, weaknesses, and the circumstances of life. He deliberately planned his life so that he would carry me with him and obtain pardon for my sins. He would provide for every weakness that I had in myself or made for myself. He would provide grace for every occasion for dealing with the enemies of my soul. In fact, he so arranged his life so that nothing should be wanting to me.

Our Lord's personal interest in you is so great that he delivered himself for you. He went through his whole life here on earth thinking of me, providing for my needs, and providing for all the things I needed to give to the Father, the infinite love and worship and everything else of which I am incapable of myself. Our Lord went so far as suffering in the Garden at Gethsemani, being scourged at the pillar, crowned with thorns, and nailed to the cross. On the cross he did an extraordinary thing. Not only did he die for me, but he offered up a sacrifice for me.

Holy Mother Church has defined the death of Christ as a sacrifice.[1] The word *sacrifice* means "to make holy." As a Jewish ritual, sacrifice is a gift given to God in a public fashion by a

1. CCC 561, 606, 611, 613–614, 616–618.

person who is recognized by God as a priest, who has the right to offer sacrifice. A sacrifice is given as a sign of our acceptance of God as God, our source of everything we have and everything we hope for. God is the only way in which we can find happiness. To perform a sacrifice is to publicly acknowledge our sovereign Lord's right to do what he likes with us and to accept and obey his will. It is the acceptance of God as God and of us as God's creatures.

Sacrifice is not made in words but by gestures or signs. A gift given is a mark of friendship. That is what the Lord did on the cross. God had previously instructed the ancient Jews how to offer a sacrifice. It is by Jesus' sacrificial death on the cross that God redeemed us. Not by his life but death. In that sacrificial death is contained the whole of his life of service.

## Obedient with Christ

The night before Jesus dies, he gives us a sign of the sacrifice he was to make on the cross. It is a sign that represents the separation of body and blood, namely a consecration of bread and wine. He changed the bread into his body and wine into his blood. As far as the words he used is concerned—"This is my body, and this is my blood"—he was separating body and blood and signifying death.[2]

We know that our Lord is present in the Blessed Sacrament. Somewhere around Palestine about 2,000 years ago, our Lord was actually present here on earth in his own physical body. We could see, touch, feel, and talk to him. As our Lord's presence in Jerusalem and Palestine so many thousands of years ago, so is his presence here in the tabernacle now.

The sacrifice of our Lord on Calvary is related to what takes place every time a priest consecrates bread and wine in the Mass. The sacrifice of Calvary is present at every consecration. And it is all yours. Why? The Council of Trent says, For us that the

2. Mk 14:22-25.

merits of his passion might be applied to our daily sins and our daily needs of graces.[3]

The sacrament of the Eucharist contains the sacrifice of the Mass and what is generally called Holy Communion. They are two different aspects of the same thing. The sacrament of the Mass is a sacrament of a sacrifice. It gives us something to give to God. The other sacraments and Holy Communion give something from God to us.

You are as near to the crucifixion when you are at Mass as our Lady was at the foot of her dying son. The fact that you are baptized means that every Mass you assist at, to say nothing of every other Mass offered up in the Church, is yours.

Pope Pius XII told us that Christ offered not only himself but all his faithful members whom he carries in his loving heart. On Calvary, Christ offered up you and me to God the Father.

> By means of the Eucharistic Sacrifice Christ our Lord willed to give to the faithful a striking manifestation of our union among ourselves and with our divine Head, wonderful as it is and beyond all praise. For in this Sacrifice the sacred minister acts as the vicegerent not only of our Savior but of the whole Mystical Body and of each one of the faithful. In this act of Sacrifice through the hands of the priest, by whose word alone the Immaculate Lamb is present on the altar, the faithful themselves, united with him in prayer and desire, offer to the Eternal Father a most acceptable victim of praise and propitiation for the needs of the whole Church. And as the Divine Redeemer, when dying on the Cross, offered Himself to the Eternal Father as Head of the whole human race, so "in this clean oblation" (Mal 1:11) He offers to the heavenly Father not only Himself as Head of the Church, but in Himself

3. "[Christ], our Lord and God, was once and for all to offer himself to God the Father by his death on the altar of the cross, to accomplish there an everlasting redemption. But because his priesthood was not to end with his death, at the Last Supper 'on the night when he was betrayed,' [he wanted] to leave to his beloved spouse the Church a visible sacrifice (as the nature of man demands) by which the bloody sacrifice which he was to accomplish once for all on the cross would be re-presented, its memory perpetuated until the end of the world, and its salutary power be applied to the forgiveness of the sins we daily commit (Council of Trent 1562; Denzinger-Schonmetzer 1740; cf. 1 Cor 11:23; Heb 7:24, 27)." CCC 1366.

> His mystical members also, since He holds them all, even those who are weak and ailing, in His most loving Heart.[4]

Do not say that I am romancing when I say that Christ was distinctly thinking of me, Brother Eugene. He was. There is proof of it. The pope says that I was most lovingly carried in Jesus' heart on the cross and so were you. The point is this: The same thing happens at Mass. Each time Mass was offered this morning, each one of us was offered to God the Father just as Christ offered up himself.[5] The meaning of that offering is the carrying out of that same policy that Christ carried out himself: the life of obedience to the will of God.

We cannot possibly return our Lord's love unless we are willing to share his sentiments and to identify our sentiments with his. Saint Paul put it another way, *Have this mind in you which was also in Christ Jesus* (Phil 2:5).

When the abbot says, "Father, you give up teaching theology and go down to the carpenter's shop," do you remember what you said to our Lord this morning? Do you remember you said, "I offer myself up with Christ?" The whole life of obedience is tied up with the offering of ourselves at Mass. Might I respectfully submit, that is the reason why Saint Benedict makes us put our schedule of profession at the altar. It is to remind us that every time Mass is said, our profession is there—our promise of obedience. It is the same promise of obedience that Christ made. The Mass is the center of our life. It is only the Mass that matters. Although the Mass commits us to absolute obedience, yet in the very same act, it makes complete reparation for our disobedience.

We have committed ourselves this morning at Mass to obedience to God's will. Does the Lord think we can carry that out?

4. Pope Pius XII, Encyclical *Mystici Corporis Christi* (June 29, 1943) 82.

5. "The Church which is the Body of Christ participates in the offering of her Head. With him, she herself is offered whole and entire. She unites herself to his intercession with the Father for all men. In the Eucharist the sacrifice of Christ becomes also the sacrifice of the members of his Body. The lives of the faithful, their praise, sufferings, prayer, and work, are united with those of Christ and with his total offering, and so acquire a new value. Christ's sacrifice present on the altar makes it possible for all generations of Christians to be united with his offering." CCC 1368.

Not a bit of it. What does he do? The very same sacrifice. The very same institution that makes that sacrifice available for us. He comes down from the altar to live in our hearts so he himself may carry the whole burden of our promises. That is the love of our Lord for us. He imposes an obligation on us because of its tremendous advantages to us. When he realizes or remembers or sees that the obligation is too much for us he comes himself to carry out the obligation.

**Christ in Us**

It is in the Mass that we can get the whole pattern of our monastic life. The other pattern of the Mass is this: The Church wants to offer up a sacrifice to God. What does she do? She takes bread and wine and she offers it up to God. That is the best she can do. What does God do? He comes down and he changes that sacrifice or that offering of bread and wine into himself—his own body and blood.

What does a monk do? The monk makes a vow of obedience. He puts it on the altar with that bread and wine. That is the best he can do. The second best is the way he carries it out because he does not carry it out perfectly. That is the best he can do. If that monk is disobedient, Christ comes down himself and changes that monk into himself by obedience. Just as he changes that bread and wine into his own body and blood, so does Christ change the monk into himself. At the end of our lives, we can say, *It is now no longer I that live, but Christ lives in me* (Gal 2:20). Why? Because Christ is the only adequate lover of God the Father.

That is why he comes down. He loves us. He changes us for the same reason as he changes the Church's offering of bread and wine into his own Body and Blood in order that his Father may have due honor, glory, and praise. If you offer yourself to God by your vow of obedience, he is going to change you. Changing you means detachment. The quickest way to detach yourself is to attach yourself to something else. If you want to get to perfection quickly, fall in love again or be even more in love with our Lord.

## CONFERENCE EIGHT:
# THE MASS

### Transformed into Christ

In the Mass you have the whole of Christ's sacrificial passion and death. Because we are made members of the Mystical Body of Christ at baptism and confirmation, all that is Christ's is ours. This gives us the right not only to pray in Christ's name but to offer in our own name, as well as Christ's, the sacrifice of Christ in the Mass.

Sacrifice is a gift given to God to represent the gift of ourselves to God. That gift, which God may or may not accept, is used as a means of uniting ourselves to God. How do we become acceptable to God when we have offered ourselves at Mass? By the fire of love enkindled in our heart by the Holy Spirit. Love transforms; it makes another the center of our life. The whole of monastic life is making Christ the center of our lives instead of ourselves. This is the purpose of obedience, mortification, and prayers: to learn how to love by denying ourselves and making Christ our all.

In one gesture at Mass, the bread and wine is transformed into Christ—"This is my body. This is my blood." The transformation of ourselves into Christ is done through a lifetime of obedience.

There is one great difference between the Eucharistic food and ordinary food. When we receive Holy Communion, our Lord comes to us as our food. This food is rather unique. Instead of being changed into us, it changes us into itself. The same process of digestion goes on in monastic life. Our Lord sought out the actions which he can make part of himself—those in accordance with his Father's will.

Our Lord is limited in our souls by two things. First, he can only do the will of his Father. Secondly, he can only do it when the glory of it is given to the Father. He cannot allow us to steal his Father's glory. As long as we are obedient with the obedience of humility, he can share in our actions and make them his own. The whole of monastic life is a gradual process in which Christ works gradually in our life, mind, soul, and heart to find actions that he can make his own. If we have not got rid of all self-seeking before we go to the grave, purgatory burns it off.

Purification burns off all that is not Christ. Our Lord himself told us, *"And no one has ascended into heaven except him who has descended from heaven: the Son of Man who is in heaven"* (Jn 3:13). Saint Paul gives a description of purification, *For we the living are constantly being handed over to death for Jesus' sake, that the life also of Jesus may be made manifest in our mortal flesh* (2 Cor 4:11).

## Prefer Christ Above All

We have not a chance of getting into heaven except insofar as we are transformed into Christ by loving him. If we are sincere in our love, we do his will. It is not a matter of giving things up, it is a matter of attaching ourselves to Christ.[1]

The wrong view of celibacy and poverty is the thought of giving up something. A man who falls in love and gets married has not given up women but has chosen one woman as the person he prefers above all others. He has chosen to give affection to one person.

When we made a vow of chastity, we said to the Lord, "The pleasure of your society is something I don't want to share with anyone else. I keep all my heart for you."

When we made a vow of poverty, we said, "Lord, you're enough for me. You'll provide for me. I want to have everything from you. I don't want to have anything of my own." It is not that we have given up things. Rather, we have chosen our Lord.

1. "The essential point underlying his [Benedict's] doctrine is that as we cease to make ourselves the center of our own lives and realize the completeness of God's claim on our devotion to him, we become more and more generous in our abandonment to his will, and more and more closely resemble our model and Master, Jesus Christ." Boylan, *The Priest's Way to God*, p. 119.

We avoid whatever gets between ourselves and the Lord, who is the one we love. When you want to get rid of faults, failings, self-seeking, vices, habits, and whatever else is worrying you, try to increase your personal love for our Lord. It is not a question of trying to give this thing up. It is choosing our Lord and falling in love with him.

**Sanctification through Obedience**

Sanctification is the begetting of Christ in our souls. We are sanctified by the Mass when we receive Holy Communion; Christ comes into our soul and changes us into himself. The same thing happens in our monastic life. God's providence tends to beget Christ in our souls but we have to be obedient to God's will. That is why obedience is so important. Our vow of obedience is a way of providing a means for knowing and accepting God's will in all its details. By practicing obedience, we are cooperating with God in the work of begetting Christ in our souls.

My cross as a superior is when I do not know what God's will is. Sometimes I have to try to find out by prayer. I cannot pass the decision to somebody else. When You have been accustomed for 27 years to divining the will of God by listening to superiors and begetting Christ that way, you become fearfully uneasy about every decision you make as a superior. You have to turn to the Lord every moment and say, "For heaven's sake, clear up the mess that I've made."

In the Air Force is the phrase, "Over to you." Somebody comes into the superior's room and asks for something, or what has to be done, and I have to make a decision on the spot. I do not get a revelation to what God's will is. I have to determine what is best and immediately switch over the intercom to our Lord—"Over to you. You better look after that. I can't. I can take no responsibility for that."

Obedience converts us into Christ. It is a parallel to the action in the Mass. Since we are baptized, the adoration and thanksgiving Jesus offered to his Father is ours to offer at the Mass. How are we to give God adequate reverence? The answer is the perfect praise and thanksgiving of the Mass. Our God cannot refuse it. We kneel in the church and say to God the Father, "This is your beloved son in whom you are well pleased. Hear him. He's praising you. He's adoring you. And he's thanking you, for me as well as for the rest of humanity."[2]

The great trick in the spiritual life is to play off God against himself. If God says anything to us, turn it back to himself. "There you are. This is your beloved Son." God has said that he is well pleased with his Son. Well, here he is. Be well pleased in him. In the Mass, God hears him praising, adoring, and thanking *perfectly*. We must increase our confidence in the Mass and the merits of Christ it contains. Our Lord is there making perfect reparation for the sins of the whole world.

### Forgiveness of Sins

We approach Mass as sinners not saints. But the application of the passion and death of our Lord Jesus Christ is adequate reparation for our sins, no matter what sin we have committed. It is quite clear from the Council of Trent that from the Mass we obtain the grace of repentance and forgiveness.[3]

When a man, after hearing one Mass, believes that his sins are still an obstacle to God's grace to him—still a barrier between himself and God—he does not appreciate the meaning of the Mass and has not sufficient faith in the Mass.

I stress the point that God forgives *all* of our sins, especially those that we commit today. Examine your notion of God saving us from our sins. You may say: "Yes, God saved me from original sin, the sins of the human race before I was born, and possibly my early sins. But I've let him down since."

2. Dom Eugene is referring to the Transfiguration of the Lord in which God the Father says, "This is my beloved Son, in whom I am well pleased; hear him" (Mt 17:5).

3. The nineteenth ecumenical council opened at Trent on December 13, 1545, and closed there on December 4, 1563. Its main object was the definitive determination of the doctrines of the Church in answer to the heresies of the Protestants; a further object was the execution of a thorough reform of the inner life of the Church by removing the numerous abuses that had developed in it.

Bring God's forgiveness up to date. Do not leave a gap between past sins and those of today. You say, "Well I committed sin yesterday, I suppose. God saved up to that but he has not saved me from that particular sin I have just committed." God's redemption is up to the minute. In fact, it is beyond the minute. It is up to the end of our life.

God has made provision for our future sins. There is no limit to God's ingenuity and plans for our sanctification. There is no limit to his compassion for us. *"This man welcomes sinners and eats with them"* (Lk 15:2). There is a tremendous truth in that. He made us part of himself even knowing he had to undergo the suffering in the Garden of Gethsemani because of his association with us sinners. Yet he loved us enough to do that.

In the Mass, we have the means of making perfect reparation for our own sins and the sins of the whole world. When one thinks of the ghastly things that have been done in the world—

---

"And for as much as, in this divine sacrifice which is celebrated in the mass, that same Christ is contained and immolated in an unbloody manner, who once offered Himself in a bloody manner on the altar of the cross; the holy Synod teaches, that this sacrifice is truly propitiatory and that by means thereof this is effected, that we obtain mercy, and find grace in seasonable aid, if we draw nigh unto God, contrite and penitent, with a sincere heart and upright faith, with fear and reverence. For the Lord, appeased by the oblation thereof, and granting the grace and gift of penitence, forgives even heinous crimes and sins. For the victim is one and the same, the same now offering by the ministry of priests, who then offered Himself on the cross, the manner alone of offering being different. The fruits indeed of which oblation, of that bloody one to wit, are received most plentifully through this unbloody one; so far is this (latter) from derogating in any way from that (former oblation). Wherefore, not only for the sins, punishments, satisfactions, and other necessities of the faithful who are living, but also for those who are departed in Christ, and who are not as yet fully purified, is it rightly offered, agreeably to a tradition of the apostles." The canons and decrees of the sacred and ecumenical Council of Trent, session 22, chapter 2. See also *Catechism of the Council of Trent for Parish Priests*, 2nd rev. ed., trans. John A. McHugh and Charles J. Callan (New York: Joseph F. Wagner; Longdon: B. Herder, 1934) pp. 258–259.

"The body of Christ we receive in Holy Communion is 'given up for us,' and the blood we drink 'shed for the many for the forgiveness of sins.' For this reason the Eucharist cannot unite us to Christ without at the same time cleansing us from past sins and preserving us from future sins." CCC 1393.

campaigns against God, crimes against humanity, insults hurled at God—we cannot understand how God could tolerate the world's existence for another ten seconds. When you ask: How does he do it? The answer: the Mass.

The Mass makes more than adequate reparation for sins. We must be convinced of it and use it. Do God's will and every Mass said anywhere in the world is yours. That, again, is the importance of obedience.

The whole of the monastic life is one unit. One part involves all the other parts. You cannot come into a monastery and say: "I'll use the liturgy. The Mass is wonderful. I'll have the Mass everyday. I'll have twenty masses in that church every day. Of course, I don't need to worry about obedience at all." By keeping to your own little way, you put yourself outside the whole thing. You must take it as it is completely or not at all. You must take it as it is practiced in *this* monastery. Not as it is in Gethsemani, Roscrea, or Cîteaux. This is the monastery to which you are called. You must accept its people, customs, and traditions if you want to accept all the masses in this house.

### Penance

As a confessor, I never give a grave penance. Instead, I have the penitent use the Mass. If a man comes to me that has been twenty years away from the Church, I say, "Say a Hail Mary, and the next time you go to Mass offer up Mass for those at home and for all the saints." I always turn a penitent's attention to the Mass. If anybody blames me for giving small penances, then Saint Francis de Sales is my bad example. He and I will both claim our Lord as a bad example. What did our Lord do with the women in adultery. He told her, *"Neither will I condemn thee. Go thy way, and from now on sin no more"* (Jn 8:11). Well, that is good enough for me.

Concerning penances for grave sins, the confessor must be expedient. It is not expedient to give a man twenty years away from the Church ten rounds of the beads. He will never say them. The confessional is a place for reconciling sinners with God. It is not a place of the mathematical bureau for the exact estimation of restitution or penance. It is a place where sinners are reconciled with God and put at peace. Do not disturb your penitents. If you are going to tell them to go in peace, make sure you have not upset that peace. It is a theological maxim: You must adapt the sacrament to the men, not to the textbooks.

We have one glorious rule in Roscrea that I wish all seminaries would adopt. No man is allowed to teach theology unless he is hearing public confessions. There are too many theoretical moral theologians who are really canonists. Avoid a canon law man when it comes to moral theology. They are two entirely different approaches. One will say, "The book says that's a mortal sin. You did that, therefore it's a mortal sin." Nonsense! I have been hearing confessions for twenty years, and I have heard tough things. I could not swear to God, but I have yet to hear of one mortal sin.[4]

People tell me, "I've committed a mortal sin, Father."

My answer to myself: Only God knows if he is guilty or not. I do not know. He thinks he is. He is sorry.

That is all you can say: Only God knows.

The amazing thing about God's friends is that he often allows them to fall into things that appear to be mortal sins. In some extraordinary way that belongs to infinite mercy and delicacy of love, he leaves them with the impression that they are serious sinners. However, they are going to get a tremendous surprise on the last day.

There is no limit to the delicacy of our Lord's love. He is a perfect lover. The romance between a man and a woman is nothing compared to the delicacy of our Lord's love for us. Nothing!

4. "It is by their failure to make some attempt at seeing the penitent's point of view that so many confessors give the impression that the Church is unreasonable in her demands, that her burdens are unbearable. Our Lord's yoke is easy and His burden light. We blaspheme Him by making it otherwise. Two things are necessary to avoid these faults. One is an understanding of our penitent's outlook and circumstances, or at least, a realization that we do not understand and a readiness to make allowances for the effects of the un-understood factor. The other is a wider reading of moral theology than a single text book affords. Nowhere is the 'man of one book' so dangerous to souls than in the confessional." Boylan, *The Spiritual Life of the Priest*, p. 103.

He is infinite goodness. An infinite artist. Infinitely romantic. Infinitely thoughtful for us. The whole of our life is planned with the infinite love of God who is in love with us. All he wants is our love.

**Grace through the Mass**

During the Mass, Jesus puts the whole of his life and death at our disposal in order that we may live intensely in love with him. In the Mass, you have God's prayer to God. There is no grace you cannot obtain through the Mass. Any grace you want, use the Mass.

You can sum it up in the phrase I suggested: "This is your beloved Son, hear him." That refers to every Mass said in every altar at the moment. It is a good thing to remind yourself that this well-beloved Son has infinite merits.

Each one of us adopts our own way of talking to God. You do not need to write a book to explain your ideas to a friend. A nod is often good enough. So with God, the name of Jesus reminds him that we are his children. And the name of Jesus reminds us that God is our savior. It is a perfect prayer. You can turn it any way you would like. You can refer it to all the masses that are being said. You can refer it to your own needs as a sinner. You can refer it to the needs of the world. You can refer to God the Father in whose Son he is well pleased. There are many applications of this perfect prayer.

The Mass is ours because of our baptism in Christ. Saint Thomas Aquinas states: Through the sacraments and baptism, the passion and death of Christ are communicated to the baptized person as if he himself has suffered and died. The passion and death of Christ on the altar, writes Saint Thomas, is communicated to me. It is given to me as if I had experienced it myself. It is mine. Therefore, I can offer it to God quite independent of my own dispositions. You need not be a saint; baptism is sufficient. If you die after baptism, you go straight to heaven not by title of merit but because you are sons of God. The same way, we are sons of God and this is ours. It is a family treasure.

**Sacrifice**

From the moment of our baptism, we have a common bank account with our Lord. It is fundamental in our life to take Christ at his proper value. Otherwise, we are wandering in a desert of austerities alone. Literally a desert. It will lead us nowhere except to fill us with the pride which says, *"O God, I thank thee that I am not like the rest of men, robbers, dishonest, adulterers, or even like this publican"* (Lk 18:11).

We get up at half past two in the morning. We do not eat meat. We keep silence. It is a lifetime's work. If that does not lead us to God, it is a waste of time. If it leads us to God why boast about it? Why not boast about God? It is God we want. If anyone asks me what we do—we seek God and by God's grace we find him. He is ours and he is our God. He is our all.

Sacrifice means to make something sacred. Our life of obedience is a perpetual sacrifice in which we are conforming ourselves to God's will, and God's will is changing us into his Son. By sacrifice we show the orientation of our mind to God. Saint Benedict says that this orientation requires humility and obedience. Humility recognizes all things as coming from God. Obedience directs everything toward the will of God. That is the exact parallel between the monastic life and the sacrifice of the Mass.

Our life of obedience and humility is a sacrifice that takes its meaning and value from Christ on the cross. It is the perfect way of conforming ourselves to that sacrifice.

We are offered to God in every Mass by our Lord. We were offered on Calvary. Jesus held us most lovingly in his heart. Exactly the same thing is done at Mass. When we offer the bread and wine, we are offering ourselves, too.

Pope Pius XI says, "The faithful are to offer themselves a living sacrifice holy and pleasing unto God. Therefore Saint Cyprian dared to affirm that the sacrifice of Christ is not complete as far as our sanctification is concerned."[5]

5. Pope Pius XI, Encyclical *Miserentissimus Redemptor* (May 8, 1928) 9.

As far as our praise of God is concerned, yes, the Mass is perfect praise. As far as our sanctification is concerned, *our* offerings and *our* sacrifice need to correspond to his passion.

## Carrying the Cross

How does the priest offer the bread and wine at the Mass? Through the sign of the cross. In the same way, it is by the cross that we give ourselves to God. It is by the cross, therefore, that we will go to God in this monastic life of ours. The whole of it is to return to God by the way of obedience.

Is that not what Saint Benedict says in the fourth degree of humility? "The fourth degree of humility is to keep patience in the exercise of obedience, and not to lose it or depart from it, either because of the difficulty of the thing commanded or the injuries to which one may be subjected. . ."[6] The fourth degree is the perfect way of conforming ourselves to the sacrifice of Christ. It is a commentary on true devotion to the Mass.

The reason we put up with the trials and tribulations in our life is because God loved us and because we offered ourselves this morning at Mass. We said to God what Christ said to God, "Eternal Father, I offer you myself and all these, my beloved members. They're all yours." I know the Lord did not use those words, but I think it is an adequate statement of what he meant. We laid ourselves completely at God's disposition.

Our offering of ourselves must correspond to the offering of Christ. We must prefer to be *obedient to death, even to death on a cross* (Phil 2:8). It is to be nailed to the cross with Christ. Jesus himself has promised us, "*For my yoke is easy, and my burden light*" (Mt 11:30). He comes to help us carry our cross. That is the whole point about the Mass. Once the Lord has induced us to imitate him by offering ourselves, he immediately comes back to us in Holy Communion in order to bare the burden of the cross he is going to impose on us. He is so impatient to help us that he cannot be kept back. As soon as we offer him up, he comes back down to the altar in order to carry out what he has promised to do in our name.

6. RB 7,35-36.

Our Lord is a perfect high priest. He has compassion on us. He suffered and endured weakness, so he knows what we are made of. He knows our needs. His very association with us produced tears and the sweat of blood in the agony of the garden. Yet he loves us.

We have to renew our confidence in our Lord and stop being afraid of what he is going to ask us to do next. The more the Lord asks us to do or the heavier cross he asks us to bear, the more willing he is to come and bear it with us and the closer the union we enter into with him. It is the cross that brings me to our Lord and unites me with him.

Our Lord sends us crosses but they are marks of his love. It is a rose in disguise. The crosses give him an excuse for entering into closer union with us. They are a message of a lover to somebody whom he loves and with whom he wants to be more intimate and more closely united. He wants to shape us according to his own mind and heart so that he can share our life completely. If he has given us a greater cross, he wants, so to speak, to have an excuse for giving us more of his strength.

Did you ever see a monk under a heavy cross who was not happy? Have you ever seen a monk who has not any crosses who was happy? There was a famous character in Roscrea Abbey. He was a secular priest in northern Ireland before entering the monastery. It was the abbot's jubilee, and we had permission to speak at a meal. I said, "Father Vincent, what on earth brought you into the monastery?" "I was procurator of the whole province," he said. "I had everything I wanted, but I was never happy. I came in here and have nothing, but I'm as happy as the day's long."[7] It is true that the cross brings the greatest joy on earth *if* we accept it. Our monastic life is only a means of uniting our-

7. Father Vincent Flood, OCSO, was ordained a diocesan priest in 1896 by William Walsh, archbishop of Dublin. After eight years serving in the diocese of Clogher in Ireland, Father Vincent joined the Vincentians. Seven years later, in 1911, he entered Roscrea Abbey where he worked on the poultry farm. He died December 11, 1938. "Dom Eugene once jokingly said of him, 'He tried to reform the secular clergy and failed. Then he tried to reform the Vincentians and failed. Finally, he died trying to reform us.'" Ciaran O. Sabhaois, Roscrea Abbey, "Dom Eugene Boylan," June 30, 2006, personal email (July 1, 2006).

selves to our Lord. If we accept it as such, it will not be a cross but a source of great joy.

## CONFERENCE NINE:
# CHARITY

### Doing unto Christ

The law of charity is that Christ has identified himself with each person. Whatever we do to our neighbor we do to Christ. Our Lord is definite about it.[1] All we say, do, or even think about our brethren is said, done, or thought about Christ himself. When we are unkind to somebody, we are unkind to Christ. Insofar as we are unkind, unjust, or uncharitable, we are being unkind, unjust, or uncharitable to Christ. Likewise, when we are helping another, we are helping and being kind to Christ.

Christ indeed lived on earth nearly 2,000 years ago. However, consider Christ as living now in all his mysteries, especially the mystery of his agony in the garden. Our Lord's sufferings in the Garden of Gethsemani should always be alive to us. It is literally true that his suffering is going on now and can be influenced by what we say or do today. You will find it in the encyclical on Reparation to the Sacred Heart by Pope Pius XI.

> And so even now, in a wondrous yet true manner, we can and ought to console that Most Sacred Heart which is continually wounded by the sins of thankless men, since—as we also read in the sacred liturgy—Christ himself, by the mouth of the Psalmist complains that he is forsaken by his friends: "My Heart hath expected reproach and misery, and I looked for one that would grieve together with me, but there was none: and for one that would comfort me, and I found none" (Ps 68[69]:20-21).[2]

1. Mt 25:44-45.
2. *Miserentissimus Redemptor* 13.

If we are kind to our brethren we literally relieve the sufferings of Christ in the Garden of Gethsemani. If we are unkind to them, we add to them.

There is no sentimental piety about that. It is solid theology. Lack of fraternal charity is an obstacle to union with Christ. Our Lord spoke of the man coming to offer sacrifice that had something against his brother. What did our Lord say? "*. . . leave thy gift before the altar and go first to be reconciled to thy brother, and then come and offer thy gift*" (Mt 5:24).

## Love One Another

Our Lord told us that his disciples are to be known because of their charity.[3] It is not by doing miracles or by austerities such as living on a Trappist diet. It is love for another. If you find a monastic house without charity, the members are not being monks or Christians.

What did the archbishop of Paris say about the nuns at Port Royal who started the heresies? "I found them as pure as angels but as proud as devils."[4, 5] Rigidity and savage austerity is always associated with pride and lack of charity. Cistercian houses should be known by their charity if they are living out the Lord's commandment to love one another. We often do not see the

3. Jn 13:35.

4. Port-Royal, a Benedictine abbey (later Cistercian), was founded in 1204, 16 miles west of Paris. In 1608 the abbess, Angélique Arnauld, sought to reform her own lax monastic life as well as that of her community. She received counsel of Saint Francis of Sales and eventually the nuns of Port Royal became known for piety. Other monasteries seeking reforms even sought their advice. The abbey moved to Paris in 1626 and became a center of Jansenism under the cofounder of Jansenism, Antoine Arnauld (more popularly known as the abbot of Saint Cyran). Angélique upheld Jansenism in her word and letters and even propagated her own ideas, even to the point of condemning Saint Vincent de Paul. In 1704, the nuns were expelled by papal bull.

5. "I found them as pure as angels but as proud as devils." Marc Escholier, *Port-Royal: The Drama of the Jansenists* (New York: Hawthorne, 1968), p. 144. The archbishop of Paris, Hardouin de Péréfixe, who upon leaving the monastery after having chastised the nuns and even denying them the sacraments, was met by a supporter of the nuns who told him of her admiration for them. The archbishop responded with this statement.

charity in our own house, but coming into it as an outsider, you might be surprised.

One test I have for a community is whether there is charity in the house. Our Father Immediate has a trick of cross-examining you so that either you gave him the information he wants or you feel an absolute fool.[6] He tackled me about the community [at Roscrea] one day. "Father Eugene, I'm afraid this community of yours is getting too active," he said. "You have a college over there with a lot of activities going on. The confession is crowded down there. Everybody seems to be doing something. I'm afraid there is no supernatural life in this house at all. There is a lack of interior life."

"Listen, Reverend Father. I can't agree with that at all," I replied. "I can see no evidence of it. On the contrary, I think I can offer you evidence that there is a very deep supernatural life in our monastery."

"How's that?" he said.

"Reverend Father, you will remember your own visitation card last time. You said that you were impressed by the extraordinary spirit of charity displayed by the community."

"Yes," he said. "And I meant every word of it."

"Well, Reverend Father, can you imagine a hundred men living together in that charity without a very deep supernatural life? That charity can only be produced by the Holy Spirit."

"Yes," he said, "you're perfectly right."

For me, the one test of a Cistercian community is its charity. Other things may be wrong but if you have charity, they will be put right and you will not have to try to put them right. The main thing is that if there is charity in the house, there is supernatural life. If there is no charity, the supernatural life has gone wrong somewhere. I have the problem of welding men of different na-

6. The father immediate (abbot of Mount Melleray Abbey in Cappoquin, County Waterford, Ireland) at the time when Dom Eugene was abbot of Roscrea was Dom Finbar Cashman, elected eighth abbot of Mount Melleray on April 26, 1957. Dom Finbar was abbot until May 6, 1971. Of interest, Dom Eugene preached the community retreat at Mount Melleray at the beginning of 1962.

tionalities and diverse ideas. The only way I can do it is by insisting on a deeper supernatural life.

## Jesus' Commandments to Love

When Jesus is instituting the Mass, he comes back to this question of charity. The night before he died he said to his disciples, *"A new commandment I give you, that you love one another: that as I have loved you, you also love one another"* (Jn 13:34). To love others *as I have loved you*. He went on to institute the sacrifice of the Mass. Our Lord seems to tie up our union with him and our neighbor with the power of prayer before the Father in heaven. A condition of our going to God in the sacrifice of the Mass, or in prayer, is that we be united to our neighbor in charity.

Charity is the most important of the virtues, because the same charity by which we love our neighbor is the charity by which we love God. All Saint John the Evangelist could say in his old age was, *Beloved, let us love one another, because love is from God; everyone who loves is born of God and knows God* (1 Jn 4:7). That comes from someone who knew the Lord perhaps more intimately than anyone else other than our Lord's mother. Saint John also wrote, *And this commandment we have from him, that he who loves God should love his brother also* (1 Jn 4:21).

Our primary duty in the monastery is toward God. If we spend our lives praising God and serving him, we do not need any further justification. If we give ourselves completely to God the fruit of our life is God's business. *De facto*, as a matter of fact, the more you give yourself to God, the more good you do to your neighbor. Direct service to God comes before the love of your neighbor.

## Law of Charity

The trouble with the word *love* in English is that it is capable of a variety of meanings. It means literally "to wish well" or having "good will." It does not mean "to like." You are not bound to like every person. You cannot. You are bound, however, to wish everyone well.

I incurred the censure of my brother, my good Carthusian brother, because I wrote in a book that we are not bound to like one another. He holds you are. I hold you are not. And I stick to it, despite my Carthusian brother. There are natural sympathies and natural antipathies. Some people rub you the wrong way. Other people are people with whom you find you are completely at ease, or, at least, you are more or less at your ease. To some extent you can modify that, and you certainly *must* see that your natural likes and dislikes do not interfere with your charitable relations with your community and with those with whom you deal. Community life is probably for most of us the greatest cross. Contact with your brother keeps your feet on the ground. It also means that you have got to rise to the stars occasionally to pull down the extra grace needed to put up with them and for them to put up with you. You have to be prudent. Instinctive likes and dislikes are partly, at least, outside our control. There is a type of person to whom you are allergic. To force intimacy, or to try to be overly nice, is asking for trouble. It is only going to cause a reaction. Our Lord himself liked certain people more than others. He liked Saint John more than anybody, but he made Saint Peter the pope.[7, 8]

## Finding Christ in Your Neighbor

You will find Christ in your neighbor when you cannot find him elsewhere. There are times when you go into the church and God is a word of three letters. There is no one in the tabernacle as far you can see. You sit down to pray but God seems distant. You open a book and see dry words. That is the time to look for God in your neighbor.

When we were novices, we were forbidden to be in church for more than fifteen minutes after communion. Even though masses were going on, we had to leave even before the consecration. We were only allowed to be in the church five minutes during the day outside the time of Office. There is no place in

7. Jn 19:26; 20:2; 21:7; 21:20.

8. Mt 16:18.

the monastery to pray. There were no prie-dieus. There were no quiet corners you can get to pray. You were living in a common room, with a minimum of furniture. I remember tackling my novice master, "How on earth are we to pray? You won't let us into church, and there's no place round here to pray. What are we to do?" "Listen, brother," he said. "If you can't learn to say your prayers, or learn to pray while you're going round the house doing your jobs, it's high time you went home, me boy." Now people are shocked by the easy way we disappear out of the church and make thanksgiving walking round the enclosure or doing something like that. The point is this, you can find God anywhere where charity or obedience tells you to be.

The only extraordinary graces of prayer I have gotten have been when I was servant of the refectory. When we serve in the refectory at Roscrea, the two servers get out soup at two minutes till twelve. You have got to put out the soup plates, pour out the soup, cover the soup. It has to be done by twelve. Then you get the potatoes out and bring the vegetables around. Brother Patrick would come in at one minute till twelve. "For sure, Father, the day is long," he would say. It is one minute until twelve and you are pouring down sweat and the plates burning your hands. Anyhow, as you know, being servant of the refectory under those conditions does not always mean to be recollected. Yet, I knew that Christ was in every person I was feeding and that Christ was in me serving them.

**Kindness and Mutual Service**

Kindness and mutual service are examples of charity. In the monastery in Ireland, each man does his own washing every Monday morning. The white washing coming in from a muddy field can be a dirty job. I was a public confessor and a bell would go frequently Monday morning during the washing. Five strokes were rung. I had to hide my washing, or it would be done when I got back.

In Roscrea, in the days when we got up at two o'clock and when we got up at half past one on Sundays, there was a public Mass at half past eleven. I would some days have to say that

Mass and preach. At five o'clock the night before you would get two ounces of dry bread and a cup of tea. You got up and you sang vigils. You endured an interval until prime. You sang prime. You endured, God forgive me, the Mass. You endured a period further where the young men were giving thanksgiving. Then you went into chapter and you endured three-quarters of an hour listening to the abbot. Then you existed until the High Mass. You got through to sext in a stifling church. There were about four hundred lay people in the church and the atmosphere was getting thicker. There was no ventilation in the church. You had a splitting head and a stomach that was beginning to turn upside down and you went out to say the half past eleven Mass. You had to preach. You got your breakfast by one o'clock. You are probably a sick man for the next three days. It only happened three or four times a year. Some men did not mind it. Personally, I was knocked out for a week.

On Saturday night you could go around the Roscrea monastery and stop any priest you met. "Father, could you take the dinner Mass tomorrow?" That is the phrase we had. "Will you take the late Mass tomorrow?" "Certainly" was the response, without the slightest hesitation. Any other Mass he had, he would go and get somebody else to do it for him. Never a hesitation to it. That is an example of charity.

Christ gives himself to us in the measure we give ourselves to him in our neighbor. The whole of our contact with our brethren should be a spiritual communion with Christ. We should approach our brethren in the same degree of faith as we approach the abbot, realizing our relations with them are different. It is Christ you are dealing with. The real test of a man's love for God is the love in practice, not in theory. Let us consider some faults against our neighbor.

### Obstacles to Charity

*Unkindness.* There is no need to explain the meaning of unkindness. Some people are deliberately unkind. They persuade themselves that it is for people's good to snub them. "Oh, he had it coming to him. It is high time somebody sat on that fellow."

That is not charity. If you want to correct your brethren, do it first of all by prayer and secondly do it kindly while it has to be done. Unkindness is *never* a sign of supernatural action.[9]

*Anger.* We need to control our tempers. I do not believe the Irish are the only people who have a temper to control. They may have a little less control of it than others, but we all have to control our temper. For that reason, we have to be ready to forgive people who lose their temper.

The older you get, the less control you have over the external manifestations of your anger. I do not know what the medical explanation is. I think it has something to do with the hardening of your arteries. The blood vessels are normally elastic and when you are excited or upset the extra pressure of the blood is taken up by the blood vessels. When you get old these things get hard. The pressure is referred back to the brain and affects the nerve endings. I have noticed that as I have gotten older, I frequently find myself trembling with anger. Yet inside I am quite peaceful. We need to allow for elderly men who often seem angrier than they are. It is a purely physical thing. In their heart they are probably praying to God for you at the moment.

*Thoughtlessness.* Unreasonable requests of one another shows thoughtlessness. There is always the type of person in a religious house who says, "My brothers are so charitable. I have only to ask them to do anything for me." You find he has no hesitation about passing on a job to somebody else for whom it is far more inconvenient to do than it is for himself. We have to accept the fact that we are a burden to one another. That can be one of the great mortifications of religious life, especially when you are old and infirm. You have the consolation: the bigger burden you are to your community, the bigger blessing you bring down on them.

Dom Sortais made a criticism of our foundation at Nunraw.[10] He said, "You made two mistakes. You sent no sick men and no

9. "The really spiritual man is known by the kindness of his speech and still more by the kindness of his silence." Boylan, *This Tremendous Lover*, p. 200.

10. Mount Saint Joseph (Roscrea) founded Sancta Maria Abbey Nunraw in Scotland in 1946.

old men. There should always be sick men on a foundation so that the young monks may realize that a man can be a perfect monk even though he is not able to attend all the exercises. Secondly, there should always be old men, so the young men can learn from the very beginning what the infirmities of old age are and learn to make due allowance for them with compassion." By bearing one another's burdens, we fulfill the law of Christ. Nevertheless, we should not add to that burden. We should accept the burden, accept the humiliation of being dependent on other people. On the other hand, as I said, we should not add to the burden by unreasonable requests or demanding unnecessary services to one another.

*Teasing and Provoking.* We Irish are supposed to have a great sense of humor. I have to admit that in Irish humor, it seems to be almost indispensable that it should hurt somebody. If you are a priest in a diocese in Ireland and on some patron's feast you are singing the High Mass and put in the wrong preface, as soon as you get back to the presbyter, someone rings you up. "Hello, Fr. John. How are you getting on? I hear you are studying a new Ambrosian Rite down in your parish. Of course, originality in the liturgy is not exactly encouraged, Reverend Father." That is alright for the first time. It is a good joke. But by the time the twentieth man has called you up to tell you this, it ceases to be a joke. The same thing goes for a community. If you pull a leg of some man about something he did, it is great fun. When forty other fellows do it, it ceases to be fun. For that reason we have to be gentle in our humor at another's expense. A laugh in a community is not a laugh *at* a man, it is a laugh *with* a man which is an entirely different thing. You are covering up a man's mistake. That is charity. Laughing at a man is different.

We cannot blame people for laughing at us, but still we expect them to moderate their fun. Teasing and provoking a man is definitely against charity. It represents a certain amount of thoughtlessness, but still it is a thing to be avoided by a monk that has a supernatural instinct for the presence of Christ in another man.

*Spreading Rumors.* It is extraordinary how you can upset men in a monastery. Pass the word around that the abbot is going to have all the windows in the church sealed and there will be no ventilation. There is going to be no central heating in the church next winter. Even minor things. A tremendous amount of speculation goes on in some monasteries. It is not easy for us to realize how liable we are to be carried away by rumors.

Rumors were rampant in our part of the world during the war when newspapers were cut off. The rumors that ran around and the people that accepted them and built up the rumor were extraordinary. The Germans had landed about fifty times during the war. Four times the whole English navy was destroyed. Everybody believed it.

Things that upset us and cause us agony in the monastery are frequently trifles that on the outside we would have laughed at. We seem to be stripped of our defense in here. That is why you have to have infinite tact in dealing with your brethren. That infinite tact sometimes comes from the Holy Spirit.

*Mischief Making.* There is a type of man that cannot avoid passing on information that should not be passed on. He comes along, "Oh, Father, do you know what so-and-so said about you?" I had to deal with a situation like that and I must confess that I blew my top in chapter about it. At our monastery a senior priest is the cook. To get him to the High Mass on Sundays, one of the brothers takes over. A certain brother came to me who does that Sunday kitchen relief work. This is a very competent brother and quite a good cook but he does not want to cook.

"It would be much better if you got some of the novices to do the cooking, Reverend Father," he said. I blew up.

I said, "I'm already worried enough about the cooking. I've had to complain about the guesthouse supper. The cook in our life is the essential thing. Your old friend Napoleon said, "A soldier marches on his stomach." So does a monk! Any change I make in the kitchen will be to improve the cooking not to disimprove it. I'm not going to have novices cooking for the community, and I'm not going to put the novices into that strain at all. That's no place for them."

He started talking in French, and I said something about our diet is not sufficient. Ten minutes afterwards, one of the two priests in the kitchen came to me. He is a man who does not speak English well. He is rather a simple soul.

"Benedicite," he said.

"Dominus," I replied.

"I'm just beginning to understand, Reverend Father, that you're not satisfied with the food we're giving to the community."

I said, "Who told you that?"

"Well Brother was down and told us that," he said.

So I soothed it over with Father. I went straight out to Brother and I just blew my top.

"Did you tell them in the kitchen that I said I wasn't satisfied with the food?"

"Yes."

"Well you better see your confessor," I said. "I dare not talk to you at the moment. I'm too angry about it."

That sort of thing, to my mind, is absolutely outrageous in a monastic life. There are men who have that kink that they want to make trouble. Before you pass on information, please use prudence. Is it necessary to pass it on? Is it useful? Is it kind? Is it going to do harm?

Remember that what we do to anybody else in the community is done to Christ. Further, what we do has to be shared by Christ. Christ will not share a lack of charity. Therefore when we fail in charity we are putting Christ, for the moment, out of our life. Not merely are we putting Christ out of our life in our own soul but we are refusing to recognize his life in the souls of others. He has warned us that he will judge us on our relations with our brothers. It is essential to practice charity and to examine our conscience in a prudent way on our relations with our community.

Relations with our brethren based on faith is a continual spiritual communion. It means uniting our life to Christ and developing his life in us. Our community life affords us endless opportunities at sanctification—of mystical union with Christ through charity and service of our brethren.

*Calumny and Detraction.* We are not entitled to tell the truth about our neighbor when that truth is to his detriment *unless* there is some reason for it. The mere fact that a man has committed sin does not give us the right to proclaim to the world what he has done.

It is a grave matter to reveal the mortal sins of our neighbor without some good reason. However, there are times when we must draw attention to our neighbor's failings, even his sins. Sometimes they will have to be reported to a superior or we will have to answer questions about our brethren from superiors. First, you are bound to tell the truth. You must not merely say what happened but you give the superior every possible excuse that can be made for that man.

*Criticism of One Another.* Since what we do to our neighbor is done to Christ, you have got to be fearfully careful what you say about your neighbor. Unless we are on our guard, even the greatest virtue that you have could be lost through criticism of another. If your attention is drawn to a brother's action that is giving you scandal or causing trouble, perhaps he does not realize what he is doing. You can always ask him. Try to save the man as much as you can. Make any reasonable excuse just as you would expect a man to make excuses for you.

I had the problem of dealing with men who had been trained to make a virtue of spying on one another and reporting to superiors. And they came in long reports about what Father X did ten years ago, and what Father Y did twelve years ago. I just flew into full Celtic wrath, appeared quite rude and nasty to them. I got so annoyed by the thing. The abbot general [Dom Gabriel Sortais], having made a visitation, met all the members of the community and sent for me, as he always does, at the end of visitations to tell me what I have been doing wrong. "L'un contre l'autre. Pas un mot d'excuse." "One man against another," he says, "and not a word of an excuse for the other."

Secondly, if you have to go to a superior to talk about another member of the community, go first into the church and say to our Lord all you intend to say to the superior. Be sure you can face the Lord with that tale first before you bring it to a superior. Is what I am about to say based on absolute objectivity?

We should be on our guard when we talk about our brethren to anybody but especially to superiors. A monk's life is closely affected by his relations with his abbot. We must be scrupulously careful lest anything we say or do would in any way influence that devotion and approach in faith to a superior. Am I in any way making it more difficult for the man to approach him by lessening his status in the eyes of a superior? If our Lord was so drastic in condemning scandals, I think he would be equally drastic in condemning anybody who interfered between the abbot and any member of the community. The abbot for each member of the community is a special source of grace in the spiritual life.

I will not tolerate men talking to me about anybody else. I am merely warning you of the dangerous implications of even what seems to be a casual discussion with a superior about another man.

A superior does have a right to make inquiries. You have a right to be candid with him, especially when it is a question of putting a man in a particular position. For example, the superior wants to know how people will regard a particular monk if you put him in a position.

At a visitation we superiors are frequently presented with a list of comments about what is wrong in the monastery. Superiors have a duty sometimes to protest and to make representations. I am tempted to say to the visitor: "But, Reverend Father, don't the regulations and the directory say that it should have been first of all reported to me. My attention was never drawn to those before. I admit that whoever the person is may have had some reason for not coming to me but I would rather doubt with such a list that there are so many reasons that I am so unapproachable that they had to keep all these things for you."

I would suggest to abbots making visitations that when a monk says, "Well such and such a thing has to be done," ask the good man, "Have you brought this to the attention of the local superior? Has he been given an opportunity to correct it? And if not, why not?" Although you may discover the local superior is seen as being a difficult man to whom to report things, you may also be able to point out that the superior should not be put into the unfair position for being blamed for not correcting things to which his attention has never been drawn.

We superiors frequently have to let things go uncorrected because we know it is a question of the lesser of two evils. It does not make it any easier to sleep at night, nor does it make our conscience any more peaceful. We have got to live dangerously, if you like, and make a virtue of it.

If you draw attention to the human qualities of a superior, even his good ones, you may be interfering with the supernatural faith and supernatural approach of a member to his superior. You are stopping a priest from giving a sacramental. All our contacts with the abbot are sacramentals. As Benedict says, the abbot is considered as representing the person of Christ.[11] I am not trying to build up a superior, but it is you yourselves I am thinking of. If you bring the abbot below the plane that Saint Benedict puts him, you are interfering with your own supernatural life. It is all very well to talk about democracies and everything else, but we *must* remember that there is a distinction. Once a man's been blessed or appointed abbot, he is a source of grace for everybody in the community *if* we have the faith that sees Christ in him. It is our faith that makes the action of Christ in the superior on our soul effective. Anything we say or do to one another that will interfere with that faith interferes with supernatural life.

Coming into chapter and listening to my abbot, Dom Justin, I had to see Christ in him and to accept all that came from the abbatial chair as coming from Christ.[12] It was easy to do. He was a man of few words. If you go to him with an urgent case—"Reverend Father, what are we to do?"—he would say, "Think about it." If I persisted, "But Reverend Father, it *must* be settled now." He would reply, "Brother, I'll consider it." That was it. You could not rush him. You would go to him and kneel beside his table. "Reverend Father, I want permission to do so-and-so." "Why?" he replied. He would listen to you most patiently. "Well have you anything else to say?" Then he would stop and look at the crucifix in front of him. He never rushed into a decision. Yet, I could always approach him in an attitude of faith.

11. RB 2,2; 63,13.

12. Dom Justin McCarthy, the second abbot of Mount Saint Joseph (Roscrea), was elected in 1911 following the death of Dom Camillus Beardwood (d. July 12, 1911) who was elected in 1887. Dom Justin was abbot from 1911 to his death at age 83 on September 6, 1944. Dom Camillus Claffey was subsequently elected as the third abbot of Mount Saint Joseph Abbey.

*Rash Judgment.* If you judge rashly, it is Christ you are judging. What right have you to judge? You have no right to sit in judgment of any man. You may say, "It's rather obvious that the man's committing a sin. It's in the books. It's obvious."

There were some very holy nuns of great prayer and penance. In the city was a woman who had a son out of wedlock. These nuns would draw their skirts aside when she would pass. "Oh, you see what she's up to now. You know about so-and-so." Before these good nuns died, the body of that woman, Saint Margaret of Cortona, was exposed under their high altar for veneration as a canonized saint.[13]

If you think your brethren are committing sin at the moment, you do not know what God's going to do with them next. That is one way of putting a break on your judgments.

There is, however, another answer. How can you judge anybody if you do not know what grace they have at the moment? You think that their conscience would tell them that their action is wrong. I know that any man, no matter how holy, goes through periods when his conscience just blanks out, especially between the ages forty and fifty. You can take it for granted that between forty and fifty you are going to pass through a phase of madness—of complete irresponsibility. If you do not know that, you have no right to be hearing confessions. If you do not know it from personal experience, accept my word for it. The older men will know what I am talking about. We all have our blind spots. There are forms of neurosis that we all, to some extent, share in that interfere with our responsibility.

13. "Margaret died in 1297, being just fifty years of age. Her confessor and first biographer tells us that one day, shortly before her death, she had a vision of Saint Mary Magdalene, 'most faithful of Christ's apostles, clothed in a robe as it were of silver, and crowned with a crown of precious gems, surrounded by the holy angels.' And whilst she was in this ecstasy Christ spoke to Margaret, saying: 'My Eternal Father said of Me to the Baptist: This is My beloved Son; so do I say to you of Magdalene: This is my beloved daughter.' On another occasion we are told that 'she was taken in spirit to the feet of Christ, which she washed with her tears as did Magdalene of old; and as she wiped His feet she desired greatly to behold His face, and prayed to the Lord to grant her this favor.'" Alan Goodier, *Saints for Sinners* (Garden City: Image, 1959), p. 44.

You do not know what grace a man has. There is no sin in the calendar that you and I could not commit were it not for the grace of God. That is why holy men are such kind confessors. They are not shocked by what you tell them because they know that if they have not done it themselves, it is only the grace of God that keeps them from doing it.

I warn you. Do not sit in judgment on another man's sins. God may show you the possibility of such things happening by letting you fall into them yourself. If You have never learned the hard way early, you may have to learn the hard way after, so be charitable in your judgments. You do not know what graces another man has.

If God has given you the grace to control your temper all your life, to give a soft answer, and you have to deal with a man who has a fiery temperament, and has not had the experience of self-control, you cannot judge him by your standards. Please remember, God does not put a premium on success. God judges and rewards the effort, not the achievement. You *cannot* judge another man's effort. You have no right to because you cannot see it. You do not know another's graces, temptations, or inherited weaknesses. Also, you do not know his glandular system. All these things come into that judgment. Have you had another man's experiences? Another man's upbringing? Another man's inherited traits? Even if you had, have you the other man's grace? If God has given you the grace to be good, you have no assurance that he has given the same measure to somebody else. Remember, God's grace is a grace. It is a free gift.

*Rigidity.* There is another weakness in the matter of charity. That is the efficacious type of person who tells you the latest rules of the abbot and reminds you, "Oh, you can't do that." There are various ways of leading other men to sin. One way is reminding them of their obligations when it is unnecessary.

Some monasteries have trouble with monks telling the superior what to do—how to run the monastery. The superior sometimes has to react strongly: "I'm the superior. That's the way it is going to be done." That sounds very drastic, but in some situations it must be clearly stated who it is that Saint Benedict has put in charge of the monastery and of the souls for whom he must give an account.[14]

When I was appointed superior at Caldey Island, I made no changes for six months. I told the abbot general that I was going to do nothing for six months. He said, "You're right." I asked my two other superiors and my own confessor, "What am I to do?"

"Father," one of them said, "you've got to show you're the superior and show your strength. Be unreasonable. Refuse to argue or discuss things. That's that and that's all about it."

The abbot general told me that when he was appointed to a monastery as superior where there were problems: "I did nothing for six months and studied the situation. Then I decided changes had to be made. I made quite a lot of changes one Sunday morning in chapter. As soon as I got out of the room, somebody knocked at the door. 'I'll kill you! If you change me out of that job, I'll kill you!' the brother said thumping the table. I said, 'Yup. I'm going to change you. Carry on and kill me. I won't change my change.'" God has his own ways of sanctifying superiors.

*Cliques.* Cliques and particular friendships in a monastery are fatal for fraternal charity. We are bound to love all men and to treat all our brethren equally. We may have our likes and our dislikes, but we must not let them affect our behavior. It is certainly true that there are always some men with whom we are more at ease. They look at things the same way as we do. They understand us better. We do not need to explain ourselves to them. There is nothing wrong in being attracted to them or having that feeling about them. Our Lord had special friends. In the community, however, it is certainly wrong to let such personal sentiments affect our conduct, especially where it starts excluding others or seeking particular people out.

*Immaturity.* One or two difficult characters can upset the happiness, charity, peace, and the family spirit of a Cistercian house. The immature monk has never established himself in his own eyes. He is like a small boy putting on "airs." As soon as you give him the slightest authority, he immediately makes himself difficult. If he is in charge of some tools, he will say, "What do

14. RB 2,34.

you want that for? No, you don't want that. You need something else." He will give you a fork to dig the earth and a spade to pitch hay. There was a master of novices once in an Irish house who broke his novices in that way. He would tell them to take the handles of their toothbrushes to scrap the wax off the seats in the church. Charity is essential. The type of man who cannot use authority charitably can be a nuisance in a monastery.

*Mockery.* There is the type of man who relishes in seeing other men slip. He justifies himself in mocking them. He is a bit put-out when the other men start to pull up their socks and to do things better. The reaction is one of jeering or making it difficult for another man to turn to our Lord. Our Lord takes a very drastic view of being a source of spiritual retardation to others.[15] We should be careful lest we interfere with the conversion of another man. It is all the more serious if the particular fault the man is trying to cure himself of is a serious one and You have a partner with him in his infidelity.

## Personal Differences

Charity is exercised through being kind and sympathetic. You make allowance for another man's point of view. Monks have different backgrounds, experiences, upbringings, personal habits, and tastes. You cannot expect another man to conform to your standards. See things from his view and do not be surprised if his reactions are different than yours. This is a land of liberty. Every man has a right to his own opinions and feelings. Respect that right. Be on guard when you find yourself demanding that another should think as you do.

## Forgiveness

Another part of charity is pardon. You know how far our Lord exercised pardoning. He died for those who offended him. That is the measure he has given us. Our Lord has insisted that the measure of the forgiveness that we ask from God is measured by the forgiveness we give to those who offend us. ". . . *and*

15. Mt 25:45.

*forgive us our sins, for we also forgive everyone who is indebted to us"* (Lk 11:4). It is not an easy thing to forgive. However, the more we understand another, the easier it is to forgive. Although it is difficult, it must be done. When there are differences of opinion in a monastery—personal disagreements—Saint Benedict made provision for it by the public recitation of the *Pater noster*.

Your first reaction to injury, insult, anger, or slight is forgiveness. There may be a reason to adopt a distant manner. It is dangerous but it may be necessary. Interiorly, anyhow, you should forgive.

On the outside world, a man needs prudence if a man has betrayed or injured him seriously. It would be imprudent to keep giving him his confidence. Interiorly, the perfect Christian—and we are of course to be perfect Christians—must forgive from his heart. We used to have a custom in Roscrea that if you were proclaimed in chapter, you said a Hail Mary for the man who proclaimed you. The attitude should be the same to anybody who has injured you even slightly. Literally pray for him just as our Lord did. You cannot study the life of our Lord with any interest or affection, to say nothing of love, without realizing that this was a fundamentally characteristic virtue of our Lord's. It is one that he expects and demands we imitate.

Forgiveness applies not merely in the monastery but to those occasions when those outside a monastery offend us. We must never exclude anybody from that charity. The people who most need the charity of our prayers are those in mortal sin. We have a duty to pray for sinners because they cannot help themselves. Their need is greater than souls in purgatory. The souls in purgatory cannot help themselves but their salvation is assured. A man in mortal sin cannot help himself without a grace from God. The step into the state of grace is a supernatural step. Even with the sacraments, he needs supernatural sorrow for his sins. He cannot get that from himself because he has driven God out of his soul. He is no longer in a state of grace. He is only capable of natural actions. Unless God gives him a special grace, which he need not give him, that man cannot repent of his sins.

It is a tremendous danger to say, "Yes, I'll commit that sin and go to confession afterwards." You cannot be sure. As far as you are concerned, you have no claim on God's grace. If you realize what God's mercy is, you could almost be sure that you will get grace. God owes it to himself occasionally to hold his hand back. That is why the Church puts on our lips the prayer in the Hail Mary, "Pray for us sinners now and at the hour of our death. Amen."

## Praying for One Another

There is the question of adaptation to one another, without which family spirit is impossible. Our cenobitic vocation calls us to be monks as a family. It is in the family that we are sanctified. It demands an effort on each one of us to have an ever-increasing degree of charity based on the fact that, first of all, what we do to our brethren is done to Christ. Secondly, that all our actions have to be shared by Christ. He will not share actions that are against charity.

Anything we do to anybody—*one of these least ones*—we do to the Lord.[16] This means that we must have faith to see Christ in our brethren. The just man lives by faith.[17] Even being rude to a man who is outside of the faith is done to Christ. Christ gives himself to us in the measure that we give ourselves to him in our brethren.

Lack of charity even against one person can be a tremendous obstacle to our spiritual advance. It interferes with the whole sacrifice of the Mass. Our Lord is quite definite about that. "*So when you are offering your gift at the altar, if you remember that your brother or sister has something against you, leave your gift there before the altar and go; first be reconciled to your brother or sister, and then come and offer your gift*" (Mt 5:23-24).

The Church never prays in the first person singular. We always pray as a mystical body united in Christ. If you are at war with a member of Christ, you are at war with Christ.

The two things that regulate your healthy union with the Body of Christ are your obedience, because you must be subject to the

16. Mt 25:45.
17. Rom 1:17.

Holy Spirit, and charity. A person without charity or obedience is a cancer in the Mystical Body of Christ. The only way of dealing with someone like that is by patience and prayer.

That is why Queen Elizabeth I (1533–1603) is probably going to heaven, if she is not in heaven already. Nobody who has martyred so many people could possibly go to hell. Why? Those martyred by her have prayed for her. That is an example of the way God works. I am taking her as an example of a persecutor of the Church. You will see that God glorifies himself by making these people saints. They cannot get into heaven unless through the prayers of the people they persecuted. Just as the Lord himself dying on the cross prayed for the people who crucified him, so the martyrs prayed for those who subjected them to death. Well, if God will not hear the prayers of a dying martyr, who is he going to hear?

It may offend our first reaction as to the suitability of what is just and right. When you think of the fact that we are living in a Christian economy, it would be one of the glories and mercy to make such people saints through the very evil they did. We should at least apply that principle to our minor persecutors and pray for them. God wants somebody to be prayed for. In that case, God lets them annoy a good, holy Cistercian monk, knowing that the good, holy Cistercian monk will pray for him.

When the good superior annoys you, pray for him. One of the simple souls in our monastery says three rounds of the beads every day for the superior. It is a great consolation for me that he does because he is a holy man and very close to God.

We came to the monastery to seek God. There are times, however, when you cannot find God in the church, in books, in prayer. You cannot find God anywhere. It is then that you will find God in your neighbor by faith.

There are times when you are overwhelmed by the majesty of God, who is self-sufficient and needs nothing from us for completeness. One of the great sufferings of the mystics is when they realize how completely satisfactory and sufficient God is to himself. God does not need me. There is nothing I can do for God, who is infinitely perfect. You are paralyzed by this absolute helplessness in dealing with God. You realize that God need not hear you. God need not worry about you at all. You have no rights where God is concerned. There is nothing you can do to touch God. At least it seems to you that way. But where then are you to look for God? In your neighbor. Perform acts of fraternal charity and pray for your brethren, and you will be close to God.

## Obstacles to Praying for Others

There are subtle and rather harmful obstacles to praying for our brethren. We pray that our brothers advance in virtue. Possibly our prayer is first for their conversion. Nevertheless, in the back of our mind is a little reservation: "But don't make him quite as good as I am." For example, you are praying for the grace of prayer. "O God, teach me to pray. Give me the grace of being united to You." Then you realize you are a member of this community. Why should I not ask that for all my brethren? "And give it to all the others, too." Then you say, "Now be careful, don't be too generous." It creeps into you prayers. Suppose you are saying Mass and you just received Communion. Full of fervor you turn toward the Lord and ask for some special grace. Our Lord suddenly suggests to you, "What about your brethren?" Immediately, being so close to our Lord, you say, "Yes, certainly, give it to them all." And then you think, "Have I said too much?"

Our tendency is to see life as a competition. That attitude does not belong in Christianity. We are a community of saints; the sanctity of one is the sanctity of all. You certainly will not lose by helping to sanctify another man through your prayers even if he surpasses you. We should be generous in our prayers for our brethren's sanctity.

Lack of, or failure in, fraternal charity is not only an obstacle to the fruit of the Mass in our souls, it is also an obstacle to the graces that we should receive from Holy Communion. Communion itself signifies union with God and the brethren. Obviously, if we are going to receive Holy Communion and are at variance with the brethren, we are giving a lie to the significance of what we do. We are putting a great obstacle in the way of Christ's life in us and of his pouring grace into our souls. As a preparation for Holy Communion it is essential to pray generously and sincerely for your brethren. Before every Mass, *go first and be reconciled to thy brother* by praying for all those who have anything against you.[18] We must be sure that our heart bears no malice and is full of good will to people. We must wish them well, which is the meaning of love.

## Grace of Charity

All of this demands humility and an intense personal love of our Lord. That is the secret for all these problems. Instead of tackling our failures directly, the best way is to tackle them indirectly by going to our Lord—reading about him, thinking about him, and talking to him and his mother. Ask our Lady to give you the grace of close familiar friendship with our Lord.

It is good to reflect on why God has called you to monastic life. God brought you to the monastery to love him. You show that love by loving your brethren with a supernatural love based on love for his Son, our Lord Jesus Christ.

If you lack charity, you find the cure at Holy Communion. In the Blessed Sacrament is our Lord who supplies every single need of your soul. The figure of the Blessed Sacrament was the manna in the desert provided by God for the Israelites to meet their physical needs.[19] In the Blessed Eucharist, you have the source of all graces. You can bring to Holy Communion all your weaknesses of nature, character, or bad habits. Go to our Lord and remind him that you are a sinner in need of his grace to avoid sin.

The journey of the Israelites from Egypt into the Promised Land, with all their infidelities and their rebellions, is a picture of your own spiritual progress toward the Promised Land of divine union. If you have sufficient grace, you will see yourself doing all the things the Jews did: rebelling against the men that God has set over you, accusing God of having led you out into the desert, letting you down on every occasion, and even worse,

18. Mt 5:24.
19. Ex 16:14-15.

you have a golden calf occasionally. You will find all those mistakes repeating themselves or tending to repeat themselves in various degrees in your life. If you do not find them, you have not lived very long in the spiritual life.

Charity is the test set by God himself. Through your charity you are known as his disciples. We have the consolation that every act of charity, however tiny, is an act of personal service to God.

## CONFERENCE TEN:
# THE DIVINE OFFICE

### Putting on Christ

Our aspiration as monks is union with Jesus Christ that leads to the adoration and love of God. Therefore, our search for Christ is for God's sake, not ours. The trouble is that you tend to want union with God as a means to perfection for your own sake. It is a holy ambition, but it is still a personal ambition. You are still looking at things from your point of view. God is not going to give himself to you completely until you seek union with God as a means of pleasing him rather than pleasing yourself, until you aim at sanctity not as a personal achievement but as a means of pleasing God.

All of our religious life—our religious regularity—is only a means to an end of uniting us to God and of pleasing God. Unfortunately we stop to make them an end. We have lots of monks who make "regular life" an end in itself. They boast of the fact that they were up at two o'clock every morning for the last twenty years, that they were never outside the monastery, that they never eat meat, they have never missed an Office. I think it is impossible to sanctify a man in a perfectly regular house because he is patting himself on the back and saying, "What a wonderful person I am! I am a perfectly regular Cistercian." He is pleasing himself. It is not God we are pleasing, it is our own sense of regularity.

Reverence for God is fundamental in Saint Benedict's Rule. It is expressed, says Saint Benedict, by humility—our acceptance of the truth about our dependence on God and our incapacity to do anything of ourselves.[1]

1. *Reverentia* (reverence) is used by Saint Benedict to denote worship and adoration of God: reverence for the Holy Trinity (RB 9,7), reverence in prayer (RB

Union with Christ involves a purification whereby obstacles—namely, self-love—are removed and we shift the center of our life from ourselves to our Lord Jesus. A personal love of our Lord is the ideal way to deal with our excessive self-love. This love can be described in various ways. Pope Pius XII in the encyclical *Haurietis Aquas* described it as the devotion to the Sacred Heart. As a monastic family, our personal love for the Lord is found in the worship and reverence given to God in the Divine Office.

The important thing at the Divine Office is that we put on Christ. Apart from the saying of Mass there is no surer way of putting on Christ than taking part in the Divine Office. This question of putting on Christ is fundamental. Dom Marmion says an interesting thing. When he was a young monk, his abbot said to him, "If the monk goes to the Office recollected, he will soon be raised to contemplation." Marmion said, "I didn't believe him at first. Now I know it to be true."[2] The recollected recitation of the Divine Office is undoubtedly one of the principal ways to higher graces of prayer. Apart from that, it fashions our prayer. It makes us cease to be self-centered. It gives a model in the formation of how we should address God.

The Divine Office, therefore, promotes our union with Christ. That is the significance for us of the short form of our Lady's Office. It is really a prayer addressed to our Lady to be a mother to us and to Christ. It is a prayer to unite us to Christ in saying the Divine Office so that her son may say it in us. She gives him to us, and she gives us to him.

---

20), and leaving the Divine Office in silence and reverence (RB 52,2). Reverence is implied in his chapters on the abbot (a monk's attitude toward authority) and humility. *Reverentia* certainly has its expression in physical gestures of bowing and kneeling before the cross or Blessed Tabernacle.

2. "At the beginning of my monastic life, the abbot, Dom Placid [Wolter], said that when one goes to the choir detached from everything and absorbed in the presence of God, one arrives, almost without suspecting it, at contemplation: at that time I could hardly believe it: now I *know* that it is true" [emphasis retained]. Marmion in a conference to Benedictine nuns, Dom Raymund Thibault, *Abbot Columba Marmion: A Master of the Spiritual Life, 1858–1923* (St. Louis, Mo.: Herder, 1949), p. 452 n.

## Praising God

Saint Benedict tells us that nothing is to be preferred to the Divine Office.[3] Yet, he did not think of an abbey as primarily a place for its public recitation. For him, the monastery was a place to seek God and practice virtue in the workshop of virtues. The Church, of course, has since then committed to us, in a very special way, the public duty of praising God in her name.[4]

In the Divine Office, we speak not merely in our own name but in the name of the Church. The Church has given us the Divine Office, almost completely composed of Scripture, as a suitable form of address to God. It is a prayer dictated by the Holy Spirit either directly in the form of the inspiration of Scripture or indirectly through the action of the Church. Everything in the Divine Office, including the writings of the Church Fathers, has the Church's approval.

## Devotions

We must not condemn public devotions such as the rosary, novenas, and litanies. The pope has even warned that while liturgical prayer is of primary importance, we must give due place, but not excessive, to other devotions. If a group in a parish church finds the recitation of the rosary or litany of our Lady has associations for them that goes back to their childhood and brings them together in devotion, we must not condemn that because we do not consider it liturgical.

Contemplative orders, including our own, have a history of adding forms of devotion to the Divine Office. Ten years ago, I spent three days visiting my brother in the Carthusian monastery. I asked the prior about the private prayer of the monks. He told me something interesting about the contemplative prayer in the order.

3. RB 43,3.

4. "Nothing is to be preferred to the Work of God. Accordingly, the Liturgy of the Hours is to be celebrated by the community which, in union with the Church, fulfils Christ's priestly function offering to God a sacrifice of praise and making intercession for the salvation of the whole world." *Constitutions and Statutes* C.19.1.

"It's rather interesting, Father, that you should ask about that now," he said. "We're just coming to the end of an era of devotions. The whole life of prayer of our order was overrun with an overgrowth of devotions. Six Hail Marys for this and seven Our Fathers for that."

That is rather shocking to hear of in the Carthusians. They were in danger of losing the dimension of contemplative prayer. Just as, with all respect, our order nearly lost it. We owe a tremendous lot to Dom Vital Lehodey and his book *The Ways of Mental Prayer*.[5, 6] He had to be guarded in his writings. We were forbidden to read his book as novices because his teaching could be misunderstood.[7]

## Prayer of Jesus Christ

The Divine Office is the work of God, not that it is given to God but that it is a work of God. In the Divine Office we are asked to share in the life of the Blessed Trinity. We put on Christ and say "Christ" to God.

I do not know whether You have had the experience of going up to a church where there are devotions or a service going on. You open the door, slip into your place, take your beads or prayer book and fit in with what is going on. Going into choir to say

5. Vitalis Lehodey, *The Ways of Mental Prayer* (Dublin: M.H. Gill, 1951).

6. Dom Lehodey (1857–1948) entered Notre Dame de Grâce in Bricquebec in France after nine years as a diocesan priest. He was elected abbot of Notre Dame de Grâce (Bricquebec) on July 8, 1895 and served until 1929. His three great works are *The Ways of Mental Prayer* (1908), *A Spiritual Directory for Religious* (1910) and *Holy Abandonment* (1919).

7. "A milestone on the road leading toward the resumption of genuinely Cistercian traditions was the publication of a revised version of the Trappist Spiritual Directory in 1910, prepared by Dom Vital Lehodey (1857–1948), abbot of Bricquebec. It was an outgrowth of the author's deep understanding of mental prayers (*The Ways of Mental Prayer*, 1908), which in any genuine monastic life ought to take precedence over observances of external asceticism. The merits of the new Directory lay in a progressive liberation from a somewhat rigoristic pessimism characteristic of the nineteenth-century Trappist milieu and the breaking of a fresh path returning to the classical traditions of mysticism." Louis J. Lekai, *The Cistercians: Ideals and Reality* (Kent State University Press, 1977), pp. 211–212.

your Office is exactly like that. This prayer of Christ has continued since the moment he was conceived, and it will go on here until the end of time. Saint Augustine has marvelous expressions about it. "Who is this man who rings out throughout the centuries and who is heard over the world?"[8, 9] Christ is always praying in the Church.

Every time we start our Office, we enter into Christ praying to his Father. As my good Father Master said, "Son, when a monk opens his Breviary, almighty God has got to listen, whether he likes it or not." When you open your Breviary, you are saying, in fact, to God, "This is *your* beloved son in whom you are well pleased. Hear him."[10] It sounds scandalous to say but even though we are in mortal sin God must listen to us. That is why the Divine Office is such a wonderful prayer. It is the prayer of Christ himself to God. The beauty of our vocation is the very obligation of praying to God in the name of the Church, which, of course, is the Body of Christ.

We cannot distinguish the Church from Christ. It is Christ himself who prays. Unless we adopt that attitude toward the

8. "The body of Christ, the unity of Christ, is crying out in its anguish, its weariness, its affliction, in the stress of its ordeal. It is one single person, a unity grounded in an individual body, and in the distress of its soul it cries from the bounds of the earth: *from the ends of the earth I have called to you, as my soul grew faint* (Ps 60[61]:3). It is one, but the oneness is unity made from many; it is one, but not because of confinement to any one place, for this is one person crying out to the ends of the earth. How could one individual cry out from the ends of the earth, unless that individual were one from many?" Saint Augustine's exposition on Psalm 54, *The Works of Saint Augustine: A Translation for the 21st Century*, vol. 3, ed. John E. Rotelle, trans. Maria Boulding (Hyde Park, NY: New City, 2002), pp. 70–71.

9. "One single person spans the ages to the end of time, and it is still the members of Christ who go on crying out, though some of them are already at rest in him, others are raising their cry now, others will cry out when we have gone to rest, and others again after them. God hears the voice of Christ's entire body saying, *I have cried to you all day long.*" Saint Augustine's exposition on Psalm 85, *The Works of Saint Augustine: A Translation for the 21st Century*, vol. 4, ed. John E. Rotelle, trans. Maria Boulding (Hyde Park, NY: New City, 2002), p. 225.

10. Compare with Mt 17:5, the Transfiguration of Jesus, when God proclaims, "This is *my* beloved Son, in whom I am well pleased; hear him" [emphasis added].

Divine Office, we miss its full significance. You will find that all of our monastic exercises can be and should be viewed as a means of putting on Christ, of uniting ourselves to Christ and giving Christ a chance to live and love in us. The act of our Lord in the Divine Office is the act of praise, adoration, and prayer to his Father. We give him our lips. We give him our bodies. We give him everything we have got. Marmion writes:

> To be truly devout in the Divine Office is to strive with all one's being to celebrate it well; it is to go to the choir every day and several times a day, with all the zeal, strength and energy that we can bring, in order to accomplish the Work of God as perfectly as possible; it is to persevere in doing this, not only when feeling consolation but whatever be the state of our mind, the weariness of our body, the inward repugnance that God sometimes allows us to experience.[11]

We must remember that we are not praying personally. That is, we are not praying in the first person. We are praying in the name of Christ; it is Christ praying in us.[12]

Many of the expressions in the Psalms apply to the life of Christ himself. Christ on the cross. Christ in the Garden of Gethsemani. Christ being scourged. Christ in his mother's womb. There are a number of expressions in the Psalms that are his. Jesus himself said to his disciples after his resurrection, *"These are the words which I spoke to you while I was yet with you, that all things must be fulfilled that are written in the Law of Moses and the Prophets and the Psalms concerning me"* (Lk 24:44). In the Divine

11. Marmion, *Christ the Ideal of the Monk,* p. 333.

12. "No monk can attend choir seven times a day without realizing that it is not merely a matter of a number of men joining together to discharge simultaneously their individual and separate obligations of reciting the Breviary, a group of men, so to speak, each praying in the first person singular. The important thing about the monastic choir is that it is a unit, not a collection of units. It is the choir who prays—if you will—in the first person singular, but if it does, that singular first Person is Christ Himself. Dom Marmion himself sums it up: 'Christ in uniting Himself to His Church gives her His Power of adoring and praising the Father.' (*Christ, the Ideal of the Monk,* c. XIII, p. 297)." Boylan, "Benedictine Influence in the Doctrine of Abbot Marmion," in *Abbot Marmion: An Irish Tribute,* p. 50.

Office, our Lord is praying them in us to his Father. Although they do not apply to us at the moment, they apply to him.

Our Lady is the same way. A lot of the older abbots were heartbroken when the Little Office of the Blessed Virgin was either shortened or removed. Many expressions in the Divine Office are our Lady's prayer for herself and her children. Our Cistercian devotion to our Lady is not a side-chapel devotion. We have our Lady over the high altar. The same is true of the Divine Office.

**Attraction to the Divine Office**

Some monks take a special delight in the daily recitation of the Psalms. The Psalms give them a sense of inner peace and harmony. Others are attracted to the Gregorian chant and liturgical ceremonies. For others, that is not so. I was brought up in a musical household. Later in life, I earned my living for a while as a music critic and developed a rather keen ear for rhythm. Then I found a Trappist vocation. I bitterly regret to this day that I ever developed a musical ear. The chant can grate on some men if it is not properly sung. One has to watch in a vocation that the attraction to the monastic life is not a mere aesthetic taste finding its satisfaction in the form of liturgical worship. The monastic life does draw a particular type of man for that reason, but you have to be sure there is something more fundamental there than a mere external attraction.

**Distractions during the Divine Office**

Have no hesitation. The Divine Office will demand the practice of virtues—fortitude, faith, hope, and charity. And sometimes this practice is to an heroic degree. If you are an organist, you know the limitations that are put on you at the organ if you stick to diatonic harmonies.

Devotion at the Divine Office requires that we give of ourselves. It costs something, no doubt. It requires attention and avoidance of distractions. You cannot pray for five hours in a church without distractions. What are you to do? What are you to attend to? Are you to follow the meaning of the Psalms? Some monks, I think, strain too much at their efforts to follow the meaning of the Psalms. It is certainly true that the study of the Psalms and an understanding of their meaning aid the Divine Office. However, that is a work to be done outside the Office.

For most of us, our attention is given to a phrase here and there during the Divine Office. It catches our mind either as an old friend or as a new friend that suddenly turns up. It is amazing when a word suddenly lights up with new meaning for you. This has happened to me countless times at the office of prime. Instead of paying attention to the Office, I am trying to figure out what I am going to say to the community in chapter. I catch myself and decide, "Well that's that. I shouldn't be thinking of that now." So I commit myself to God and stick to the Office. Suddenly one word lights up and I have my conference for the morning's chapter. In the same way, you may discover an illumination as you sing a phrase in the Psalms. For most, however, it is a word here and there that holds our attention and gives us something to hang onto during the Psalms.

Obviously we must use ordinary human prudence to avoid distractions. We must pull ourselves together at the Divine Office. If we find that our distractions are always turning to the same thing, then we may be unduly attached or occupied. Therefore, cut distractions off at their source.

**Divine Office as Intercession**

All the saints are praying in the Office. We are praying in the name of every member of the Church. In other words, everything that is said in the Office is said on behalf of somebody who is either living now, lived in the past, or yet to be born. There is no succession of before and after in the Mystical Body of Christ. Rather, the succession of the before and after has to be modified because of the association with the Father.

The Divine Office is not a private prayer. It is the prayer of Christ praying on behalf of his members. The same Christ who is interceding for us at the right hand of God is with us in the Divine Office. This is important when the question of attention arises. What if you find it difficult to attend to the text? General attention to Christ is, in my mind, the principal form of attention in the Divine Office. Remember that Christ is at the center of the monastic life. It is our gentle devotion to our Lord that aids our attention in choir.

Do not forget that the "I" of the Office is Christ. It is Christ who is crying for us, either on his own behalf or for some person. In one sense, he is still on the cross. Do not get the idea that the life of Christ is over. It appears so in one sense, but we are kept in touch with it by the sacraments. We have cut out not only the space interval between Palestine and today, but also the time interval. You can say the Office in the name of Christ in any mystery you like—Christ on the cross, in agony in the garden, as a child, as a workman, as a preacher, healer, and others.

## Graces of the Divine Office

The beginning of the Office should be a spiritual communion with our Lord. It is an appeal to God to come and remain with us so that we may praise him orderly. When a parish priest tells me there is something wrong with the parish, the first question I ask him is, "Father, how do you say the Office? Because remember the flow of grace to every soul in your parish depends on you saying the Office and how you say it." The way I want to say the Divine Office is in union with Christ. It is to realize that behind the Office we have the merits of Christ, the blood of Christ calling down the grace of God in heaven. When we stand in choir we offer God the Body and Blood of our Lord and all his merits.

The example of Moses is obvious. *As long as Moses kept his hands raised up, Israel had the better of the fight, but when he let his hands rest, Amalec had the better of the fight* (Ex 17:11). Why? Merely to remind us that all we have comes from God. We do not pray to God to remind him of our needs. We pray to remind ourselves of our need for him and to give him his due recognition for his goodness to us. This is basis for the fact that our life is probably the most efficacious means of the apostolate. You will find that around every monastery there is an atmosphere of grace. People who come to the monastery do, indeed, get a grace.

At Roscrea we would send out conventional letters at Christmas, just casual Christmas wishes. People would write back, "Father, your letter gave me such consolation. I've carried it around for the past two or three months. Every time I look at it, it brings me grace." That is literally true. Now where does that grace come from? From the good writing or the wonderful words we use? Nonsense. I suggest two sources: the Divine Office and the holiness of the lay brothers.[13]

## Holiness of Lay Brothers

If you want to look for mystics, look among the lay brothers. The most humiliating thing in my life is to say Mass with the lay brother serving. I hold the Lord in my hand, but I know perfectly well that he is far most interested and has far more reason to be interested in the man kneeling behind me. It is the most humiliating thing I know. I am speaking of life in a monastery where I know the brothers because I hear most of the confessions one way or another. I know what goes on. Every man who wears a brown habit has mystical graces *if* he is humble. If he is not humble, he has lost everything. We priests have to stand back in awe before the holiness of the lay brother. I can only speak of my own experience and those of other priests of the order with whom I have had contact.

## Praying by Faith

You can get into the carelessness that is the result of familiarity with the Office. We must not forget the reverence that is due to the details—the ceremonies of choir—that unite us to Christ. When we bow, it is Christ who bows. In our obedience to the rubrics, we are again fulfilling the law of our union with Christ and uniting ourselves to him by our conformity to liturgical laws

13. Before the reforms of Vatican II, there were two categories of monks in Cistercian monasteries: choir monks and lay brothers. Choir monks were devoted to the Divine Office (Opus Dei) and to studies. Lay brothers professed religious vows but their day was given to manual labor such as agriculture. The lay brothers were distinguished by their brown scapulars compared to the black of the choir religious.

and rules. That applies particularly, for example, to the chant. The cantor may have his own ideas of the chant. They may not be ours, but in keeping with him and following his instructions, we are giving Christ a new way of singing his Father's glories. That is one thing I always felt about the choirs that get a regular rhythm from side to side. The uniform rhythm is a perfect example of the union of the whole choir in Christ. It effects what it signifies by keeping us together in Christ. But all these mechanical details and artistic details of the chant must be seen against the bigger background as a means of uniting us to one another and above all *in* and *to* Christ.

We need to be ready to give ourselves completely to God when we go to the Divine Office. As time goes on, we may lose our sense of devotion. As one abbot said to me when I was a novice: "It becomes a question of thrashing out the Psalms."[14] His statement shocked me. Only later did I realize how true it was. We have finally to fall back on faith. The just man lives by faith and he prays by faith. There are times when we are only conscious of men around us. We cannot see anything extraordinary in the Office unless we make a deliberate effort to stir up our faith by the gifts of the sacraments.

We must be prepared to be reduced to the sheer nothingness of faith. To live by faith, hope, and charity is fundamental to our life. Faith is the practical one because you have to believe in your hope and charity. If faith is the only thing you have got, you have to almost believe in your faith. You have to be prepared to live by faith otherwise you will get nowhere in the spiritual life.

The Office is not a question of feelings, artistic attraction, or natural satisfaction. If you have all those things, they help. Even if you have them, they may be taken away and you are left with nothing else except that dry faith to appreciate Christ present in the Office and Christ praying the Office. That faith should put the Office in its place of primary importance in our life.

14. Perhaps it was a visiting abbot to Mount Saint Joseph Abbey in Roscrea who said this to Eugene. Or, it may have been the abbot of Roscrea, Dom Justin McCarthy.

The danger is when a man gets a job or a responsibility and says, "Oh, what's the use? This is more important. Somebody else can say the Office for me." It is the problem of every superior. It is the problem of every man with a heavy charge in a busy house. He has to exempt himself from the Office sometimes. We must be careful to keep before us the importance of the Office. As Saint Benedict said: That to which nothing is to be preferred.[15]

15. RB 43,3.

## CONFERENCE ELEVEN:

# PRAYER

### Developing the Life of Christ in Us

The monastic life is a union with Christ in order to praise and adore the Father. From our Lord's own insistence and from the teaching of Saint Paul, union with Christ is based on love and faith. While our love for the Lord must show itself in our love for God and our brethren, the Divine Office is a place where we can find Christ and unite ourselves to him. It is a place that is the least dependent on his grace. The very fact that we are in choir, standing before God in the name of his Church, is to some extent independent of our own disposition. However, we still must work at developing the life of Christ inside us.

We must feed the life of Christ in us by the exercises of the interior life. Saint Benedict's Rule provides for such an interior life through intervals of work, prayer, and reading. Modern writers on the spiritual life use two words when referring to the interior life: meditation and mental prayer. I wish they could be banished from their vocabulary. However, they are both used in ecclesiastical documents, so I have to speak with a certain reserve about them.

All the sacraments give us Christ. When you receive absolution, you receive the Holy Spirit. In the sacrament of matrimony, a man and woman give each other the Holy Spirit. The sacraments give us the life of God in association with Christ.

One way of developing the life of Christ that we receive from the sacraments is by increasing our knowledge of Christ. For most of us, that knowledge comes through reading. Spiritual reading is reading about our Lord or about our Lord's doctrine purely for one purpose—to improve your relations with our Lord and to make himself and his teachings real to you, to form convictions. You cannot pray unless you read. You may substitute for reading, listening. Saint Benedict says, Listen readily to holy reading.[1]

In the history of my own country the census of one hundred years ago showed ninety percent of the population as illiterate. Schools were forbidden. However, these people had a vocal tradition of language, Gaelic. That is the reason for the stained glass windows in the church. The windows aided in the vocal stories of Christ's faithful ministries.

We must reflect on what we have read. Like digesting the food, you must digest what You have read by reflection. In particular, with regard to Christ, we have to read about him and make ourselves familiar with his life and teaching. We must develop and deepen our knowledge and understanding of him by making his life real to our own life.

To make his life real, we must talk to Christ in personal prayer. Saint Benedict tells us to devote ourselves often to prayer.[2] Also, he says that if someone chooses to pray privately, he may simply go in the church and pray, not in a loud voice, but with tears and heartfelt devotion.[3] It is the prayer of a monk seeking God. The Lord tells us that we will not be heard for our long speaking and many words.[4] Saint Benedict's rule is a preparation for prayer through reverence, humility, compunction of heart, and perseverance.

## Mental and Vocal Prayer

The monks of old were not reading any treatises on prayer, detailed spiritual direction, or analysis of scripture. Yet, they rose to mystical union with God. The simple monk does what Saint Benedict tells them—enter and pray.

Monks were monks and then they started to be preachers. Religious were initially confined to the monastic orders. The

1. RB 4,55.
2. RB 4,56-57.
3. RB 4,57.
4. Mt 6:7.

Dominican Friars, however, were founded to preach the Gospel, and the work of the various religious congregations developed. They found they could not keep up the spiritual life, so they started to organize exercises—reading, reflection, and private prayer—into one exercise. It was called meditation. Eventually, they squashed out the reading and prayer but kept a point-by-point system of reflection. Then someone started this thing of mental prayer and vocal prayer.

Saint Teresa of Avila (1515–1582) said that a prayer with wonderful words but no thought makes very bad music before God.[5] Vocal prayer is certainly not prayer unless our mind is turned to God. Mental prayer does not cease to be mental prayer because you are expressing yourself in words. You can pray vocally by reciting a set formula, but you must try to mean it either by what each particular word means or by what the general meaning of the prayer is. In vocal prayer, we try to mean what we say. In mental prayer, we mean something and we try to say it. It is a difference of attitude.

### Saint Ignatius

The press of work on the religious congregations required a certain time set apart for personal prayer. Unfortunately, it was identified with reflection that is only preparation for prayer. This seems to be the fate of many congregations. Saint Ignatius is blamed for it but there is no greater injustice done to Saint Ignatius.

Saint Ignatius of Loyola (1491–1556) is one of the great mystics in the Church who has seemed to suggest devotion to the soul

5. "You will now understand how different it is from mental prayer, which I have already described, and which consists in thinking of what we are saying, understanding it, and realizing Whom we are addressing, and who we are that are daring to address so great a Lord. . . . To recite the Paternoster and the Ave Maria, or any other petition you like, is vocal prayer. But think how harsh your music will be without what must come first; sometimes even the words will get into the wrong order. In these two kinds of prayer, with God's help, we may accomplish something ourselves. In the contemplation which I have just described we can do nothing. It is His Majesty Who does everything; the work is His alone and far transcends human nature." Teresa of Avila, *The Way of Perfection*, trans. and ed. E. Allison Peers (New York: Image, 1964, 1991), p. 171.

of Christ. Saint Ignatius never proposed a method of prayer and never had daily meditations in his monasteries. Saint Ignatius wrote spiritual exercises for a man who had to make a very serious decision such as getting married, getting ordained, entering an order, or converting his life. At such an occasion he had to put before himself in an orderly fashion all the truth of faith. Saint Ignatius provided for that with masterly skill and courage. Someone that succeeded Saint Ignatius took his idea and applied it to the daily prayer.

### Prayer and Grace

Prayer and all of the supernatural life is not possible without God's grace. To expect a lamp to go on lighting after you cut the electricity off is the same as to expect the soul to go on living once the stream of grace stops. Our Lady and the saints pray that we have those graces. God insists that we realize our need of him by asking for some grace.

The person who put the theology of prayer best is the Queen Elizabeth II. I had to preach a sermon at Saint Mary's Cathedral in Sydney. It is an enormous gothic building. I went up into the pulpit before Mass to prepare a sermon. I opened the notice book and found that I would be announcing a Pontifical Mass the next Thursday for Her Majesty the Queen. The cardinal would preside.

The cardinal had done a very clever thing. Queen Elizabeth II was arriving on Wednesday and the Anglican people would be having a service that she would attend on Thursday. The Prime Minister, the lord mayor of Sydney, the chief of police, and other officials were Catholic. They were in a bit of a jam. If they did not attend the service a cry would go out, "These Catholics are disloyal." If they went, it was a scandal of Catholics attending non-Catholic worship. The cardinal scheduled a Pontifical Mass for Her Majesty at the same time. I said in my sermon: "My dear brethren, please give me the occasion of reminding you of your obligations in regard to the Queen's upcoming visit. Her Majesty comes to this country as a representative of Christ in things temporal and must be received with the respect due to such a person."

The Communists nearly had a hold of Australia. They practically got the Labor Party but a system of Catholic groups broke it up. The Communists were studiously propagating a technique of disrespect. I dealt in the sermon with the duty of respect and loyalty. The communists were undermining all civil loyalty. I pointed out the fourth commandment that gave us the patriotic devotion to the powers that be—to the office sovereign.

I said: "There may be people here from Ireland like myself who feel that Her Majesty's right to govern parts of our country is open to question. That has absolutely nothing to do with her position in Australia where she is the lawful sovereign. She is, as I said, the representative of Christ in things temporal."

I went on to deal with the duty of prayer: "We have to pray for Her Majesty. Saint Paul says to pray for those in high places. The queen is a person who needs our prayers. You in Australia have a forty-hour workweek. The Queen has a twenty-eight hour day for a seven-day week. Her work has to be done under the glaring eyes of the people. If she raises her eyebrow, everyone wants to know why. She is also the mother of a young family. She is a young woman carrying a heavy burden."

Finally, I said: "On the night of her coronation [June 2, 1953], she herself tore up the speech written for her by her ministers and put the theology of prayer better than any Catholic priest. She said, 'Today, I dedicate myself before the altar of God to the service of my people. It is an enormous task, impossible for human nature. It is only possible to carry it out by grace. The grace of God is only got by prayer. I ask you all to pray for me. May God bless you all.' That is the theology of prayer."

We have a task to perform: to bear and develop the life of Christ within us. It is only possible by God's grace. We have to pray for one another and ourselves.

Our prayer as we know it is based on the merits of Christ. We can obtain any grace necessary for our salvation or for our sanctification by his merits. Our Lord himself has promised us that anything we ask in his name will be given us.[6]

6. Jn 14:13.

## Praying the Merits of Christ

I suggest one form of prayer that expresses this attitude of praying in Jesus' name. The Holy Spirit pours into our hearts the love of God.[7] It is by the Spirit that we love God. If you would, stand before the Eternal Father and say: "Father, this is your beloved Son in whom you are well pleased, hear him. I ask you by his merits to give me your Holy Spirit so that I may love your Son as he desires and deserves to be loved." That is a prayer God cannot refuse to answer. It is a prayer in the name of his Son based on his Son's merits for something his Son deserves and desires. There is nothing of ourselves in it. Our Lord told us that if we ask anything of the Father in his name, his Father and our Father will give it.[8]

We can use many forms of prayer but above all is the prayer taught by the Lord himself, the Our Father. This covers every need we have, both spiritual and temporal. We pray for God's glory, the advance of his kingdom, the doing of his will, and for our temporal necessities. It is a prayer in the first person plural, not in the first person singular. It is a prayer addressed not to God our master, but God our Father. Our Lord, when asked how we are to pray, said, *"Our Father who art in heaven. . . .'"* (Mt 6:9). I think our Lord would agree with me that if we were to ask him how we are to live, we are to live exactly in the same spirit—as a child dependent on his Father in heaven.

## Friendship with the Lord

As far as special periods of prayer are concerned for us monks, if we have done our spiritual reading and have been sufficiently interested in what we have read, we will automatically think about it while we are working.[9] The whole idea of our manual work is to leave our minds free to work gently on what we know

7. Rom 5:5.

8. Jn 14:13-14.

9. "Prayer is merely one way of expressing your heart to God. Whether you express it by going off and answering a telephone, or going off and taking a class when God wants you to do it, makes no difference. It is still prayer. It is a lifting up of your heart and mind to God. That is the true contemplative life, by the

and hear about Christ. I insist that the essence of the spiritual life is to cultivate personal friendship and love with our Lord. For this, we can pray without a method or technique.

Be sincere in what you say to God. It does not matter how you say it or even whether you use words. It does not matter whether you speak Greek, Latin, or American slang; the good Lord understands. Talk to our Lord as you would talk to a friend. As that friendship grows, the formula for expression, or the lack of formula, looks after itself. It molds itself according to the friendship.

The secret of prayer is to share what we are doing with our Lord, whether it is joy or suffering. If you do not agree with that, read Saint Gertrude (1256–1302).[10] She was one of those mortified nuns. She would not take grapes when the infirmarian came along. Our Lord appeared to her and said, "I want those grapes, if you don't want them. I want the pleasure of those grapes and you had better eat them to give me the pleasure." Remember that the next time something turns up in addition to the main meal. If you do not want to enjoy what is provided—if you are one of those mortified men—do not mortify our Lord please.

There is a simplicity about true devotion to our Lord that does not stop to think whether our actions bring us pleasure or bring us pain as long as it is pleasing to him. The whole spiritual life is delightfully simple. Unfortunately, some spiritual writers have complicated the question of prayer.

Prayer is talking to our Lord. We remind ourselves who he is. We get hold of some aspect of our Lord—something we have been reading about or something we have been thinking about. It may be a mystery of our Lord's life. It may be just about himself. It may be a vague concept of God. We put everything else out of our mind and we talk to him.

---

way, a life of activity done out of a sense of getting in contact with God." Boylan, talk to Sisters, 6,8.

10. See Gertrude the Great of Helfta, *The Herald of God's Loving-Kindness: Books One and Two*, trans. and annotated Alexandra Barratt, Cistercian Fathers Series, vol. 35 (Kalamazoo, Mi.: Cistercian Publications, 1991) and Miriam Schmitt, "Gertrud of Helfta: Her Monastic Milieu and Her Spirituality," in *Hidden Springs: Cistercian Monastic Women, Book Two* (Cistercian Publications, 1995), pp. 471–496.

**Seeking God**

I can speak from my personal contact with men who have given themselves completely to God and whom you would expect to be men of great prayer. Ask these men what they do at their time for mental prayer and you might be surprised to hear that for most of the mental prayer they are distracted. The only person that can save that prayer is our Lord. He has promised us that he will come and save us. You will never be men of prayer until you have found out that you cannot pray. You have got to die daily to yourself.

When we were baptized, the Holy Spirit took up residence in our souls. He wants to pray there. Saint Paul told us that we cannot pray of ourselves, but the Holy Spirit prays for us.[11] God removes the orange skins, so to speak. There are about a hundred of them. He peels them until at the depth is the Holy Spirit. Then You have got mystical prayer. You are out of the picture and will not be able to say, "*I* have the prayer of contemplation." You realize that you have been let in on something much bigger. You quietly, like the Arabs folding their tents and slipping away, leave God talking to God. This is mystical prayer.

The advance in the monastic life consists in gradually getting rid of self-seeking. Some seek power; others seek comfort. Still others seek favor with their brethren or with superiors. We must know ourselves. Grace will always show us where we are going wrong if we pray for light. God's providence is continually whittling away these attachments to self and self-seeking, gradually forcing us back to a forgetting of ourselves and a seeking of him. He is helping us to seek him for his own sake, making him the center of our lives.

God whittles everything down so that there is nothing left but sheer faith. Saint John of the Cross is quite definite that faith is the basis of all our purifications. The transformation that must go on in us is a work of faith, although charity really is the consuming fire. Faith is where we can make efforts to advance in prayer, not at prayer itself. Do not start doing mental gymnastics.

11. Rom 8:26.

Do not start forcing yourself: "I'm going to think of God. I'm going to think of God." Prayer is a gentle thing. When distracted, we just turn straight to God. Leave them there; do not deal with them. To avert to a distraction is to make it more distracting.

## Living Your Prayer

Prayer, whether expressed in thoughts or words, whether you are kneeling or standing, depends on our sincerity. It is being before God and exposing to him our complete poverty. It is a manifestation to God of our life.

Lehodey, in *The Ways of Mental Prayer*, says there is no technique of praying but of living.[12] What you do is to start examining the way you live. What sort of a monk are you? How sincere are you in your search of God? Lehodey uses purity of heart to describe the sincerity of life that affects prayer.[13] It is custody of the heart that matters, not custody of the eyes. Is your heart given to God alone? How about your attachments? Are there undue attachments that could interfere with prayer? What is the normal course of your thoughts during the day? Do you let your thoughts run wild? I am not talking about distractions. I am talking about the deliberate course of our thoughts.

What is the motive behind your doings? Is it self-seeking? Self-satisfaction? Looking for admiration? Trying to get in with superiors? Trying to plan or work out a monastic career for yourself? All of these are ways that we seek ourselves.

12. "[Prayer's] principal object is not to instruct us, pious reading would suffice for that; it is rather to inflame the heart, that it may discharge better its duty towards God, and especially to conform our will to that of God, so that prayer may detach us from everything else, attach us to Him alone, and so transform our habits and our life." Lehodey, *The Ways of Mental Prayer*, p. 16.

13. "Our heart is pure when we love only God, or according to God. We must, therefore, banish every culpable affection, sever every tie of which the Divine Master is not the beginning and the end, and which is not regulated according to His will. . . . If on the other hand, our heart belongs to God alone, our thoughts and affections move at ease in prayer, as a fish does in water. The heart carries the soul to God . . ." Lehodey, *The Ways of Mental Prayer*, p. 36.

**Difficulties in Prayer**

In the beginning stages of prayer, God manifests himself in a quiet way. You have a sensation that God is somewhere around. Eventually, that feeling ceases to make an appeal to the imagination. God may begin to appeal somewhere in the intellect. The result is that the imagination has no food at all and starts rambling. The answer is to leave them alone. The same thing can happen to your intellect. God leaves our imagination and intellect without any satisfaction; we are forced to live by faith.

I will not let anyone discourage the use of vocal prayer, but our Holy Father has said that we were overburdened with vocal prayers. There is certainly a prudent limit to our vocal prayers. If you start forcing yourself to say vocal prayers all day, you may kill the grace of prayer that is something quieter. Saying aspirations, for example, is a wonderful way of sanctifying your work but one aspiration is enough.

Vocal prayer is a way of keeping our mind on God. However, you can read your Breviary, recite the Office in choir, say rosary after rosary, say Hail Mary after Hail Mary, read every prayer in the prayerbooks and *still* have your mind made up to commit sin. You can even say Mass and have your mind made up to commit sin. There is one thing you *cannot* do. You cannot kneel before our Lord and not catch our Lord's eye.

At least one time during the day, or during our prayer, we should stop all talking and just quietly be mindful of God to see if he has anything to say to us. You cannot do that and have your mind made up to betray him. You definitely will not stray far. If you do not do that, you can do everything else in the monastic life and still commit infidelities.

Arid prayer can be nothing more than facing our Lord and allowing him to correct us. You must be willing to hear him speak—"Speak, Lord, your servant hears."[14] Monastic life brings us to the heights of union with God without any complication if we faithfully and patiently listen to the Lord.

14. 1 Sm 3:10.

## CONFERENCE TWELVE:
# CONTEMPLATION

### In the Presence of God

Reading about Christ's life and teaching, reflecting on it, and talking to him are essential to the spiritual life. Our reading about Christ is a personal matter between you and God. You read with care, although every page may not help you. When you do read something helpful, take it easy. Put down the book and think it over. The slow reading of Scripture is reflection. If you start your reading with a prayer to God, and read in God's presence, you will find yourself talking to God about what you are reading. Then you are praying. And it should be a prayer.

You can easily develop a sense of God's presence. It is an awareness that allows you free action to do what you are doing. It is not so easy if you are not doing God's will, if what you are doing is done for your sake and not for his. The more you empty yourself in what you are doing, the easier it is to avert to him, and the more readily God manifests himself to you. Remember, both things are happening: You are seeking God and God is avidly seeking you.

God is not distantly passive in the heavens. God is burning with love, just eager to get a chance of uniting us to himself. The dynamic nature of God's love for us—the goodness of God—is appealing. When we see it, we are terrified of the obstacles we have placed before it. We do not realize that all we have to do is to get out of the way. When we do so, the heights of sanctity are opened to us in five seconds. However, we have to move slowly, being what we are.

The perception of God's presence is a tremendous help if you can cultivate it while you are reading. That is why we kneel for a few moments before we read. In the same way, a reflection can be turned into a prayer. For example, we reflect on our Lord's agony in the garden, not only wondering what the Lord felt but talking to him about it. That is the beginning of prayer. After all, there is probably far more praying going on than you realize, because prayer is the lifting up of your heart and mind to God. Even though you are reading or sitting quietly, your heart is saying things to God. Think of a mother sitting by the baby's cot. The mother's looking at her baby and is not saying anything. Yet her heart is full of love for that child. God is a mother who looks upon us with infinite love.

**Our Uniqueness**

In prayer, we are speaking to a loving father. If you like to speak in English, very well. If you speak in Arabic, then pray in Arabic. If you prefer to express you sentiments in popular songs, then do so. Use whatever language makes it easy for you to talk to God and do not imitate anybody else. Each of us is unique in our life of prayer.

Our love for God and the way we personally give it to him is unique. No one else can give it to him the way we as individuals do. Even the way he leads us is unique. No two men go the same way. Never worry about another person's way to God. Mind your own business. The pace at which you go to God is his business and yours, no one else's. If God wants to rush somebody on, let him. He may slow him up afterwards and push you on a piece. If he wants a man to climb up steadily every year higher two or three degrees, then good. That is his business. If he wants you to hang around in mud for ten years and suddenly shoot you in an elevator up to the top, that is his business. You cannot change it. He will sanctify you his way and not your way. There is no good in comparing your progress to anybody else's.

There is no good in trying to find out where you are. God is not going to tell you. There is no ladder of numbered steps and subdivided compartments. Books on progress in prayer are written by persons. Each is giving their personal pattern—the way he or she went to God. Saint Teresa gives hers. Saint John of the

Cross gives his. They are not the same. Other people give theirs. Each is unique.

Stop worrying about where you are, whether you are in the second mansion or the fifth. All that matters is you want God and you are determined to get near to him. When you talk to our Lord, use any words you like. Do not use words that you do not like. The mere fact that you are in there on your knees with a personal love for our Lord is a prayer. Often, you can do no more than that.

## Learning to Love

You go to prayer to worship God, giving him all honor and glory. The fact that you consecrate thirty minutes for doing nothing else except kneeling there is an act of divine worship. Also, you go to prayer to talk to our Lord and to hear him talk to you. If he will not talk to you, then that is his business. If he makes a date with you and he does not turn up, well, that is his business. If you want to be sulky and go off home, you cannot say you are a true lover of his. True lovers have the habit of hanging around for quite a long while.

You learn the spiritual life from human love. There is no other way of knowing what the love of God means. That is why we are brought up in a family. Fraternal charity is of tremendous importance. The history of our personal relations is a preparation for our spiritual life with God. The romantic dreams we have had, the times our hearts beat twice as fast because someone's coming down the street, are part of God's preparation for our love with him. Do not think that human love is evil. We would not be here if it was not for human love. God created human love as an image, a faint representation of his own divine love for us. That is where we learn to love God. That is the importance of having a happy home. For most people the sacrament of marriage is where they are going to learn what love is and how to love God.

The language of human love is the language of prayer. It may need purification, but love seeks union. We are seeking union with God. If our Lord does not turn up during your prayer, that is his business. We can, at least, adore him and show our love by staying ever mindful of him.

It is extraordinary how acute your vision becomes when you are walking in the dark. You see things you never saw before. Before entering the monastery, I was in Vienna as a Rockefeller fellow doing research in atomic disintegration. In those days, we were trying to count the number of atomic particles that were smashed up by a bombardment. We did it with a florescent screen. You had to sit for twenty minutes in the dark before you could see one of these. You could see about five in a minute. Wait for another ten minutes in the dark and you would see about fifty in a minute. Wait for another five or ten minutes and the number would go up to sixty. It was extraordinary how your eye developed perception for faint specks of light in the dark. God keeps us in the dark to recognize his way of approaching us.

You can see your mother when she comes to greet you but when she takes you into her arms and embraces you, you cannot see her. When God takes us in his arms, as he does, and presses us to his breast, we cannot see him. We are embraced in God's love. You cannot be sure what God is doing. You need trust and patient abandonment to God's providence.

### Dedicated Prayer

When a monk sits for 30 minutes of mental prayer but has 28 minutes of distraction, the question arises: Is it not a waste of time? With studies to do, conferences or classes to prepare, and overtime work, why waste half an hour in the morning? Why not at least do some spiritual reading? That question has been put to me frequently. As a confessor, my answer depends on the man who asks me. Sometimes I say, "Father, suppose we compromise. Do your spiritual reading during that time for the next week or two. But come back and tell me about it."

He comes back and says: "Well, there is no trouble about that half hour. I do my reading but I have to admit there is something gone wrong with the rest of the day. It used to be I would find myself saying prayers around the house and making aspirations. I used to find it fairly easy to work in the presence of God. All of that is gone now. I never think of saying a prayer during the day."

It is not unusual to find in our houses that the time monks pray least is during mental prayer. The time they pray most is casually knocking around the house or at work. We sow in the morning by our effort to remain there in the church and keep our mind on God despite aridity. God does not give us the fruit of our sowing in the morning. You find that God reminds you of the Divine Presence during the day. The Holy Spirit moves you to make aspirations to God. Tiny little phrases come up during the day—something you hear in the refectory, the abbot's chapter talk, or in the reading before Compline. What you hear has a special meaning for you. It brings you to God or clears up some trouble for you. All those things tend to cease if you do not devote yourself to God in the morning or at the times appointed for prayer. Devoting yourself to God does not mean forcing your mind but putting aside other things.

I remember my vocation being saved once by a text welling up like that. Somewhat early in my days I realized the complete frustration of the Cistercian life. I thought it was absolute madness to waste a lifetime at it. I could not see any purpose in it whatsoever. It was during vigils that I happened to be looking at the book while the hebdomadary was singing the prayer and the words jumped out from the prayer of the Holy Innocents: "Not by words but by dying."[1] I suddenly realized the whole meaning of the life. It was to die to your self. You were to confess to God, work for God, and praise God not by speaking but by dying. That was and is our life.

1. "Sed moriéndo conféssi sunt [Not by speaking but by dying]" is found in the collect prayer for the Mass in the Latin missal (New York, Sheed and Ward, 1949, p. 47). The modern day equivalent is in the concluding prayer of the Mass on the feast of the Holy Innocents which is on December 28: "By their silent profession of faith. . . ." In the Liturgy of the Hours (New York: Catholic Books Publishing, 1975) for the feast of the Holy Innocents, is the Morning Prayer (Lauds) antiphon: "These children cry out their praises to the Lord; by their death they have proclaimed what they could not preach with their infant voices." In the intercessory prayers for Lauds: "The Holy Innocents gave witness not by words but by their life's blood."

The Jews in the old days had to offer sacrifices—their first fruits.[2] The best animals of their flock were offered as sacrifices. So it is with that half hour of the day. It is given to God. We get nothing out of it. At least we decide that we will not look for anything else during that time. We keep that period for God day after day, year after year. However, under the pressure of an overloaded timetable, you begin to wonder if there is any meaning in it?

On the contrary, it is the most precious half hour of the day. Unless we are men of interior prayer—unless we set a definite time apart every day for personal prayer—our spiritual life is doomed to extinction. We cannot be men of God without being men of prayer.

## Gentleness in Prayer

A look at our Lord can speak volumes. Think of a husband and wife who know one another's mind intimately. They understand one another perfectly even without words. We should be with God on those terms. Just as human friendship develops from formal speech to familiar speech, and from familiar speech to silence, so is our relationship with God. We can become quite happy to be in God's presence like a husband and wife knowing each other intimately sitting quietly beside a fire.

There is a natural development in friendship with our Lord that manifests itself in prayer. You may tend to talk a lot in the beginning, but gradually you are in absolute silence with our Lord. That is the normal development. By keeping up your reading about the Lord and being with him, there is ordinary grace working there that follows the course of natural friendship.

At times you may find that you cannot even think of God. Twenty-eight minutes of distraction, two minutes of turning back to God. Even souls who have devoted themselves to prayer for a long time do not always have the inclination to meditate. Many would say: "I used to have a desire for prayer, but now, unfortunately, it is gone. Meditation has become a weariness to me. I

2. Ex 23:19.

cannot find one good thought to touch my heart or to fill it with love of God." Our hearts may become dry and void of every feeling. We even are afraid to tell God of our love for him because we are afraid of telling him a lie.[3]

When souls reach this crisis they shall soon become contemplatives. God is now manifesting himself to the soul at a new level. We may think of God using our imagination or intellect but we cannot meet our Lord on our own terms. We must bring the plane of our life down from the imagination and intellect and be prepared to live at a level of faith. Put another way, it is the prayer of the Holy Spirit. All the natural workings of our imagination and intellect have to be paralyzed and let wither in order to allow the fire of prayer from the Holy Spirit to burn inside us. We unite ourselves with the Spirit by faith.

If you start forcing your mind during prayer you are going to do damage to yourself. Prayer must be effortless. There is no madness and slamming at distractions but a gentle turning back to what you are doing. Being gentle is essential in the spiritual life. Violent effort gets you nowhere. Occasionally, in dealing with temptations, you will have to be direct.

Our Lord said, *But from the days of John the Baptist until now the kingdom of heaven has been enduring violent assault, and the violent have been seizing it by force* (Mt 11:12). However, that is a different sort of violence. You cannot do violence to your own mind without damage. Quiet, gentle control is needed.

Remember that Christ is always ready to intercede for us. The prayer of Christ to his Father is living. It is always going on in heaven and in the Church—in his Mystical Body. You can offer

3. "Further, your inability to pray is a perfect prayer. If prayer is the expression of the truth about yourself, your inability to pray is a perfect expression. Your distractions are a perfect prayer. They show what you are when you are left to yourself. What you have to do is to use yourself and your inability to pray—your distractions—as a blind man uses his blindness when he is begging. He just shows it to other people, or shows the wounds in his hands or whatever injury he is suffering, which has disabled him, and he wants your help. You are a beggar knocking before God, hoping he will be moved by your incapacity to do something for you. There is nothing more you can do about it. You have to accept it." Boylan, talk to Sisters, 6,6.

that prayer of Christ to God. It is Jesus whom you allow to do the talking to the Father in heaven. You will not get much satisfaction out of that period of prayer; it may be impossible to realize what you are doing. Yet, you patiently and gradually center your prayer and your life on Christ rather than on yourself. It is not so much praying *to* him but praying *with* him to the Father.

**Acceptance**

There is no use in trying to find a pattern for your prayer. There is none. There may be a gradual development, a slow, gradual appreciation of God's action on your soul. God may raise you up and drop you down with a bump. Just when you think you have got a pattern or are conforming to a pattern, something turns up to make you realize that you indeed have no pattern. God is not going to let you see his work in your soul. He will leave some faults that you have been praying to him to take away. You will be riddled by temptations. You will be rebellious. You will fall into faults. He will even let you fall into sin occasionally if necessary to hide from you what he is doing because he wants you to turn to him in poverty of spirit.

I personally hold that there are saints in heaven who would not be in heaven if they had not sinned mortally. Sin is sometimes a necessary purification for our pride. Those of us who have sinned must be prepared to accept the fact that we have sinned. Such sin was a manifestation about ourselves to God. We are sorry for having offended God, but we accept the humiliation of having sinned.

One essential act of the spiritual life, and you will never find God if you do not make it, is to accept yourself as you are and as you have made yourself. It is an act of great confidence in God that despite the fact that I am what I am, God can still make me a saint. Accept yourself with all your faults and all your failings. That is essential because Christ is going to replace you by himself in your prayer.

The whole of monastic life is a gradual replacing of ourselves with Christ. *It is now no longer I that live, but Christ lives in me*

(Gal 2:20). We can help ourselves through humility, obedience, charity, Divine Office, and some attempt at prayer, but we are dependent on God.

## Contemplatives

There is a controversy as to whether we are all called to contemplation. You can get into an argument about ordinary and extraordinary contemplation, normal and abnormal contemplation, and contemplation according to Saint Teresa of Avila and Saint John of the Cross. It does not get you anywhere.

First, I defy anyone here to say that he or she is not called to contemplation. Secondly, I can assure you that if contemplation is necessary to bring you to the sanctity that God has destined for you, you will get it. Thirdly, if you do not get it, you will not lose by not getting it. *If*, I say. It is a very big *if*. Monks are not canonized for mystical prayer. They are canonized for heroic charity. There is no definite ratio between the degree of our charity and the degree of our prayer. Some imperfect souls have infused contemplation. Some of the most holy souls, very close to God, apparently have no infused prayer. If you suddenly find yourself a contemplative in infused prayer, do not go around looking for a halo. You may be very low down without any virtue. And if God leaves you to your own devices at prayer, you will get discouraged.

Saint Teresa of Avila tried to get her nuns to approach contemplation in confidence and yet not in presumption.[4] She did not want them to take it for granted. It is a very difficult thing to do. As I see it, infused contemplation comes through grace and the gifts of the Holy Spirit, especially the gift of wisdom. How-

4. "The most common yet most hidden temptation is our lack of faith. It expresses itself less by declared incredulity than by our actual preferences. When we begin to pray, a thousand labors or cares thought to be urgent vie for priority; once again, it is the moment of truth for the heart: what is its real love? Sometimes we turn to the Lord as a last resort, but do we really believe he is? Sometimes we enlist the Lord as an ally, but our heart remains presumptuous. In each case, our lack of faith reveals that we do not yet share in the disposition of a humble heart: 'Apart from me, you can do nothing' (Jn 15:5)" CCC 2732.

ever, these are God's secrets, and the graces he gives is his own business. We must abandon ourselves into his hands in quiet resignation.

There is a point where you can say to God, "Well, if you don't want me to be a great saint, I'm quite content. I only want to be holy enough to please you." There is a period in our purification where our hopes of sanctity have to be lowered, because there is still a certain amount of self-seeking in our search for God and holiness.

The answer is the fourth degree of humility; it is the whole of the spiritual life. To receive the gift of contemplation, ordinarily the soul will have had to make a profound act of humility recognizing the fact that our existence depends upon God. To continue to exist is only by his grace. We have sinned frequently and are unprofitable servants.[5] We must recognize these things.

God has to bring us down to earth—to cut us down. It is a painful process. You have to die daily. If we fight God, he has to either leave us in peace and settle for less (which is the most prudent thing) or use drastic measures. Those drastic measures may include serious sins. We confessors have to be careful in a monastery when monks come to us with serious sin. It can happen to anyone. We must encourage men to accept the humiliation of having sinned but not to lessen their confidence in God's mercy, goodness, and grace.

The essential purification is the humility that expresses itself by accepting ourselves. We have to accept everything that God sends us. If we are to understand what Saint Benedict demands of us in his ladder of humility, we cannot hide the truth from ourselves. And the truth is that we are our own stumbling blocks.

God wants to provide us with occasions of going up higher. He asks of us nothing that is greater than our strength and always gives us the needed grace. To correspond to that grace, we have to make an effort. However, we sometimes refuse to give effort, suggesting to ourselves that it is too hard and even not fair. Soon we begin to increase the number of "might have been saints."

5. Mt 25:30.

God has in mind our progress. He intends to help us when he sends us trials. It is not a question of a prayer technique. It is a question of dying to ourselves. God continues to offer us opportunities. Are we to continue to say, "That's too much"?

Unless you have turned away from the high road, he will keep on giving you chances. Sooner or later, if you want to reach contemplation, you have got to accept yourself as you are with all your sins, with all the humiliation of being yourself as you know you are. Accept God's will when it seems most unfair. It is the cross in its full measure. We have to be obedient unto death, even to the death on the cross.[6] If we do that, God will raise us up.

6. Phil 2:8.

## CONFERENCE THIRTEEN:
# OUR LADY

### The Immaculate Conception

Talking about our Lady is a difficult task. Our Lady's association with the redemption, the incarnation, and with sanctification is an extraordinary mystery. Our Lady put it best at Lourdes: "I am the Immaculate Conception." Notice the curious use of the phrase. Not that I had the privilege of an Immaculate Conception or that I was immaculately conceived, but that I *am* the Immaculate Conception.[1]

Each of us corresponds to an idea in God's mind. By our sins, defects, and self-will, we have blemished God's work in representing himself. We departed from God by disobedience. Our work as monks is to restore that image of God in ourselves. How do you do that? At every point in the spiritual life, we come back to Saint Benedict's humility and obedience. There is an extraordinary spiritual genius at work in Saint Benedict's rule. We as Cistercians have no excuse for not reaching sanctity. We have the blueprint.

God is continually trying to re-create us in Christ. Our Lady is his masterpiece. First of all, God's design for her was the greatest that he had in creation, except for the human nature of our Lord. Our Lady was designed to be the most wonderful human person he was going to make. It came off perfectly; his idea was

1. Our Lady first appeared to Bernadette Soubiroux, a poor, fourteen-year-old girl, in Lourdes, France, on February 11, 1858. On March 25, 1858, the day of the sixteenth Apparition, Bernadette went to the Grotto, and on the instigation of the parish priest, Abbé Peyramale, she asked the Lady for her name. Three times Bernadette asked the question. On the fourth request, our Lady responded, "I am the Immaculate Conception."

completely realized. The concept in his mind was rendered by our Lady's cooperation as immaculate. She is the Immaculate Conception.

Our Lady started her existence free from the curse of original sin. In her life, she never committed sin. We know that she grew in grace from the first moment that she was conceived. Her grace at the end of her life certainly exceeded the grace of every other soul in the Church—angel or human. Even more, it has been said that her final grace surpassed the total of grace found in all the angels and saints.[2] Some say that she started that way.

We are members of the same communion of saints. The love that our Lady has for God is ours to offer God if we only know how to use it. God received from her the measure of praise and love that he demanded. She never once let him down. She always responded completely to what God wanted from her. Our Lady was the most wonderful creature God ever made, yet she never fell once into pride. That represents tremendous humility.

The Litany of Loretto is one of the wonderful devotions to our Lady. Each title of our Lady offers a starting point for mental prayer. One title is Refuge for Sinners. Our Lady has a tremendous compassion for sinners. Every confessor should pray to our Lady for such compassion. An understanding confessor will never be shocked by your sins if he is holy. He knows that he would commit any sin in the canon law were it not for the grace of God. If his life has been innocent, it is only because of the preventing grace of God. God saves some people by preventing them from falling into sin. He saves others by lifting them up, restoring them to grace after they have committed sin. Where sin abounded, grace may more abound.[3]

## Our Mother

We have to consider two aspects of our Lady. First of all, she is the mother of God. Notice what her maternity involved. She provided a body for our Lord. Uniquely, by the conception in a virgin birth, there is no cooperation from any other created agent,

2. Dogmatic Constitution on the Church *Lumen Gentium* 55.

3. Rom 5:20.

so that our Lord's body came completely from his mother. Our Lord's early training came completely from his mother. There was a resemblance between our Lord and his mother because she was his mother.

While our Lady was the mother of Our Lord's body, God created the soul. The same for us: our body came from our parents; God created our souls. Yet, our father and mother are truly father and mother not of our body but of our whole person. Now, our Lady is also our mother. That is Catholic doctrine.[4] We have two lives in us: supernatural life and a natural life. Our natural life came through our human parents. Our supernatural life is through our Lady. When we call our Lady "Our Mother," it is not merely a title of an honor, affection, interest, or intimacy. It is based on a very real maternal relation to us. She *is* our Mother. Since the supernatural is much more real than the natural, she is more our mother than the mother who birthed our physical body.[5, 6]

### Mediatrix of Graces

Our Lady is the mediatrix of graces. Graces from heaven pass through her hands. Therefore, she has influence on that stream of grace. She obtains the graces by her *impetrations*. I was once refused an imprimatur for using that word in an article on our Lady. Whatever God can do by his power, our Lady can do by her prayers. She can merit for us because she is our spiritual mother.

I cannot conceive how we can call our Lady "Our Mother" if all she does for us is to pray for our life and to merit it for us. I hold that she is also a physical cause of grace. I refuse to believe

4. "Mary gave her consent in faith at the Annunciation and maintained it without hesitation at the foot of the Cross. Ever since, her motherhood has extended to the brothers and sisters of her Son 'who still journey on earth surrounded by dangers and difficulties.' Jesus, the only mediator, is the way of our prayer; Mary, his mother and ours, is wholly transparent to him: she 'shows the way,' and is herself 'the Sign' of the way, according to the traditional iconography of East and West." CCC 2674.

5. Pope John Paul II, Encyclical *Redemptoris Mater* (March 25, 1987) 23.

6. Pope Pius X, Encyclical *Ad Diem Laetissimum* (February 2, 1904) 10.

that I as a priest am not a physical cause of grace. When I say, "I forgive you your sins," your sins are forgiven. I do not ask God to forgive them. When I say, "This is my body," it is turned into the body of Christ. When I put water on the head of a child, "I baptize thee," the Holy Spirit is poured into the soul of that child. I hold that I am a physical cause of grace, an instrumental cause in the hands of Christ, a ministerial cause. I cannot conceive our Lady being any less.[7]

Our Lady's part in our life is that of a mother. She is a scheming mother because not only is she our mother, but she is the Queen of Heaven. She has the actual power to tell angels to come, go, and get things done.

Our Lady has the whole of heaven at her disposal. Whether by asking or commanding does not matter. The point is that she can get things done. She is a true mother because mothers know how to get things done. She is certainly pushing our interest all of the time. Our Lady has a hand in every grace that comes down from heaven. We do not need to ask her for every grace, but it would seem we need to ask her for some graces lest we should take her intervention for granted. There is absolutely no need why our Lady should be in the thing at all. None. God could act on us directly and put aside all mediation, all other channels of grace. God could have become man without any human cooperation but he did not. He came to us by our Lady. He expects us to do the same by going to him through our Lady.

## Devotion to Our Lady

Saint Bernard says, "God wills that we should have all things through Mary."[8] However, we have certain duties to our Lady.

7. *Redemptoris Mater* 40.

8. "Therefore, my dearest brethren, with every fibre, every feeling of our hearts, with all the affections of our minds, and with all the ardour of our souls, let us honour Mary, because such is the will of God, Who would have us to obtain everything through the hands of Mary. Such, I say, is the will of God, but intending our advantage." "Sermon for the Feast of the Nativity of the Blessed Virgin Mary" in *St. Bernard's Sermons for the Seasons and Principal Festivals of the Year*, trans. priest of Mount Melleray, vol. 3 (Westminster, Md.: Carroll, 1950), p. 289.

In what does devotion to our Lady consist? True devotion to our Lady is living a good Catholic life.

Our first duty to our Lady is to praise her. To praise all the work that God has done in her. It is a duty of praise and certainly of love. We are bound to love her with a filial love. We should love her, too, because she is so pleasing to God. Also, we love her because she loved and loves us so much. Her cooperation in the work of our redemption was a painful one. When she was asked to become the mother of our Lord she knew what was to be involved. She knew she was to be the companion of the redeemer in his painful work of redemption. Yet, she loved God enough to accept his will and embrace it.

At the cross, we see our Lady standing beside the crucified Christ, her son.[9] Look at her attitude. There is never a moment of suggestion to God, "This is not necessary. You know as well as I do that a single act of my son is sufficient to save the whole world. Why this torture of the cross?" There was never a protest against God's way of redeeming the world, even though it involved the torture of her son on the cross and the torture of her own heart beside it. She is standing beside the cross, completely accepting God's will and God's way of redeeming the world. Hers was true submission to God and a personal love for us.

Just as our Lord showed us the nature of sin and the extraordinary depth of his love in his willingness to help sinners by being crucified, so our Lady was quite willing to share in the agony of his death for you and me because she saw our needs. We owe her our love and gratitude. God made his whole plan for the incarnation of redemption dependent on her consent. What would have happened if she said no? She did not say no. She said yes at a cost to herself. She knew it was of tremendous dignity to say yes, but she knew also she was to be the queen of sorrows.

## Imitation of Our Lady's Ordinariness

We have the duty of imitation of our Lady. What was characteristic of our Lady's life? Ordinary, obscure, and laborious. What

9. Jn 19:25-27.

is the characteristics of the life of a Cistercian? It is ordinary, obscure, and laborious.[10] She was a perfect Cistercian and a perfect example for us.

Saint Joseph, who most closely imitated her, lived exactly the same life: ordinary, obscure, and laborious. He is the greatest saint in heaven after our Lady. We are called to exactly the same life. Sometimes we may resent the frustration of monastic life. We may wish we could get out and do apostolic works. Yet, our life as Cistercians is the life lived by our Lady, her husband, and our Lord for his first thirty years: ordinary, obscure, and laborious.

Note how little of the extraordinary there is in the life of our Lady. An angel appears to her once and that is the end of it. She is in the background. Our Lady is a quiet, reserved woman, knowing more about our Lord than anybody on the earth. After his death, she knows far more about his message and revelation than the twelve apostles. She has more gifts of mystical union with God and prophecy. She was the queen of prophets. No one had the salvation of men so much at heart than our Lady. What does she do? She keeps house for Saint John and says her rosary beside the fire.

The silence of our Lady is of extraordinary significance. She did more for souls by the humble doing of God's will and by union with him than by the most wonderful preaching or miracles or anything else in the world. That applies to our interior life in the monastery.[11] If you read the lives of Cistercian saints, they lived a life of ordinariness even when they are extraordinarily holy. Our life is a community life. It is not a life of solo flights. It is formation flying the whole time. Even when God is giving us extraordinary graces, he keeps us on the common track.

We have to accept the ordinariness and obscurity of our life as an act of devotion to our Lady. It is hard. We want to have something to show for our lives. We have nothing to show for our progress. External progress is quite unreal in our order. It

10. *Constitutions and Statutes* C. 3.5.

11. "By fidelity to their monastic way of life, which has its own *hidden mode of apostolic fruitfulness*, monks perform a service for God's people and the whole human race" [emphasis added]. *Constitutions and Statutes* C. 3.4.

corresponds to no advance whatsoever. As far as Cistercian monastic value is concerned, talk of advance is utterly meaningless. The only thing that matters is our union with God. That is the thing that you cannot manifest in the external form unless God manifests it by miracles. I do not think he is going to do that if you are a Cistercian. You have got to be prepared to die daily, even in the eyes of your friends. It is part of our life.[12]

I can assure you that when God does put a man in an abbatial chair, God immediately provides plenty of ways to show him that he is still an ordinary man. From my own experience, I know God looks after the humiliations of superiors quite effectively. I live in dread in my chapter every morning that somebody would get up and say, "Why don't you do it yourself?"

This imitation of our Lady is of tremendous importance to our devotion to her because she expresses in her whole life the full Cistercian life and the Cistercian ideal. As a matter of practice, I suggest one form of devotion to our Lady that I think is extremely pleasing to her. That devotion is to thank God for the graces and love he has given her, especially her Immaculate Conception and Assumption. Then we should come back to ourselves and thank God for the wonderful mother he has given us.

## Our Lady's Obedience for Love of Us

When our Lady gave her fiat—"*Behold the handmaid of the Lord; be it done to me according to thy word*" (Lk 1:38)—she exposed herself completely to the providence of God. Our Lady's *fiat* was not merely in her name but in our name as well. She, like her son, has offered us up to the will of God. We have been consecrated by our Savior and his mother to do God's will. We carry out the *fiat* pronounced by our Lady through our vows, daily offering of ourselves in Mass, obedience, humility, acceptance of ourselves, and our acceptance of God's will.

12. "Living in solitude and silence they aspire to that interior quiet in which wisdom is born. They practice self-denial in order to follow Christ. Through humility and obedience they struggle against pride and the rebellion of sin. In simplicity and labor they seek the blessedness promised to the poor." *Constitutions and Statutes* C. 3.3.

Our Lady is a perfect example of charity as she stands beside the cross.[13] Not only does she forgive those who have offended her and her son—we ourselves are the cause of her son's sufferings—but she offers up the terrible sufferings of her son and her own sufferings for our salvation.

When the moment of her son's birth comes, she finds there are orders made by the Roman emperor: *a decree went forth from Caesar Augustus that a census of the whole world should be taken* (Lk 2:1). Joseph and Mary go to Bethlehem to register because Joseph *was of the house and family of David* (Lk 2:4). But what does he find? There is no where for her to live, not even at the inn.[14] She might have easily have said to God, "Surely, you could have made better arrangements, not for me, but for the birth of your son." Yet, she was quite willing to bring forth her son in a stable outside Bethlehem. *And she brought forth her firstborn son, and wrapped him in swaddling clothes, and laid him in a manger, because there was no room for them in the inn* (Lk 2:7).

The Holy Family had to flee into Egypt.[15] From that moment on, her life is marked by the cross. She sees her son being misunderstood, misrepresented, and betrayed. Finally, she sees him on the cross. In the eyes of many, Our Lord had died a failure.

On Palm Sunday, Jesus was given wonderful acclaim and devotion. They took branches of palm trees and went out to meet him, shouting, *"Hosanna! Blessed is he who comes in the name of the Lord, the king of Israel!"* (Jn 12:13). On Good Friday, the crowds are hollering for his crucifixion.[16] Our Lady accepted all of that.

In the apparent wreck of our Lord's plans, the greatest plan was achieved. It was on the cross that the world was saved. God saved the world, not by his preaching, not by his miracles, not by his wonderful works, not by his wonderful power, but when he was absolutely frustrated, nailed to a cross. He was incapable of moving a hand or foot except in the spasms of the agonies of

13. Jn 19:25.
14. Lk 2:7.
15. Mt 2:13-14.
16. Jn 19:15-16.

a tortured death. Yet, then he was most powerful. Then he overcame the world. He overthrew the devil and his kingdom.

When we are tempted to resent the frustrations of the monastic life, to feel that we could do more for souls and something better with our lives than wither away in a Cistercian monastery, our answer is to look at our Lady, Saint Joseph, and our Lord as perfect examples. It is in our imitation of their obedience and abandonment to God that we achieve our vocation and give glory to God.[17] Our fate is that of the martyrs. Every day, through obedience to God's will, we have to shed our blood drop by drop and die to ourselves.

### Our Lady's Humility

Our Lady's humility calls for our attention. She has a perfect promptitude by which she recognizes the truth about herself and defers all the good that she finds in herself to God. It is spontaneous and immediate in her case. Saint Elizabeth reminds her that she is God's greatest creature. What is our Lady's answer? *"My soul magnifies the Lord, and my spirit rejoices in God my Savior"* (Lk 1:46-47).

Saint Bernard points out that it was by her humility that our Lady drew God to earth and united him to herself and to the rest of the human race. That is the answer to all of our difficulties. It is not our virtue that draws down God. It is the acceptance of our lack of virtue—all of our past sins and failings—that gives us the most important of virtues: humility. Humility is the basis for our union with God. Even our sins, says Saint Augustine.

### Our Spiritual Mother

Our Lady is the spiritual mother of all. At the crucifixion, you find Saint John reporting our Lord's own words on the cross. *When Jesus, therefore, saw his mother and the disciple standing by,*

17. "By the vow of obedience a brother desiring to live under a rule and an abbot promises to fulfill all that lawful superiors command in accordance with these Constitutions. In thus renouncing his own will he follows the example of Christ who was obedient until death, and commits himself to the school of the Lord's service." *Constitutions and Statutes* C. 11.

*whom he loved, he said to his mother, "Woman, behold thy son" Then he said to the disciple, "Behold, thy mother"* (Jn 19:26-27). Pope Leo XIII says that the whole tradition of the Church is that Saint John represented the human race. Our Lord is proclaiming the maternity of Our Lady.

> As we contemplate Him in the last and most piteous of those Mysteries, there stood by the Cross of Jesus His Mother, who, in a miracle of charity, so that she might receive us as her sons, offered generously to Divine Justice her own Son, and died in her heart with Him, stabbed with the sword of sorrow.[18]

No one is more efficacious in uniting us to Christ than our Lady. We have to cooperate with her maternity as we beget Christ in our own souls. All the graces she has come to her from Christ. She was preserved from original sin by the foreseen merits of her son. She is only a creature, yet she is the head of the angels and saints in heaven. This is a tremendous source of confidence and encouragement for us. Despite the limitations of human nature, the grace of God is powerful enough to raise human nature above the angelic nature. The angelic nature is so tremendously beyond and above human nature, but our Lady by grace is queen of the angels.

We, too, have our role to play to fit into heaven. We are to fill the places of the fallen angels. In one sense, perhaps, it is true that some of us, by the grace of God, will be raised above the angels. At least we know that the grace of God can raise human nature up to share in his divinity. Whether above or below other people or other creatures does not matter.

### "Do Whatever He Tells You"

How are we to cooperate with our Lady? The answer is by humility and obedience to the will of God. Christ said, *"For whoever does the will of my Father in heaven, he is my brother and sister and mother"* (Mt 12:50). Also, Jesus spoke of his food as doing the will of God: *"My food is to do the will of him who sent me, to accom-*

18. Pope Leo XIII, Encyclical *Iucunda Semper Expectatione* (September 8, 1894) 3.

*plish his work"* (Jn 4:34). We feed Christ in us by doing the will of his Father in heaven. This is the importance of obedience. It begets Christ in us.

At the wedding feast of Cana, our Lady addressed the human beings with a message that applies to the whole human race.[19] They were having quite a good time, drinking wine fairly heavily. A wedding feast in those days lasted four or five days. They had drunk every drop of wine in the house. She realizes that the host and hostess are embarrassed that the wine has run out after some hefty amount of feasting. What does our Lady say? She turns to our Lord and says, "They have no wine." There is every reason for our Lady saying, "Well that's enough. You have had a good time, so now close down." Yet, she turns to our Lord and makes a request to save embarrassment to the hostess.

You would think that the most unsuitable place for a miracle, the least reasonable request ever made to God, would be at a wedding feast where the people have already had too much to drink. Our tendency is to say, "Thank God, anyhow, his providence has interfered and put an end to these goings on." Our Lady turned to our Lord and said quite simply, "They have no wine." The Lord answered her in a phrase that is somewhat hard to understand: *"What wouldst thou have me do, woman? My hour has not yet come"* (Jn 2:4). Consider the phrase as meaning: do not let that trouble you and me, do not let that come between us, my time has not yet come.

What does our Lady do? She just goes on and says to the waiters, *"Do whatever he tells you"* (Jn 2:5).

"Very well," he said. "Fill up those empty vessels there with water. Bring them to the steward of the feast." And they found that the best wine had been kept for the last. The water was turned into wine.

What our Lady said at the wedding feast is important. *"Do whatever he tells you."* If I had to preach on the occasion of the blessing of an abbot, that is the text I would take. Those words of our Lady apply to all superiors, to all ecclesiastical authority. I assure you that if you follow our Lady's words as the waiters

19. Jn 2:1-10.

did, you would get exactly the same results. The water of your own life, of your own actions, of your own fervor, of your own feelings and dispositions, will be changed into the wine of the Christ-life with his love and his fervor; all your actions would become his.

*"Do whatever he tells you"* is our Lady's commandment to us. She imparts to us the secret of our Christian vocation. The woman who is queen of the prophets and queen of the apostles, who knew all the secrets of God—certainly the secret of the redemption and our sanctification—sums it up for us: *"Do whatever he tells you."*

How does our Lady's words apply to the abbot or to a superior? Saint Benedict's rule tells us that we are to believe that the abbot plays the part of Christ in a monastery.[20, 21] The superior says, "Go out there and weed those cabbages." Well, whatever he says, go and do it. What happens? Who weeds the cabbage when you do it? Christ. What does God say when he looks at you weeding cabbages? *"This is my beloved Son, in whom I am well pleased"* (Mt 3:17). What do you do when you weed cabbages? You bring forth Christ here on earth. You give him a new body, new hands to serve his Father with a new heart to love him, new lips to praise him. It is the whole of monastic life. It is why we have come to the monastery.

The only fruit we can bring forth worthy of God is Christ himself.[22] The only way to bring it forth is obedience. At the Incarnation, what happened? What did our Lady say? *"Behold the handmaid of the Lord; be it done to me according to thy word"* (Lk 1:38).

20. RB 2,2; 63,13.

21. *Constitutions and Statutes* C. 33.1.

22. "The fruit of a religious house is not the education that it gives, not its reputation for learning, not its reputation for regularity, not its reputation for penance, not its reputation for poverty, not its historical fame, or anything else. All these things have their place and God forbid that we should neglect them. But it is the degree to which that house brings forth Christ. We bring forth Christ by a life of humility and obedience. There is no other way. . . . Saint Augustine tells us that every Christian—and we have got to be good Christians, even though we are religious—every Christian, doing the will of God is a mother to Christ. So that your vocation and my vocation, even though I am a man, is to share in the maternity of our Lady: to bring forth Christ." Boylan, talk to Sisters, 1,5.

What does our Lord say? *"Sacrifice and oblation thou wouldst not, but a body thou hast fitted to me: in holocausts and sin-offerings thou hast had no pleasure. Then said I, "Behold, I come—(in the head of the book it is written of me)—to do thy will, O God"* (Heb 10:5-7). The depth of the meaning of those words! *Behold, I come to do thy will, O God.* The Incarnation was accompanied by a solemn act of obedience by our Lady and our Lord. We make the Incarnation our own by obedience carried out in our every action.

Note that phrase, *"but a body thou hast fitted to me."* You can take it as referring to the body God was providing through our Lady for our Lord. However, its meaning could be seen as the body of the whole of Christ. Our Lord accepted his union with each one of us when he took upon himself the task of living our life for us and taking upon himself the burden of our sins. From that moment on he lived in our name just as our Lady had accepted the will of God in our name. Jesus took on our obligations to God—all our responsibilities—and discharged them. Not only did he accomplish the work of our redemption, but he also accomplished the work of our sanctification. It is only a question of handing it over to us. How does he do it? By our obedience.

## Partnership with Christ

The Christian life is a partnership with Christ.[23] Christ is the senior partner. He has already done the work of our sanctification. All of his infinite merits are at our disposal provided we do his will. To the monks sent out to weed the garden, Christ says, "If you do that, I'll do all the rest. Leave the rest to me." The same applies to everything we have done. It is a secret of all monastic happiness and peace. You are given a job to do, go and do it. The rest is done by Christ. The rest is not your business. If you want to be a holy saint, a great monk, perfect Christian, a happy man,

23. "The whole spiritual life is a partnership with Christ and His Spirit; prayer is, as it were, the meetings or interview—one might well call it a lover's tryst—where we assure God of our love and of our co-operation, where we manifest our union with Him and even find joy in that union." Boylan, *Difficulties in Mental Prayer*, p. 50.

and a man intimately united to God, do what you are told and mind your own business. All of monastic perfection is there.

I have to frequently tell men who come to me as their superior, "Brother, what business is that of yours? Mind your own business." If I am told a monk is wasting money up there on the farm, I have to say, "What business of that is yours? You weren't appointed to look after that. That's my business and the cellerar's." The same way if someone comes to me and says, "Reverend Father, the novices are not being done properly." I reply very simply, "That's none of your business. The master of novices has been appointed to look after them."

### Leave It to God

All monastic families have the same troubles: people who will not mind their own business. I am not questioning the right of anybody in the house to draw the attention of the superior to a state of affairs. Sometimes it is the duty of the member of the community to do so. However, once his attention is drawn to it, that is the end of it. If certain things are going wrong, put it to the superior. Leave the solution to him. You are not asked to provide the solution. Leave it there peacefully and cultivate indifference immediately as to what he does about it.

Even in prayer, we must be careful. We must pray for sinners, trouble in families, world crises. Be careful, however, about forcing our own solution before God. Draw his attention to the problem, suggest a solution you would like, but leave it to God's will. Often people will make novena after novena that a crisis be solved their way. Underlying it is a secret desire to control the lives of other people.

I was a postgraduate student in Vienna for three years. One evening, I escorted to a party the daughter of the famous Professor Adler (1870–1937), founder of the school of individual psychology. I knew of the Adlers, but I had never met the professor. I presented myself at their residence with my best bib and tucker and a book under my arm, in keeping with Austrian courtesy. I asked to speak to the father Adler. The servant said, "I am sorry. There is a party in the house tonight. Would you mind waiting in the consulting room. All the other rooms are occupied." I was shown into Dr. Adler's famous consulting room with the couch where you commune with the ceiling and where he gives you absolution in modern psychological form. I sat patiently until there appeared Adler himself. We exchanged pleasantries, and he said, "You're Irish."

"Yes," I said.

"You're a scientist."

"Well, not exactly," I said. "I am doing research at the institute of physics. I hope to become one. I wouldn't yet call myself one even though I have published a few papers."

"Well, you have modesty to your credit," he said. "I understand you are a Catholic."

"Yes," I said. "I'm Irish."

"Are you a practicing Catholic?" he said.

"Of course, I am."

"Do you pray?" he said.

"Of course I do."

"But why? It is madness," he said. "How can you be a Catholic if you are a scientist?"

"It is because I am scientist that I am Catholic," I said.

"But how can you pray? Can't you see that it is purely a will to power. You have an inferiority complex. You're trying to compensate for it through your prayers." He started on a long explanation of the individual psychology of prayer.

Finally, I had to look at my watch and say, "Professor, it is a wonderful privilege to have from you a personal explanation of your wonderful theory of psychology. I cannot express my personal appreciation and gratitude. Unfortunately I have other obligations. I am supposed to have your daughter to the party at eight o'clock. It is now 25 minutes past. Do you think you could allow me to take your daughter?"

"Oh, if you're praying for her, you can have her all the time. If you're mad enough to pray, you're dumb enough to be trusted with anything."

Although his ideas about prayer were wrong, there was something in what he said. Inside some of us is the desire or need to rule other people's lives by praying for them and dictating solutions to God. There is a certain amount of self-seeking in the desire to control another's life. There is the same will to power that can frequently be seen in parents.

God knows the right solution, the right time to give grace to a sinner, the right time to convert the man, the right vocation to give a man. Leave it to God. There must be a fundamental reserve in our prayer.

**Our Lady's Guidance**

The function of our Lady is to unite us to Christ and to bring us forth in Christ. The only model we have of how she does that is the way she produced the human body of Christ. Where did the body of Christ come from? Every particle of our Lord's body when it was born had originally been part of our Lady's body. Every cell of it. With us, there is at least one cell that is an exception to that. In the case of our Lord there is no exception. Every particle of his body came from our Lady. He was fed at his mother's breast, living on her substance. After he was weaned, our Lady's hands prepared his food.

We must go through somewhat the same process. Our Lady must mold us with her hands and make us her possession. Is there any more direct way of cooperating with our Lady than by consecrating ourselves completely to her care? Does it not seem the obvious shortcut to the obvious formation of Christ in us?

The zeal of our Lady's heart is tremendous. She is longing to change us into Christ. If we give her a free hand, she will take advantage of the offer. It implies that we see our Lady's hand in all that happens. We need not be afraid because our Lady is a perfect mirror of God's providence. Her maternal guidance is really a reflection of God's providence. It means, for example, that when the soup turns up tomorrow, perhaps a bit distasteful, you realize that our Lady had provided this soup and are grateful. It means that when the abbot decides that we have to drop theology classes today because of the extra work, you see our Lady's hand in that.

There are a number of people going around talking in lovely terms about devotion to our Lady. They speak of being slaves to our Lady. When things do not go their way, however, they gripe and murmur. They do not see our Lady's hand in what happens. When you are praying hard for some particular intention, she has the right to change that prayer to something else because you have consecrated your life to our Lady. You have, of course, the assurance that your prayers could not be better applied than when our Lady applies them. That means if somebody prays for you, she can divert those prayers to somebody else. As far as you are concerned, you are giving her the right to do so. Insofar as you can, you strip yourself and give our Lady the complete right to do what she likes with everything that you can call yours.

The closest way to cooperate with our Lady's maternity is by giving her a free hand to change us into the body of Christ as she changed the very food she ate into the body of Christ. It requires dependence on our Lady. How that comes about is not always easy or as expected. In the active orders, you will see men and women being allowed to do wonderful work in God's vineyard. Then comes some obstacle—poor health, some misunderstanding with superiors, difficulties with communities. It reduces the power of serving him. What happens next is either dependence on your own strength or turning to our Lady and leaning on her maternal care.

It is death to ourselves so that her son can live in us. We each have a certain amount of self-seeking and self-glorification in our lives. You frequently see the work of sanctification in the active orders and of priests being held up by their zeal for activity. In a monastery, he lets some people achieve office and achieve works that they are interested in. If it is purely for the love of God, well and good. If it is self-seeking, our Lady knows that and is ready to help us when the time comes. Do not be surprised if the very jobs you are looking for are always outside your reach. I warn you. Devotion to our Lady involves thorns. It is not a sentimental thing that is all roses.

Our Lady is a woman of courage, fortitude, and obedience. She demands the same from us. We are to die daily, but cheerfully and patiently. If you die to yourself, you live for Christ. You will be able to say with Saint Paul, *It is now no longer I that live, but Christ lives in me* (Gal 2:20). There is no one who can bring that about more perfectly than our Lady. Consecrating ourselves to her is the most effective way of reaching sanctity. It is a matter not of a prayer but the attitude of abandonment that has to be carried out sincerely, courageously, and completely at all times.

## CONFERENCE FOURTEEN:
# POVERTY

*Dominus Est*

The vows of obedience and poverty unite us to Christ. I am not talking about poverty in regards to our institute but a personal lack of ownership that essentially means detachment. Our vow of poverty means that we give up the right to own property or to use it without the permission of a superior. We have sold everything—every attachment—to follow him.

Being detached from possessions is the negative aspect of poverty. However, negative piety or negative spirituality gets you nowhere. It is true that the commandments are framed in a negative form, but their intentions are positive. God was definite when he said, *"Thou shalt love the Lord thy God with thy whole heart, and with thy whole soul, and with thy whole mind . . . Thou shalt love thy neighbor as thyself"* (Mt 22:37, 39). The obligation of poverty is the negative aspect of this positive command to love God with your everything.

Just as prayer is a conversation with God whom we know loves us, so our virtue of poverty is abandonment into the hands of God whom we know loves us and has provided for us. We say to our Lord and to our God, "I choose you. I love you. I hope in you. I believe in you. You are all I want. I am quite satisfied with all you provide for me." It is an act of abandonment into the hands of a loving God. Jesus tells us that not a hair of our head falls without his providence.[1]

When changes are made in the house—when things happen or something goes wrong—God has arranged that. It is *not* a

1. Mt 10:30.

question of being resigned to God's will. It is poor comfort to God to be resigned to his will. "Well, I'll put up with this manifestation of God's love." You do not "put up" with it, you *embrace* God's will.

There is a lack of love and even respect in being simply resigned to the will of God. "I know the better solution to this problem, but if God wants it that way then well and good. He can have his way." That is not love nor abandonment. The attitude of someone seeking God and expecting to find all from God is to recognize God's love—*dominus est*, this is God. This is the Lord doing this and he loves me. He knows what he is doing. It is not my way, but his way that matters.

**Vice of Private Ownership**

I was asked to write an article for a symposium on Dom Marmion and the Rule of Saint Benedict as sources of a spiritual doctrine. I stated that Dom Marmion's success with his doctrine was due to his spirit of poverty.[2] He had nothing of his own and expected to receive all things in the spiritual life from the father of the monastery, namely God.

In the Rule of Saint Benedict, monks have a right to expect all things from superiors.

> In order to prevent even the least violation of poverty, let the Abbot supply every brother with all things necessary; namely, a robe, a cowl, shoes and stockings, a girdle, knife, pens and paper, a handkerchief, needle and thread, so that there may be no ground or the excuse of necessity.[3]

However, there is a dangerous obligation there. If we are going to go wrong as monks it generally starts with the vow of poverty.

2. "This seems to be specially true of one influence which we feel to be the underlying principle of all that Abbot Marmion taught and lived, and one from which his work derives its greatness, its richness and its power, namely that filial abandonment to God and emptying of himself inculcated by the Scriptures and translated by monastic rule and observance as poverty of spirit and utter simplicity of life." Boylan, "Benedictine Influence in the Doctrine of Abbot Marmion," in *Abbot Marmion: An Irish Tribute*, p. 53.

3. RB 55,18.

You appropriate something and hold onto it. You may take it in good faith saying to yourself that you have a right to it. The next time, you begin to have doubts. Every time you pray it comes between you and God. Though you took it in good faith, it is a continual source of trouble between you and God. That is why I would ask superiors, procurators, and especially librarians to be lenient in granting a request because sooner or later if you do not give a man what he thinks he needs, he will take it. If he takes it, it is an obstacle between himself and God. The multiplication of rules and multiplication of prohibitions about taking things only creates barriers between souls and God. They are occasions of sin and scruples.

If you are a monk, you took a vow. It is presumed that you meant what you said. Now it is up to you to keep it. When I became superior, I said to the community, "I am a superior. That is, the father of the house. I am not a policeman. If you want a policeman, I won't do any policing. I presume you meant what you said when you took your vows and that you intend to keep them. I am not going to see you do it. If you have difficulty in keeping them and want help, I will give you all the help I can. If you give scandal and get other men in trouble, I'll interfere. Otherwise, I am not going around to see that you do what you should do or that you avoid what you don't do." The more you trust monks, I believe, the more trust you will get.

We say to our Lord, "You are all I want." The vow of poverty really involves the virtues of faith, hope, and charity. If you are going to say you must have those books, these tools, or an extra habit, you have not sufficient faith in God. You do not love him enough to trust him that he provides all these things. Instead, you take it upon yourself to provide for yourself. It is a lack of faith in God's providence.

One of the difficulties about the spiritual life is that we erect, so to speak, a little church where we have the high altar for God and a side altar where we put ourselves. We render ourselves a rather lower form of worship but there is definitely some form of self-worship, of self-seeking on the side altar. The spiritual life consists in getting rid of that side chapel and concentrating on the central altar. It is a matter of poverty.

In the world outside the monastery, people measure their success by their bank account and possessions. People measure themselves by what they have. Our purpose in coming to the monastery is to decrease our self-centeredness so Christ may increase in us. Ownership involves pride. We want to get rid of anything that feeds this pride and keeps us from seeking God.

Our Lord's poverty was not merely material. His doctrine was not his own. It was the doctrine of his father. His will was not his own, although he had the most perfect human will ever created. It was the will of his father that he sought. His strength was not his own. He lived on complete dependence on the Holy Spirit. Notice that Saint Paul said he sacrificed himself by the Holy Spirit, not by his own strength. Who raised him up from the dead? God himself. It was a complete dependence on the Blessed Trinity.

Did you ever notice the radical poverty of the Blessed Trinity? There are three persons in the Blessed Trinity and one divine nature. The three persons can make a distinction between I, thee, and thou. They can make no distinction between mine and thine. Everything is held in common. The only distinctions are the distinctions of relationship. There is an extraordinary poverty in God. God is infinitely complete without this distinction between mine and thine.

## Spiritual Childhood

Even our prayer is not our own but God's. Every bit of *your* prayer is going to be stripped, and God is going to substitute the prayer of his Spirit until you are convinced that you have nothing of your own. The Spirit prays in us. We alone cannot pray. The more we try to make prayer our own, the more harm we do. Our poverty is to allow the Spirit to take over our prayer.

No one practiced spiritual poverty better than Dom Marmion, and no one wrote about the theology of spiritual poverty as well as he.[4] I hold he was raised up by God to reconvert us to live the

4. "Another example [of humility and spiritual childhood] is that of Dom Marmion, the Dublin priest who became a Benedictine abbot and wrote what I think I may justly call the theology of spiritual childhood. Time and time again

true spiritual life. Our life is not a matter of long prayers and practices of fierce endurance and stoicism. That is not Christianity.

While Dom Marmion wrote the theology of the spiritual life, the revelation of what the spiritual life is comes from Saint Thérèse of Lisieux.[5] On August 14, 1921, Pope Benedict XV declared that Sister Thérèse of Lisieux had manifested heroic virtue. Obviously, he says, anybody who knows Thérèse knows her life was characterized by spiritual childhood.

> There lies the secret of holiness . . . spiritual childhood fostered by confidence in God and filial abandonment into his hands. . . . Spiritual childhood fostered by confidence in God and trustful abandonment into His hands. . . . Spiritual childhood excludes first the sentiment of pride in oneself, the presumption of expecting to attain by human means a supernatural end, and the deceptive fancy of being self-sufficient in the hour of danger and temptation. On the other hand, it supposes a lively faith in the existence of God, a practical acknowledgment of His power and mercy, confident recourse to Him who grants the grace to avoid all evil and obtain all good. Thus, the qualities of this spiritual childhood are admirable . . . and we understand why our Savior Jesus Christ has laid it down as a necessary condition for gaining eternal life. One day the Savior took a little child from the crowd,

---

he insists in his writings that we must find all in Christ. Time and time again he urges us to lay down our will and judgment, our own way of seeing things, at the feet of Christ, and to tell him that we do not want anything except what comes from him, that we do not desire to do anything except what he, as the Word, from all eternity has decided for us: that in fact we should try to live in the spirit of Saint Paul's words: 'Vivo autem, jam non ego: vivit vero in me Christus' [It is now no longer I that live, but Christ lives in me] (Gal 2:20)." Boylan, *The Priest's Way to God*, pp. 130–131.

5. A Church is infallible, but members of the Church, even theologians, can make mistakes. It would seem that a mistaken notion of sanctity had grown up in the Church in the last three or four hundred years. . . We have the notion—at the least the notion that has been banded—that sanctity consists in being tough with yourself and live a life of hard penance, long prayers, fasting, hair shirts, flagellation, or else doing extraordinary deeds, extraordinary accomplishments. God raised up two people to bring the Church back to a proper concept of sanctity. One is Saint Thérèse of Lisieux. . . God raised up a man, even though he is an Irishman, to write the theology of her doctrine. That was Columba Marmion." Boylan, talk to Sisters, 3,1.

> and showing him to His disciples, He said: "Amen I say to you; unless you be converted and become as little children you shall not enter into the kingdom of heaven." . . . "Who, do you think, is the greater in the kingdom of heaven?" . . . "Whosoever shall humble himself as this little child, he is the greater in the kingdom of heaven." And again on another day, Jesus said: "Suffer little children to come to me, and forbid them not; the kingdom of heaven is for such. Amen I say to you, whosoever shall not receive the kingdom of God as a child shall not enter into it."

Notice the importance of Jesus' words. He not only says that the kingdom of heaven is for children or those who will become as little children, but he threatens exclusion from heaven for those who will not become as little children. Jesus wants us to see spiritual childhood as necessary for our entrance into heaven. How do we do this? By the way of confidence in God and abandonment to God's will. The surest means of gaining God's heart is to be a child in his eyes—to recognize our own nothingness in his sight and make ourselves truly little in the presence of his goodness.

In spiritual childhood, there is the recognition of our poverty and our incapacity. We see ourselves as we are and look with joy into the depths of our own lowliness. We proclaim our nothingness in regard to the greatness of the Almighty.[6]

A child's strength lies in his very weakness. God is inclined to help his creatures in proportion to their recognition and humble acceptance of their natural helplessness. The child possesses nothing of its own; everything belongs to his or her parents. Yet, the father is to provide for his child's every necessity. At each moment of our life, we can be assured of God's care. However, God will never give you a store of grace. He will only give you enough to deal with the needs of the present moment. Tomorrow must look after itself. You cannot carry tomorrow's cross with today's grace.

6. "It is God alone that all value must be attributed; there's nothing of value in my little nothingness." Thérèse, in her last months before death, confiding to Mother Agnes (her blood sister, Pauline) on August 8, 1897 in *St. Thérèse of Lisieux: Her Last Conversations*, trans. John Clarke (Washington, D.C.: Institute of Carmelite Studies, 1977), p. 141.

These are Saint Thérèse's words:

> "To love Jesus is to be the victim of his love. The more weak and miserable we are, the better disposed we are for the operations of His consuming and transforming love. . . . The sole desire of being a victim suffices; we must, however, be always willing to remain poor and weak. Herein lies the difficulty, for where are the truly poor in spirit to be found? "They must be sought for afar off," says the author of the Imitation. . . . He does not say that they must be sought for amongst the great, but afar off—that is to say, in lowliness, in nothingness . . . Ah! Let us remain far away from pomp; let us love our littleness, let us love to feel nothing. Then we shall be poor in spirit, and Jesus will come to seek us, be we so ever far away. He will transform us into flames of love.[7, 8]

Spiritual childhood is the way of confidence in God and abandonment to God. The basis of all God's work in our souls is our nothingness, our weakness, and even our sins. It is our nothingness that God wants. We broke our Lord's heart in the agony of the garden not so much by our sins or our infidelity but by our self-sufficiency.[9]

If you have ever been in love, you know the hardest thing you had to put up with was the fact that the one you loved did not need you. Not that the person did not want you but did not need you. She was sufficient to herself. That is the hardest thing. God is in love with each one of us. What hurts him more than

7. Thèrése letter to Sister Marie of the Sacred Heart on September 17, 1896 in Laveille, *St. Thérèse de L'Enfant Jésus*, pp. 258–259. Full text of the letter may be found in *Collected Letters of St. Thérèse of Lisieux*, ed. Abbé Combes, trans. F. J. Sheed (New York: Sheed and Ward, 1949), pp. 289–290.

8. "I am only a child, powerless and weak, and yet it is my weakness that gives me the boldness of offering myself as *VICTIM of Your Love, O Jesus!* . . . Yes, in order that Love be fully satisfied, it is necessary that It lower Itself, and that It lower Itself to nothingness and transform this nothingness into *fire*" [emphasis retained]. Saint Thérèse, *Story of a Soul*, p. 195.

9. "I understand very well why Saint Peter fell [Mt 26:69-75], Poor Peter, he was relying upon himself instead of relying only upon God's strength." Thérèse to Mother Agnes on August 7, 1897 in *St. Thérèse of Lisieux: Her Last Conversations*, p. 140.

anything is that our self-sufficiency is a basis and the cause of our own endless harm to ourselves. Our only hope is to empty ourselves of ourselves and trust everything to him.

The poverty that we have vowed and the poverty that is incarnated in Saint Benedict's Rule must be applied to the spiritual life. For Christ to dwell in us, we have to let God empty ourselves of ourselves and we have freely glory in our infirmities.[10]

10. 2 Cor 12:9.

## CONFERENCE FIFTEEN:
# CHASTITY

### Natural Love

While poverty is an obligation associated with the vow of obedience, chastity is another aspect of detachment that comes under the same vow. We do not mention it explicitly in our formula for profession but the obligation is there. I dread the retreat master who comes into a religious house and starts off: "Now I suppose it is not necessary to speak of holy purity or sins against holy purity in this holy house. Such things would never occur to anybody even to think of."[1] The man sets up an atmosphere of fear and hush-hush so that the monks are afraid to talk to him. Each thinks he is the only man in the house that is tempted by the devil.

We are men, not angels. We have a human body, and God has given us two extraordinary instincts. One is the instinct for food on which our life depends; the other is the instinct of sex on which the human race depends. Neither instinct becomes extinct in us, because we have put on a Cistercian cowl or Roman collar. We are men all of our lives.

Our instinct for procreation is a holy instinct created by God. I suggest that in every house a competent priest give a course of lectures on the duty and glory and wonders of married life and human love as well as the wonderful thing that parentage is. I would make it clear to every young religious: what he has given up is not anything evil but something very wonderful and holy.

1. "The first point of capital importance is: *Never to take one's chastity for granted.* The man who upon hearing of someone's fall, exclaims 'That could never happen to me!' is on proximate danger of a catastrophe" [emphasis retained]. Boylan, *The Spiritual Life of the Priest*, p. 83.

However, in coming to the monastery he has chosen a way that is also wonderful and holy. If we give up natural parentage, we must take on spiritual parentage. If we give up natural love, we must put on supernatural love.

## Temptations

This tendency for sex is a holy thing. It tends to have a physiological basis practically in our whole body. It tends to manifest throughout all of our lives in various ways—thoughts, desires, and feelings. In themselves these are not evil. We get what we call "bad thoughts and desires." There is nothing bad about them in themselves. They are just in the wrong place. We have renounced all of these things.

As monks you may find yourself being tempted to impurity in thought and desire much more than before you entered the monastery for the obvious reason that in our life there is little variety to catch our interest. Outside the monastery there is a whole stream of different events such as meeting different people and seeing different things all day. It tends to wash these things out of your mind. Living in the world, you come to terms with it, so to speak, in the sense of not being drawn away by every pair of blue eyes that you see. In the monastery, however, you are more sensitive to temptation. Thoughts and desires can get a grip on you and create problems for your prayer life. Every woman you see or think about is a temptation to you for two or three days.[2]

## Scruples

Religious can become obsessed by the whole question of morality and sex. Saint Alphonsus, for example, identifies as grave matter those things that excite the passions, but today those same

2. "Custody of the eyes is an age-old prescription which has not lost its efficacy. But it must be used with prudence. The real incitement to passion is not so much in the exterior object as it is in the real self, but as it is elaborated by the imagination." Boylan, *The Spiritual Life of the Priest*, p. 84.

things are not tremendously exciting for the majority of men.[3, 4] While we must take our principles from Saint Alphonsus and other theologians, the application of them has to be modified according to the time, place, and the circumstances in which you are living. You will find it remarkable how many of the modern theologians just copy out Saint Alphonsus's word for word on this matter.

In Ireland, some Irish priests accused me of ruining the moral life of the countryside. I was giving absolution in cases where they were insisting on refusing it. I stood my ground and asked why they were refusing it. I said, "We can't discuss actual cases but let's postulate a case. What would you do in such a case?"

They had no basis for their refusal for absolution. I stuck to my opinion. "Bring it to the bishop if you like," I said. "I'll even defend it in Rome. It is only fair to tell you that the last I heard from Rome is that the diocesan authorities would not give faculties to priests holding the opinion that you Irish priests hold. You do not know what you're talking about."

I said to one Irish priest, "Father, have you ever been out with a girl in your life?"

"Oh, no, Father," he said.

"Well, I have Father, and I very nearly married," I said. "Now you've got a most prurient mind where men and women are concerned. Learn to understand the nature of your penitents."

If you are not sure you are in mortal sin, you are in good faith. If you receive the Eucharist in good faith and with attrition—none of us want to go to hell—the sacrament gives you grace. You must know in your heart that when you come from Holy Communion, you are in a state of grace. That is the only way to deal with that situation. You may think it is drastic but I have learned the hard way that you have to be drastic. I have been there myself.

3. Saint Alphonsus M. Liguori, *The True Spouse of Christ;* 2nd ed., trans. Eugene Grimm, The Complete Ascetical Works of St. Alphonsus de Liguori, vols. 10–11 combined (Brooklyn: Redemptorist Fathers, 1929) pp. 205–248.

4. Saint Alphonsus M. Liguori, *Dignity and Duties of the Priest or Selva,* trans. Eugene Grimm, The Complete Ascetical Works of St. Alphonsus de Liguori, vol. 12 (Brooklyn: Redemptorist Fathers, 1927) pp. 362–383.

You know what our morning is like. You may have a sleepless night and you come down at two o'clock and during vigils or at the meditation period some thoughts have been on your mind all of the time, and then you would go over to the sacristy to prepare for Mass but you think, I cannot say Mass. I am sure I consented. I am sure I took pleasure in those thoughts. I got so bad once that I had to make a fixed resolution that I would never go to confession more than once a week.

Once you get into scruples, you are only making trouble for yourself. You have got to be definite that unless you swear that you deliberately decided to commit a mortal sin, you do not go to confession. The whole question that matters is the decision of your will to commit mortal sin, not the consent to a pleasure. Even if you consented, the whole question still arises: Are you guilty of mortal sin subjectively? There are several factors that affect subjective guilt, especially where habits are concerned.

## Compassion toward Penitents

As confessors, we have to be kind, understanding, and sympathetic. We must always encourage men.[5, 6] We must never be shocked no matter what happens to a monk or a priest. We must never make confession difficult for another man. It is difficult enough to go down on your knees to a man whom you live with, especially if you are a priest and confess even venial sins to say

5. "A single word from a priest inflamed with holy charity will do more good than a hundred sermons, composed by a theologian who has but little love of God." Saint Alphonsus de Liguori, *Dignity and Duties of the Priest*, pp. 301–302.

6. "You must be very, very careful how you deal with students committed to you, or anybody else committed to your charge. Your general attitude to them is going to affect and to form, to some extent, their idea of God. If you make God appear as a hard task-master, or an unreasonable judge, an exacting master, you are destroying their hope of salvation. That is why, in all things, when you use authority, you must be a mother rather than a superior, a parent rather than a teacher in dealing with children. I grant you the problem is that one has to keep a certain reserve, stand on a certain aloofness, nevertheless, kindness should characterize the whole pattern of our dealing with souls. It is the only way to win people for God. It is the only thing that has a lasting effect on other people. Kindness." Boylan, talk to Sisters, 3,2.

nothing of more serious sins. Remember the words about Christ: *"This man welcomes sinners and eats with them"* (Lk 15:2). Our chief duty as confessors is to reconcile sinners with God and to restore confidence in themselves and, above all, in God's mercy.[7]

Unfortunately there is another aspect of our work as confessors. We have to consider the suitability of certain men for monastic life and whether the circumstances in which they are living, even after profession, are the best circumstances for the salvation of their souls.

## Companionship with the Lord

Chastity means not only giving up physical pleasure but a much deeper need in us. When God made Adam, even in the garden of paradise, he said that it is not good for man to be alone. There is a fundamental need in each one of us for that particular type of companionship in sympathy, love, and admiration that a man receives from his wife. It is a unique friendship. We have deprived ourselves permanently of that by coming into a monastery. We may not realize at the time what we are doing but it is brought home to us later. Unless you find in the person of our Lord a greater companionship than the one you have given up, there is going to be trouble. Sooner or later you look for that interest and affection somewhere else. That is where people go wrong. They look for it either within the community or outside the community.

I strongly object to characterizing the vow of chastity as giving up something. A man does not give up other women when he chooses a wife. He chooses one woman and keeps his whole heart for her. We do not give up the world so much as choose God. This is the positive side of chastity.

7. "It is indeed necessary to admonish the sinner, in order to make him understand his miserable state, and the danger of damnation to which he is exposed; but he must be always admonished with charity, he must be excited to confidence in the divine mercy, and must be taught the means by which he may amend his life." Saint Alphonsus de Liguori, *Dignity and Duties of the Priest*, p. 275.

## CONFERENCE SIXTEEN:
# FAITH

### Mary's Faith

When we honor our Lady, she immediately turns that honor to God. Elizabeth gave our Lady a greeting based on faith and revelation that Mary was the mother of God: *"Blessed art thou among women and blessed is the fruit of thy womb!"*(Lk 1:42). What is the result? The *Magnificat*—the most sublime piece of sublime praise that has ever left the lips of anybody except the Lord Jesus Christ himself.[1] Any praise we give our Lady has a similar result in heaven. She sings another *Magnificat*. That is worthwhile, is it not? When we feel we cannot praise our Lord as we should, start praising our Lady instead. She praises our Lord much more magnificently than we can.

Imitation of our Lady's faith is part of our devotion to her. The virtue that seemed to touch our Lord most was the faith of people in him. What hurt our Lord most was the lack of faith, especially among his friends and the apostles.

### Faith in Jesus Christ

Let us not be deceived by the English meaning of the word *believe*. The meaning of the word in English is "to express an opinion," but in Latin it is "to know." Supernatural faith is knowledge based on the authority of God. To exercise faith is to exercise God's will. In ordinary knowledge our intellect is convinced. In the case of faith, we have to use our will to decide the question. Though our intellect can resist, our will says that God exists and is looking after our welfare.

1. Lk 1:46-55.

It is by faith in Jesus Christ that we are children of God. Saint Paul writes: *For you are all children of God through faith in Christ Jesus* (Gal 3:26). This faith is fundamental in the monastic life. Unless we have faith and are growing in faith, our monastic life is meaningless. Our faith must be in Jesus Christ who is God's only begotten son. Not only must our faith be in Christ in all his mysteries of the Gospels—in the crib, as a workman, as a teacher, preacher, in all his acts and miracles in Palestine, his public life, in the Garden of Gethsemani, on the cross, in all the tortures of the passion—but in the Christ who dwells with us now in the Blessed Sacrament.

## Faith in the Forgiveness of Sins

When the priest absolves us from our sins, we must believe that we are dealing with Christ who is God. The confessor is not a mere man who is trying to psychoanalyze us and give natural psychological peace of mind. He is a person who can speak to us in the name of God and can say, "Your sins are forgiven."

We must believe in the divinity exercising itself in and through the Church. We must also believe in the infinite value of Christ's obedience to the will of God. The plan of God's providence was accomplished by Christ's passion and death. We must believe that we are incorporated in Christ by baptism.

Our lack of confidence, especially the lack of confidence that comes from our sins, is very closely connected if not entirely due to our failure to believe properly and completely in the salvation that comes through Jesus Christ.

We are dealing with infinite goodness and forgiveness. Do we believe in God's forgiveness of our sins or do we feel that God forgives like a man? Do we think that God makes a good job of forgiveness but still holds our sins in memory? That does not apply to God. When God forgives, he forgives completely and immediately offers us a means of regaining all we have lost and undoing any harm that we have done. If he asks us to suffer the consequences of our sins, it is merely to help us advance in virtue, namely, to grow in love.

You must never give in to the feeling, "Well, I would have been a great monk or a great saint or a very holy man were it not for my sins." It is the prudence of the devil who puts that into your mind anything that contradicts the inspiration of the Holy Spirit. "It would have been alright if I'd ran straight from the beginning, but I haven't. I must now be content with my lot." That is fatal.

There is a time when you must be content with your lot not because You have sinned but because you realize your own powerlessness to extract anything from God beyond what he is prepared to give you. During the darker parts of the spiritual life when God is purifying us, he makes us very conscious of our complete powerlessness to move him or to change his plans in the least. We know that God could make us saints, but we realize that we cannot force him to make us any holier than he has decided to make us. It is then that we accept the limitations that God puts in our way. We have planned sanctity and a spiritual career for ourselves, but we find our plan not in accordance with God's. He has other plans. They do not seem at least to be quite as good or to lead quite as far as the ones we had.

### Faith in God's Providence

We have to resign ourselves to the current limits of our sanctity but the limits are never on account of our sins. If God wants us to be great saints, then our sins will make us great saints. If God wants us to be not such great saints, our sins will still have their part to play in our sanctity. It is not because of our sins that God has lessened the goal but because of his own divine wisdom and right to do what he likes.

Saint Columban (543–615), the great monk, summed it up in a glorious phrase, "We are not ours. We are Christ's possession."[2, 3]

2. *Christi Simus Non Nostri.* Translations vary: "We are Christ's not our own;" "Let us be of Christ not of ourselves."

3. "Thus let us live to Him Who while He dies for us is Life; and let us die to ourselves that we may live to Christ; for we cannot live to Him unless first we die to ourselves, that is, to our wills. *Let us be Christ's and not our own*; for we are not our own, for we are bought at a great price (1 Cor 6:19-20) and truly a great one, when the Lord is given for a slave, the King for a servant, and God for man. What ought we to render ourselves, if the Creator of the universe for us ungodly men, yet His creation, is unjustly put to death? Do you think you ought not to

God has earned the right to do what he likes with us by first creating us and then redeeming us. Everything that happens is in some sense an act of God. God makes use of everything in our life for our sanctification. An artist is drawing a design and mistakenly blots the paper. The artist can either erase the blot or get a new sheet of paper. God makes those blots—our sins—into a part of the design. The blots profit us through God's mercy. God is a Father who desires to unite us to his Son. God spoke directly to the world, *"This is my beloved Son, in whom I am well pleased; hear him"* (Mt 17:5). Trace all of your hope back to that. Our love for the Lord is love for his Father.

We must have faith in the Holy Spirit. It is from the Holy Spirit that we derive the grace of prayer and progress in holiness by abandonment into his hands. The Holy Spirit's gifts make us pliable in God's hands.

**Faith in God's Power**

We need faith not merely in God's providence but God's power. Everything is under God's control. Mark Twain said that he had many troubles but most of them never happened. One of our greatest faults in regard to faith and trust in the Father is to worry about what is going to happen next. There are a hundred and one things that animate your mind in the monastic life. We should blame ourselves first. If we mind our own business, we worry far less. Even when it is our business, there is no reason to worry. Everything is under control; God is on the job. God is a perfect father. Why worry?

It is true that where God's will is not clear there is a certain bit of anxiety, worry, or preoccupation. We must train ourselves to depend on God's providence and make the best decision we

---

die to sin? Certainly you ought. Therefore let us die, let us die for the sake of life, since Life dies for the dead, so that we may be able to say with Paul, 'I live, yet no longer I, but Christ lives in me' (Gal 2:20) [emphasis added]. Saint Columban, Sermon X in *Scriptores Latini Hiberniae*, vol. 2, ed. G.S.M. Walker (Dublin: Dublin Institute for Advanced Studies, 1957; 1970) <http://www.ucc.ie/celt/online/T201053.html> (CELT: Corpus of Electronic Texts: a project of University College, Cork College Road, Cork, Ireland, 2004).

can at the time. God knows we are not infallible and is quite prepared to see us make mistakes. As long as we admit to the need of his grace and act in conscious of our own need for him, he will back us up. He will use our mistakes for good.

The only possible approach to any spiritual problem or even the temporal administration of the monastery is, "I can't handle this, but God will help me to handle it." It is Saint Thérèse's maxim: "Jesus does everything, I do nothing."[4, 5] It is quite sound. Even there, God lets us make our mistakes. The mistakes, however, are used by him to the advantage of souls.

## Peace through Faith

We monks have to use tremendous faith. Our life is based on supernatural values and principles. We have given up everything this world has to offer and placed our lives completely in God's loving care. Our happiness and peace are evidence of Jesus' words: *"Amen I say to you, there is no one who has left house, or parents, or brothers, or wife, or children, for the sake of the kingdom of God, who shall not receive much more in the present time, and in the age to come life everlasting"* (Lk 18:29-30).

Our peace is different than the peace found in a state of intoxication which is the negative peace of having no worries for the moment because you have forgotten them in your state of stupor. The peace of Christ is a positive peace that flows inside of us like a river. It is a peace given by God as a gift for those who believe.[6]

## Faith in God's Graces

We came to the monastery with certain high purposes. From a worldly point of view, we might expect to find in monastic life a certain wisdom, organization, and competence. Each one of us

4. Saint Thérèse of Lisieux letter to her sister Céline on July 6, 1893 in *Collected Letters of Saint Thérèse of Lisieux*, p. 191.

5. Compare with the words of Jesus, *"I am the vine, you are the branches. Whoever remains in me and I in him will bear much fruit, because without me you can do nothing"* (Jn 15:5).

6. Jn 14:27.

could expect perhaps from the worldly point of view that we get a master of novices, director, or superior who understands perfectly. If we came to the monastery looking to do farming we would expect perhaps from a worldly point of view to have the best of machines and help if we needed it. But in practice we know that none of these things happen. However, we often find ourselves in the position of the Israelites who were asked to make bricks without straw. Whether you are a superior, teacher of theology, supervisor of the farm, or whether you are simply trying to practice a spiritual life, you have limited agents or instruments to help you.

When you come into the monastery and decide, "Well, this is not a bad place but it needs a little bit of reorganization," please remember that we have to correspond with the designs of God and certain dispositions are necessary. First, we need docility to the inspirations of the Holy Spirit. We are dependent on God's grace and fidelity. We wait for the moment when it shall please God to employ us as his instruments. We never anticipate his will or add our own conception to the plan marked out by Providence.

A number of men have come to me and said, "Reverend Father, I didn't come into this monastery to be so and so." I reply, "What did you come in for, Father? The best thing is to go home because the best thing I can offer you is to do what you are told and if you don't like it Father. . . ."

In the words of the famous movie about World War I, "If you know the better hole, go to it." The war was fought from the trenches where soldiers literally had to live for days under shell fire. In the terrain in front of them were deep craters from exploding shells. The craters were filled with water and mud from the rains and raked with stench from dead bodies. When you went on a raid or advance, the soldiers had to dive into a shell hole for protection from artillery fire.

In the movie, these two soldiers—one was a veteran and the other fellow was a private—got into this hole. There were shells exploding around them. Two dead men were floating in the hole. The young soldier was complaining. The veteran said, "Well, if you know the better hole, go to it." Going into another hole meant that you would go into a rain of shell and machine gun fire. That, of course, meant that you were most likely going to be killed.

That is the answer to the man who comes into the monastery and begins to complain. God is not going to let you know what he is going to do with you. He never presents you with the complete plan. He gives it to you page by page and occasionally he modifies it. We need to have generous courage in encountering the contradictions and the difficulties that disconcert our views and apparently blight our hopes. It would sometimes appear that we have totally lost sight of our end. Instead of advancing, we perceive that all is lost. But far from abandoning the work under such circumstances, we should pursue it with redoubled confidence in God. To attain his end God invariably adopts measures of apparently different tendencies. He conceals his resources. And when we believe ourselves most remote from the end, we have in fact nearly reached it.

### Faith in God's Will

Forget self-interest. It should never mingle with our efforts to carry out the work of heaven. We should be ready if such were God's pleasure to lavish our exertions, renounce our repose, and, if necessary, lay down our lives since to lose all for God is to gain all.[7] These spiritual sacrifices should extend even to those things which seem directly connected with the glory of God or with our own perfection.

Some monks think they must disobey the superior in the interest of God's honor and for their own sanctification. What is the plan of our own sanctification? God's will. What is the best thing for God's honor? God's will. What are the commands of the superior? God's will. How can they be in conflict with one another? Each one of us has private plans, ideas, and principles of our own that tend to make us unpliable in the hands of authority. For example, a monk insists in carrying out rubrics despite common custom or even direct orders about another way of doing things.

7. Phil 3:8.

Submit to the manifest will of God and leave to him the working of procuring his glory and our sanctification. After all, our sanctification is not our work but the work of God. We must exercise the faith infused in us at baptism and given us as gift in the other sacraments. It is a gift we should always pray for. It is by faith that we touch God and by charity that we are made one with him. The theology of the mystical life, mystical prayer, the dark night of the soul, the ascent to Mt. Carmel, the living flame, the divine love, the cloud of unknowing are summed up by Saint Bernard and Saint John of the Cross in the doctrine that it is by faith that we are purified and prepared for complete union with God. Saint Paul said, "The just man lives by faith."[8]

There is no other way of living in the monastery except by faith. We must believe Christ is in the abbot and our brethren. Charity, obedience, humility, faith, the Divine Office, and the use of the sacraments depend on faith. Our prayers are prayers of faith. The whole life of a monk is a life of faith. We must pray for faith. The most important prayer we have to say in that regard is the prayer of the Church to give us an increase of faith, hope, and charity. The other virtue that matters is humility which will make it possible for God to give us a great increase of faith, hope, and charity.

8. Hab 2:4; Rom 1:17; Gal 3:11; Heb 10:38.

## CONFERENCE SEVENTEEN:
# CONCLUSION

### Christ Living His Life in Us

The purpose of our life is to give glory to God by giving him Christ in us. That means our primary duty is to form Christ in ourselves. We receive him in baptism and in the sacraments, especially at Holy Communion. However, we must not keep him wrapped in swaddling clothes. We must let him live with us and gradually develop his life in us so that our life is converted into his. Our vocation is to be able to say with Saint Paul, *"It is now no longer I that live, but Christ lives in me"* (Gal 2:20). Christ's life inevitably will be given us if we live by faith in the Son of God who loved us and gave himself for us.

Saint Benedict bases his rule on reverence for God.[1] He asks us to realize that we are completely dependent upon God's mercy. All that is good in us—even the good that we seem to have produced ourselves—is ultimately to be traced to God's goodness and grace. Further, Saint Benedict expects us to accept ourselves as we have made ourselves. This requires the acceptance of all the humiliation of our past sins and our current faults.

1. "The Divine Office is an 'entering-in' to the prayer of Christ Himself continued in His Mystical Body. One can here find the association between reverence for God and union with God, which allows us to sum up Saint Benedict's whole spirituality in one word, 'reverence.' For reverence demands adequate adoration, and the only adequate adoration and praise of God is that of Christ Himself. Going in to choir, the monk finds Christ, and in uniting himself to his brethren unites himself to Him." Boylan, "Benedictine Influence in the Doctrine of Abbot Marmion," in *Abbot Marmion: An Irish Tribute,* p. 51.

In the acceptance of our sinfulness and weaknesses is the realization that we can only love God by giving him Christ. We cannot do that by ourselves. We need Christ's help. With humility and confidence in Christ's wonderfulness, we ask him for help as we aspire to the highest possible union with God, which is union with Christ.

**Humility**

We ascend into the abyss of our own nothingness and are raised to the heights of God's divinity. Thomas à Kempis (1380–1471) writes in *The Imitation of Christ* that they who know their own infirmity shall be raised to the height of God's divinity.[2, 3] Saint Peter tells us that we are to be made partakers of the divine nature.[4] Through Benedict's steps of humility, we remove the chief obstacle to the life of Christ in us, namely our tendency to put our own name to all we do. It is pride that claims for us the glory that is solely God's.

We give expression to that life of Christ within us by removing another obstacle (or, if you prefer, the continuation of the same obstacle)—our self will. Scripture warns us, *I the Lord, this is my name: I will not give my glory to another, nor my praise to graven things* (Is 42:8).

It is of central importance to pray for humility, but it is only by prayer that we get it. Everything in our life—profit or loss, sin or virtue, shame, sorrow, or joy—can be used to increase our humility. Humility is the virtue that turns even our sins into treasures. Through humility our greatest loss has become our greatest victory. Humility supplies for defects in all the other virtues. We grow in humility by the experience of God's grace.

2. Book III, chapter 20 which is titled "Of the Acknowledgement of Our Own Infirmities and the Miseries of This Life." Some translations use "weaknesses" instead of "infirmities."

3. "The more one humbly recognizes that one is weak and miserable, the more God lowers Himself toward us in order to lavish His gifts upon us with magnificence." Attributed to Saint Thérèse of Lisieux by Sister Marie of the Trinity in M.M. Philipon, *The Message of Thérèse of Lisieux*, trans. E. J. Ross (Westminster, Md.: Newman, 1954), p. 59.

4. 2 Pt 1:4.

When we fall, we might ask with Saint Paul, *Unhappy man that I am! Who will deliver me from the body of this death?* (Rom 7:24). We might get the answer given to Saint Paul by our Lord, *"My grace is sufficient for thee, for strength is made perfect in weakness"* (2 Cor 12:9). Not by justice, but by grace. In other words, God's mercy is sufficient. It is all we want and that is all we have.

The spiritual life requires that we accept our infirmities, sins, weaknesses, limitations of self and surroundings. We accept them and glory in them as Paul gloried in the cross of Christ. It is because of our infirmities and weaknesses that the power of Christ will dwell within us and sanctify us.[5]

**Obedience**

In addition to humility, obedience to God's will brings forth the life of Christ in us. We give him our hands, heart, lips, and eyes. We give him all that we have to serve, praise, and love his Father. Jesus continues to love his Father here on earth through us.

Scripture tells us: *Be sober, be watchful! For your adversary the devil, as a roaring lion, goes about seeking someone to devour* (1 Pt 5:8). The Sacred Heart goes around, so to speak, seeking whom he may devour in love so that he may take over the whole of our personality in order to make it his to serve, praise, and love his Father. Even if you but give him half a chance, he will do it. Do not think that we have to put pressure on God to come to our aid. The whole trouble is merely to avoid stopping him from coming. He is at the door. *"Behold, I stand at the door and knock. If any man listens to my voice and opens the door to me, I will come in to him and will sup with him, and he with me"* (Rv 3:20). Can you

5. "Fr. Clerissac, OP, summed it up very neatly in the introduction to his book, *The Mystery of the Church* [New York: Sheed and Ward, 1937], when he said: 'It is our emptiness and thirst that God needs, not our plenitude.' The realization of this truth is a great grace from God and it is one we priests should ask for, earnestly and insistently. Human reason and human experience may, perhaps, indicate to us the poverty of our own resource, but unless God gives us the grace we are not likely to relish our own poverty and glory in our infirmities." Boylan, *The Priest's Way to God*, p. 103.

imagine anything more intimate than that invitation of our Lord? All we have to do is open the door by humility and obedience.

Our obedience is to God's commandments. We must exercise fraternal charity because Christ cannot live in us—cannot share our actions—if we do not follow his law of fraternal charity. Monks not only find Christ in each other but in the Divine Office, where Christ goes to pray to his Father. Christ can be found there in a way that is truly sacramental (as opposed to a sacrament). We can put on Christ in the choir. We can say to the Father looking at the choir, "This is your beloved son in whom you are well pleased, hear him."[6] God must hear us because it is no longer private persons who pray, it is the authorized representatives of the Body of Christ which is the Church to which Christ himself associates himself independent of our dispositions.

There are the obligations of our vows. The vows of poverty and chastity empty our hands and hearts of all that is not Christ. That is obvious because to live in union with Christ we have to let him live with us. We must get rid of self-love and self-seeking and be content to have everything from him. We have to consider what he has done for us. What have we at our disposal? We have the power of Christ.

### God's Love for Us

How does the power of Christ come to us? First, God takes pity on us from heaven. God came down into the womb of the Virgin Mary. He comes as a cell. That is the Son of God incarnate. A child was born, and he was nursed. God grew as we all grew. God lived and worked as a poor young boy and then as a poor young man. He was a working man at Palestine. God preached and suffered the insults of the crowd and the hatred and the growing resentment of the leaders. God suffered the malice, envies, and infidelities of his friends. God suffered from others' lack of faith. God was in the midst of us and we believed him not. God's agony is seen in the Garden of Gethsemani. God was scourged at the pillar and crowned with thorns.

6. Mt 17:5.

We are tempted to overlook the tremendous sufferings of our Lord. We are tempted to say, "Well that was all over in twenty-four hours. Look at those who were in concentration camps. Look at the tortures they endured. Look at the torture of a long, drawn-out cancer. At least our Lord's sufferings were always short." Do not make that mistake. Our Lord had a body that was built for suffering. His was a perfect human body with the most sensitive nervous system. The one thing he could do in his human nature that he could not do in his divine nature was to suffer for love of us. He suffered more in twelve hours than others would suffer in twelve years. His sufferings were such that only his divinity could save him from death.

The only use the Lord made of his divinity in his passion and death was to keep conscious so that he could suffer more. The physical sufferings, not to mention the mental sufferings, of our Lord are beyond imagination. We are drawn to those sufferings of his heart in the devotion to the Sacred Heart. Christ's heart was on fire with love. His heart was pierced with a lance and wrapped with the thorns of our coldness. It is impossible to find words to represent what Christ experienced on the cross.

After Jesus instituted the Eucharist at the Last Supper, he began to be sad and troubled. He went into the Garden of Gethsemani and prayed. He suffered terrible agonies. His anguish was such that his sweat became as drops of blood. It seems to have started with the new bond with us called the Eucharist. Immediately he began to suffer and carry the burden of our sins. Yet in that very moment, his love was so urgent that he designed and planned this wonderful mystery of his presence in the Body and Blood. He wished that he might always be available to us both as a sacrifice offered his Father and as food given to our souls.

God instituted the Eucharist so he might mingle with us. In the agony of the garden we see the price Jesus was willing to pay for that union with us. He took on the burden of our sins and suffered a tortuous death. Jesus the Son of God experienced our lack of confidence and trust as he was scourged and crowned with thorns at the pillar, and as he was nailed to the cross to die.

Jesus made the effect of his death obvious when the criminal condemned to death beside him made an act of trust in him.

*"Lord, remember me when thou comest into thy kingdom"* (Lk 23:42). What is his reward? *"Amen I say to thee, this day thou shalt be with me in paradise"* (Lk 23:43). The criminal became a saint; he was canonized before his death. We wonder: when is God going to make me a saint? How can he make me a saint in the years left to me? Here we have a saint made out of a scoundrel in one second. Why? Because of his faith in Jesus Christ. We have the same sacrifice of Christ on our altars. If we only have faith in it our sanctity will be achieved as efficiently.

**Sanctified by Jesus Christ**

When we are tempted to doubt Christ's power and his willingness to help us, when we are overwhelmed by our own infidelity and sins, remember the request of the good thief and the words of our Lord in response, *"Amen I say to thee, this day thou shalt be with me in paradise"* (Lk 23:43).

Jesus is resurrected from the dead. Does it make headlines? No. Does it create faith and extraordinary enthusiasm among his disciples? No. They do not know what to make of it.[7] They are still afraid.

After rising from the dead, Jesus meets two of the disciples on the road to Emmaus.[8] They start talking. "Why are you so sad and troubled?" he asks. "Haven't you heard what has happened in Jerusalem?" they say. The two disciples had hoped for great things.

We have to be careful. Are we doing the same thing? We came into this monastery with definite plans for our own sanctification. What were the apostles expecting of Jesus? His crucifixion? There are times in our monastic life when we are tempted to say, "I had hoped for . . ." We were looking forward to living the monastic life according to our own ambitions but gradually found ourselves in the depths of aridity with the plans *we had hoped for* in shambles.[9] In the very hour that we are disappointed and almost

7. Mt 28:16-17; Mk 16:14.

8. Lk 24:13-32.

9. "St. Gertrude, despite her unceasing prayers for deliverance from certain imperfections, was never entirely set free from them. Her natural impetuosity

despairing, it is the very hour of our triumph.[10] Our Lord has already risen with our sanctification completely accomplished. We are as blind as the two disciples going down the road who did not realize that the whole plan of the incarnation was a success. The world had been saved by what they thought was a disaster. And the disasters to our hopes that occur in the monastic life are the very God-designed means for our sanctification.

### Trust in Our Lord

Is our Lord saying to us, *"O thou of little faith, why didst thou doubt?"* (Mt 14:31). We have obvious reasons to trust in our Lord, yet we try to find reasons for not trusting. You may point to the times when you thought that you let our Lord down. Was there not a famous Canaanite woman who asked our Lord to cure her daughter?[11] What does our Lord do but in a rather brisk tone, refuse her request saying that he was sent to the lost people of Israel and he compares her to a dog. And she lowered herself below the comparison and still insisted on believing him. And what does he say? *"O woman, great is thy faith! Let it be done to thee as thou wilt"* (Mt 15:28). Notice what is happening. Confidence has caused our Lord to break through a barrier laid down by God the Father.

---

caused her many a humiliation. Thus, in her zeal for exact observance of the Holy Rule, her reproaches to the negligent were often excessive. In endeavoring to rid herself of those failings, the Saint complained to Our Lord, and asked to be completely delivered from them. She was told, however, that frequently defects of this kind are left in chosen souls in order that they may bear in mind the weakness of their nature, and realize that all their purity is but an effect of God's mercy." Michael Oliver, *St. Gertrude the Great: A Cistercian Nun of the 13th Century,* (Dublin: Anthonian Press, 1930), p. 55.

10. "At the second bell for Matins, the Saint again began to praise God; and God the Father spoke thus to her: '. . . for there are certain faults in men, the knowledge of which serves to humble them, and cause a holy compunction, and these faults further their salvation.'" *The Life and Revelations of Saint Gertrude the Great (Insinuationes Divinae Pietatis)*, trans. Poor Clares of Kenmare [Ireland] (Westminster, Md.: Newman Press, 1949; Westminster: Christian Classics, 1975; Rockford: Il.: TAN, 2002), p. 288.

11. Mt 15:22-28.

Lazarus is dead. Martha says, *"Lord, if thou hadst been here my brother would not have died. But even now I know that whatever thou shalt ask of God, God will give it to thee"* (Jn 11:21-22). What does Jesus say to Martha? *"I am the resurrection and the life; he who believes in me, even if he die, shall live; and whoever lives and believes in me, shall never die. Dost thou believe this?"* (Jn 11:25-26). Even though you are dead in sin—dead in the spiritual of life—you will still live, provided that you have faith in Jesus.

Those two incidents alone should wake us up to the need and to the reward of confidence. "Yes," you say, "that's all very well if you have faith. But I haven't faith." Well, of course, there is one thing about faith. You have got to believe that you have faith. You never know you have faith. You will not feel it because the very essence of faith is the opposite of feeling. The whole purification of the spiritual life is the reduction of everything to living by faith. Faith even in the faith by which we live. It excludes any assurance of support through self-confidence. All the supports are gone except this blind decision to trust in God without apparently any reason.

Faith and hope overlap. Our hope is in God's goodness. You must keep on hoping. Why? *That whoever calls upon the name of the Lord shall be saved* (Acts 2:21; Rm 10:13; Jl 3:5). What is the name of the Lord? Jesus Christ. That is our hope. God's plan is to glorify himself by his mercy. We are miserable and only Jesus' mercy will make us saints. The other things that we hope in are merely straw. They let us down.

What if you are convinced that you have no faith? Remember what happened at Cana.[12] The wine supply almost came to a rather providential end. Although it would have certainly embarrassed the host and hostess, our Lady had every reason to say, "Let things be; it's about time they shut up and stop drinking." Our Lord even assured her that he had good reasons for letting things be. *"What wouldst thou have me do, woman? My hour has not yet come"* (Jn 2:4). Every good reason for doing nothing about it. Just as some bright genius would try to tell you, "Father, you

12. Jn 2:1-10.

may as well give up hope of being a saint. You'll probably save your soul, but you'll never become a saint."

Your answer is to go to our Lady. Tell her, "I have no wine." Tell her: "I have no faith. The whole of salvation depends on faith in your son, but here I am with no faith in him."

Is she going to say, "That's your fault"? Did she say that to the host and hostess? "That's your fault you have no wine. You gave too much to drink. You didn't buy enough." No. She will tell you exactly what she told the waiter. *"Do whatever he tells you"* (Jn 2:5). She is telling us to go to her son in complete abandonment to his will.

Our Lady will fix a deal with our Lord. He may say, "This man's had it. I have given him mercy time and time again. It is time he got no more. It is only a waste of my goodness. A waste of my suffering." The answer would be the same. She would just kindly go on and arrange the whole thing. She is one of these dominating mothers that dominates our Lord Jesus Christ himself. He is glad to be dominated by her. Our salvation is in completely safe hands when it is in the hands of the Blessed Virgin. Even if we have not faith, we can have confidence in the Mother of God.

### All Things Are Possible

All I know about the spiritual life—which is not much—is from two sources: from having fallen in love when I was a young man and from being a mile swimmer. Anyone who has done a long-distance sporting event knows about "second wind." Second wind is an important lesson in the spiritual life. You reach a stage in a long-distance event—running, skiing, swimming—where you feel absolutely convinced that you cannot go another step or take another stroke. Everything is gone. You have absolutely no energy to continue. You are convinced that you cannot. Then, out of nowhere, you find sufficient strength to put out the next foot or to take the next stroke. You decide to manage another one. Gradually you begin to find that you can do it. You can at least do another length of the pool if you are swimming. And then the guy at then end of the pool says, "Another thirty-six links." And you say, "Well, I can do another two of them." Then you begin to realize that possibly you can do the entire thirty-six. You look around the field and see that the leader is not too far ahead. I might catch him, you think. You find yourself with the front of the field, and it is a fight to the finish. That happens in the spiritual life. You are down to a position where all hopes seem to be gone. You have got to remember the doctrine of the second wind. Just keep on going. If you give up hope, you are dead. All things are possible to him that believes.[13] Belief is the act of the will. It is a decision to trust God.

## Our Love for God

Our confidence must express itself by abandonment to God's love for us. We must abandon our own plans, ideas, and personal hopes.[14] We must cease all worries. How many worries do we have that never come close to happening? God is our Father; Jesus is our Savior; the Holy Spirit is our sanctifier. We have a perfect mother in the Mother of God. The only valid reason for

13. Mk 9:23.

14. "It was the greatest grace of my life, at least one of them. It was the day I was solemnly professed. I was professed on the feast of St. Teresa of Avila [October 15, 1936]. At the High Mass that day, there was no organist, and I had to play Terce before High Mass. We use the big psalters—tremendous things. The antiphons stand out in print, a fourth of an inch high. And the words stand out. We are professed at High Mass. We go up at the offertory, and we finish up by writing out our vows on parchment and putting them on the altar with the bread and wine. We came to the end of Terce, and three words of the antiphon just stood out from the book as I was turning to leave the organ. *Dedit omnia sua.* It is a quotation from the scripture about the man who found a field in which there was a treasure lay hid (Mt 13:44). He gave up all that was his own. He sold all his goods. Everything that he could call his own. Now if you are going to be holy—if you are going to be united to our Lord—everything that you can call your own is going to go, including your prayer and your spiritual life and your collection of virtues. You have got to scrap all of those things. Rather, let them be scrapped. You cannot scrap them yourselves. Our Lord will scrap them for you. He strips you of everything you can call your own until you realize that he is yours and that having him, you have everything. That is our trouble, you see. We are still holding on to what is our own. We are still basing our confidence on our own achievement in the spiritual life." Boylan, talk to Sisters, 3,8-9.

hoping is because of God's goodness, and his goodness never changes. No matter whether we are in sin or in grace, whether we serve God faithfully or serve him viciously, our reason for hope is the same. Our hope is in God's infinite mercy and goodness.

God has planned this world to glorify himself by giving mercy to each of us. He gives us something that we have never dreamed of and which is beyond all that we deserve.[15] God has assured us that for those who love him all things will work together for good.[16] That all barriers between us might be broken, God has given us his son who spent his life and even died for us. He loved us and delivered himself for us. Remembering that, surely we can abandon ourselves to God's will. Surely we can rely on him to save us and to make us all that he wants us to be.

No matter what talents, capacities, or opportunities we may have, there is nothing we can do for God that somebody else could not do except the one thing—to love him with all the love of our heart and soul. Our personal love is something unique, and it is the one thing God wants.[17]

It is my prayer that in the name of Jesus you receive the Holy Spirit so that you may love our Lord as he desires and deserves to be loved. If we love our Lord Jesus in the Holy Spirit, Jesus will unite us to himself and fill us with himself so that with Him, in Him, and through Him in the unity of the Holy Spirit, God will find all his glory. God bless you all.

15. Is 64:4; 1 Cor 2:9.

16. Rom 8:28.

17. "You and I chose to enter religion, but our choice was the result of God's choice of us and he chooses not for the work we are going to do, but for this one thing that no one else can do. And that is to love him with our whole heart and our whole soul and all our mind and all our strength. No matter what we do for him, unless it is done through love of him, we are wasting our time. . . . It is sheer—and I want to stress the fact—it is sheer waste. Too many of us are career women and career men in religion, and too many of us have almost been trained in regard that a career in religion is the thing which we are called. That will not soothe the Sacred Heart of Jesus at all, and it is his heart that we have to love." Boylan, talk to Sisters, 1,2-3.